It's the Story That Counts

More Children's Books for Mathematical Learning, K–6

David J. Whitin
University of South Carolina

Sandra Wilde
Portland State University

HEINEMANN
Portsmouth, NH

HEINEMANN
A division of Reed Elsevier Inc.
361 Hanover Street
Portsmouth, NH 03801-3912
Offices and agents throughout the world

The publishers and the authors wish to thank the children and their parents for permission to reproduce material in this book. We are also grateful to the following:

Excerpts from *Curriculum and Evaluation Standards for School Mathematics.* ©1989 by the National Council of Teachers of Mathematics. Reprinted by permission of the publisher.

Acknowledgments for borrowed material continue on page 223, which constitutes an extension of the copyright page.

Library of Congress Cataloging-in-Publication Data
Whitin, David Jackman, 1947–
It's the story that counts : more children's books for mathematical learning, K–6 / David J. Whitin, Sandra Wilde.
p. cm.
Includes bibliographical references.
ISBN 0–435–08369–4 (acid-free)
1. Mathematics—Study and teaching (Elementary). 2. Children's literature in mathematics education. I. Wilde, Sandra. II. Title.
QA135.5.W465 1995
372.7'044—dc20 94-46291
CIP

Editor: Toby Gordon
Production: Vicki Kasabian
Cover design: Mary Cronin
Book design: Jenny Jensen Greenleaf

Printed in the United States of America on acid-free paper
99 98 97 96 95 DO 1 2 3 4 5 6 7 8 9

To Tana Hoban and David M. Schwartz, for helping readers young and old learn about speckles and spirals, millions and billions.

Contents

Acknowledgments

Both of us are tremendously grateful to our editor Toby Gordon at Heinemann, who has encouraged us to write this book ever since we finished the previous one, and to Alan Huisman, for his expertise in getting the manuscript into production (and for his patience!). We are also grateful to the production editor, Vicki Kasabian, and to all the other people who helped produce the book. Thanks also to the staffs of Heinemann Services and Heinemann Workshops (especially Leslie Schwartz, Susie Stroud, Karen Hiller, and Cherie Lebel), who have helped both of us share our ideas with many teachers in person.

From David Whitin:
I'd like to thank Lynn Gates, Andy Reeves, Joan Armistead, and Harry Tunis at the National Council of Teachers of Mathematics for the opportunity to review children's books for *Arithmetic Teacher* and *Teaching Children Mathematics.* I also thank the hundreds of teachers I've had the privilege to work with in South Carolina, particularly those in Aiken, Georgetown, Conway, Winnsboro, and Columbia. A special thank-you to John Gorman, a fifth-grade teacher in the Lakota Public Schools of Cincinnati, Ohio (and my classmate in a fifth-grade class in Connecticut a long time ago!), who invited me to work with him and his students. Thanks also to Joan Stephenson of the R. L. Bryan Book Company of Columbia. My heartiest thank-you goes to my wife, Phyllis, whose voice is in all that I write. She continually provided insightful and thoughtful readings of this book, even though she was busy completing one of her own.

From Sandra Wilde:
I'd like to thank my colleagues at Portland State University, especially Christine Chaillé and Emily de la Cruz. I am also grateful to the Multnomah County Library of Oregon for their generous borrowing and telephone renewal policies, and to Federal Express. A special thank-you goes to Bill Kruger.

Introduction

There have always been stories, even in the earliest of times. There were stories about the size of a ferocious animal or the shape of its tusks or the pattern of its hoofprints or the number in its herd. There were stories about the probability of killing it and about how the spoils would be divided. People expressed these stories through speech and through visual representations that they cut into the walls of caves or scratched with a stick in the wet sand.

It is through stories that we make and share meaning; it is the way we come to know and understand our world. It was that way *then*, and it is that way *now*.

Unfortunately, for too many children in our schools, the stories surrounding mathematical learning go something like this: "In the beginning there was . . . the quadratic formula," or "In the beginning there was . . . the invert and multiply rule." These children are missing out on the real stories that lie behind all the abstractions they are expected to memorize. Harold Rosen (1987) zeros in on the universality of storymaking when he writes:

> *All abstractions are rooted in the tissue of human experience. . . . What is geology but a vast story which geologists have been composing and revising throughout the existence of their subject? Indeed, what has the recent brouhaha about evolution been but two stories competing for the right to be the authorized version, the authentic story? . . . There are stories wherever we turn. . . . Every chemical reaction is a story compressed into the straitjacket of an equation. (p.16)*

The purpose of this book is to continue to undo that straitjacket as it appears in the field of mathematics. We believe that children's literature has a powerful role to play in restoring story to the teaching and learning of mathematics. It helps portray mathematics as it really is: a tool for helping us tell the stories of our lives.

The central role of stories

Mathematics is not a body of knowledge independent of human activity. Rather, like all forms of knowledge, it is a consequence of social interaction. Children's literature provides this human perspective about mathematics. Through stories children see people putting mathematics to good use, whether harvesting pumpkins (*Pumpkins,* Ray 1992), baking a cake (*The Biggest Birthday Cake in the World,* Spurr 1991), constructing a building (*Amazing Buildings,* Wilkinson 1993), or telling a tall tale (*A Million Fish . . . More or Less,* McKissack 1992). As teachers share mathematical stories with their students, they often find that these stories become the catalyst for further storytelling; for instance, after hearing about the sharing of cookies in *The Doorbell Rang* (Hutchins 1986), children may want to tell their own sharing stories.

However, stories from children's literature and from students themselves have not always been a valued part of classroom life. For some teachers, "a concern with stories seems frivolous and pupils' personal anecdotes an annoying and irrelevant interruption for the official matter of the curriculum" (Wells 1986, p. 203). Also, the fact that stories are everywhere cheapens their importance in the eyes of many: "Stories are as common as dirt and therefore easily dismissed, or not taken very seriously" (Rosen 1992, p. 1). For many years the mathematics community has operated from this perspective; there was an impatience with the details of stories and an insistence on "getting to the numbers" right away. Therefore, the intent of this book is to show that telling stories is not an irrelevant departure from a preordained curriculum but a cherished enterprise that enriches and extends this curriculum.

There are many who argue that storytelling ought to be the heart of any school curriculum (Rosen 1987; Smith 1990; Wells 1986). According to Barbara Hardy, telling stories is "a primal act of mind"; it is "not a conscious and deliberate activity, but the way in which the mind itself works" (in Wells 1986, p. 197) Stories are the fundamental way of making meaning. Frank Smith elaborates on the important sense-making dimension of stories: "When we say we cannot make sense of something, we mean that we cannot find the story in it, or make up a story about it. . . . This is the way we make sense of life, by making stories. It is the way we remember events: in terms of stories. Without stories, there would be no events" (1990, p. 64).

David Whitin remembers the absence of mathematical stories in his own education. When he was in middle school he learned about factorial numbers in a conventional and formulaic way. The teacher's explanation went something like this:

> *Do you see this symbol [!] here? That's a factorial sign. I know it looks like an exclamation point but it's not. This is math class, so it's a sign for factorials. Now what this means is, if you see a number with a factorial sign after it, like 4!, you multiply together all the whole numbers that are four or less. So, we multiply 1 × 2 × 3 × 4 to get 24. That's what a factorial is. Just to be sure you understand this idea, please complete the first thirty factorial problems on page 140.*

David diligently followed the rules, got mostly right answers, and thought he "understood" factorials. However, if anyone had ever asked him to tell a story that involved a factorial, he would have been hard pressed to do so. Right answers in a

FIGURE I–1

textbook are not synonymous with understanding in the real world; unless learners have stories to tell about mathematical concepts, they have no understanding of those concepts.

Children's literature is a powerful way to incorporate stories into the teaching and learning of mathematics. The concept of factorial numbers is beautifully told in *Anno's Mysterious Multiplying Jar* (Anno 1983). The author invites readers into a mysterious jar that contains an ocean and two islands, with three mountains on each island, four castles on each mountain, and so on, up to a final ten jars in each of nine cupboards. The book's portrayal of the explosive power of a geometric progression is enhanced by arrays of dots later in the book that directly illustrate the cumulative effect of continuous multiplying. After reading and discussing this story with her students, Phyllis Whitin invited her seventh graders to tell their own factorial stories. Three girls wrote and illustrated an island adventure (see Figure I–1).

Every mathematical concept ought to be backed by hundreds of stories like Anno's and like Phyllis's seventh graders'. The meaning of mathematical concepts is naturally carried through the medium of story. Learners let go of rules and algorithms that don't make sense, but they hold on to stories. We know that students have been denied a story-centered curriculum when teachers complain that they need to spend a lot of time at the beginning of each school year reviewing because "the kids just seem to lose it over the summer"; we would argue that the children never had "it" to begin with. But if they'd had stories to carry with them, the meaning would have traveled along as well. Stories are the conduit for making and sharing meaning. "Making sense of an experience is thus to a vary great extent being able to construct a plausible story about it" (Wells 1986, p. 196).

A curriculum for storytelling

The teaching and learning of mathematics in today's schools will change dramatically if we view mathematics as a tool for telling stories. Learners will see mathematics as a consequence of social interaction; they will recognize it as a tool for telling and remembering, not reciting and memorizing. Frank Smith has said, "A story is a world that can be entered and explored" (1990, p. 63). Stories are natural invitations for learners to enter and explore the mathematics of their own lives and the lives of others. Harold Rosen urges educators "to look at the whole school curriculum from the point of view of its narrative possibilities. . . . Narrative must become a more accepted way of saying, writing, thinking, presenting. . . . Narrative should be allowed its proper place in the analysis of everything" (1987, p. 19). Gordon Wells also argues that schools need to foster a curriculum of storytelling in which "stories are woven into the tapestry of a child's inner representations" (1986, p. 196). Children need stories, with all their rich and supportive details, as the primary means for representing, constructing, and understanding mathematical ideas.

Dale Andersen witnessed the power of mathematical stories when she read *Tom Fox and the Apple Pie* (Watson 1972) to her eighth graders. Because she was afraid her students might think she was treating them inappropriately by reading them a book that seemed better suited for younger children, she told them she simply felt it was a good story and wanted them to listen and enjoy. As she read and turned the first page, a big, burly (and usually her most inattentive) student raised his hand and said, "Mrs. B, please hold that book a little higher. I can't see the pictures." She knew then that using the book was going to work.

In this story, Tom Fox, the youngest in a family of sixteen foxes, sneaks off to the country fair, buys an apple pie, and heads home to share it with the rest of the family. However, on the way, he imagines his mother slicing the pie into sixteen pieces and is concerned that the pieces will be so small that he won't taste the apple part at all! He decides that if he doesn't go into the house until eight of his brothers and sisters are out looking at the stars, the eight remaining foxes can eat the pie and the pieces will be much bigger. However, still concerned about the size of the pieces, he thinks how much bigger they would be if the pie were divided into fourths—or in half. In the end, of course, he eats the whole pie himself! Pictures throughout the story show the size of the pieces increasing or decreasing as Tom Fox contemplates the number of potential eaters. During the class discussion afterward, Amy commented, "I wish my teachers had read math books to me. That's the first time I've ever really understood why the smaller bottom number is worth more [*why 1/2 of a pie is larger than 1/8 of a pie, even through 8 is greater than 2 in whole numbers*]. Are there any more books that teach math? I learn better that way."

And so we say to Amy (and to you), "Yes, there are many more books out there that can help you understand mathematics. And we invite you to find them, and read them, and enjoy them. Because you're right—we all learn better that way."

About this book

Our previous book about mathematics and children's books, *Read Any Good Math Lately?* (Heinemann 1992), is organized around mathematical topics—place value, multiplication, geometry, and so on. Each chapter explores books on a given topic and gives some examples of how the books have been used in classrooms. This sequel is structured a little differently. Part 1, Children, Teachers, and Authors, is about the people who use mathematically oriented children's books and two of the authors who create them. The first three chapters tell a series of stories about how books have been used to explore mathematical concepts, how children's spontaneous reactions influence the way teachers use these books in their classrooms, and the role of mathematical conversation. In Chapter 4, children and teachers talk about how they see the role of literature in developing mathematical understanding. Then, in Chapter 5, Tana Hoban and David M. Schwartz discuss (separately) the origins of their ideas and what they are trying to accomplish in their mathematically oriented books for young readers.

Part 2, Books, Books, and More Books, focuses on the books themselves. Chapter 6 presents a number of books on two topics that we did not deal with in *Read Any Good Math Lately?*—the number system, and statistics and probability. Chapter 7 explores an issue that is generating increased interest and concern: multicultural themes and images in mathematical children's books. Chapter 8 invites our adult readers to develop their own knowledge of mathematics through reading; we describe a number of books that explore mathematics from a variety of angles appropriate to the nonspecialist adult reader. The final chapter, Chapter 9, is a series of mini-essays on the best of the new mathematical books for young readers that we have discovered in the years since we wrote *Read Any Good Math Lately?* It includes a bibliography of over three hundred newer books, arranged by category. The twenty-two books we like best are listed at the end of this introduction. These twenty-two, plus three books aimed at adults but suitable for use with children, make up a "Top Twenty- Five" for teachers who want a quick overview of the latest and best mathematically oriented children's books.

References

Anno, Mitsumasa. 1983. *Anno's mysterious multiplying jar.* New York: Philomel.

Hutchins, Pat. 1986. *The doorbell rang.* New York: Greenwillow.

McKissack, Patricia. 1992. *A million fish . . . more or less.* New York: Knopf.

Ray, Mary Lyn. 1992. *Pumpkins.* San Diego: Harcourt Brace Jovanovich.

Rosen, Harold. 1987. *Stories and meaning.* Sheffield, England: National Association for the Teaching of English.

———. 1992. The power of story. *Teachers Networking: The Whole Language Newsletter* 11(1):1,3,6.

Smith, Frank. 1990. *To think.* New York: Teachers College.

Spurr, Elizabeth. 1991. *The biggest birthday cake in the world.* San Diego: Harcourt Brace Jovanovich.

Watson, Clyde. 1972. *Tom Fox and the apple pie.* New York: Crowell.

Wells, Gordon. 1986. *The meaning makers.* Portsmouth, NH: Heinemann.

Wilkinson, Philip. 1993. *Amazing buildings.* New York: Dorling Kindersley.

Twenty-two of the best recent mathematical books for children

Clement, Rod. 1991. *Counting on Frank.* Milwaukee: Gareth Stevens.

Clements, Andrew. 1992. *Mother Earth's counting book.* Saxonville, MA: Picture Book Studio.

Cole, Alison. 1992. *Perspective.* Eyewitness Art. New York: Dorling Kindersley.

Edmonds, William. 1994. *Big book of time.* New York: Readers Digest Kids.

Fraser, Mary Ann. 1993. *Ten Mile Day and the building of the transcontinental railroad.* New York: Henry Holt.

Heinst, Marie. 1992. *My first number book.* New York: Dorling Kindersley.

Hoban, Tana. 1992. *Spirals, curves, fanshapes and lines.* New York: Greenwillow.

Hulme, Joy. 1991. *Sea squares.* New York: Hyperion.

Kitamura, Satashi. 1986. *When sheep cannot sleep: The counting book.* New York: Farrar, Straus & Giroux.

Maestro, Betsy. 1993. *The story of money.* New York: Clarion.

Marchon-Arnaud, Catherine. 1994. *A gallery of games.* New York: Ticknor & Fields.

McKissack, Patricia. 1992. *A million fish . . . more or less.* New York: Knopf.

McMillan, Bruce. 1991. *Eating fractions.* New York: Scholastic.

Norden, Beth B., and Lynette Ruschak. 1993. *Magnification.* New York: Lodestar.

Ockenga, Starr, and Eileen Doolittle. 1988. *World of wonders: A trip through numbers.* Boston: Houghton Mifflin.

Pinczes, Elinor J. 1993. *One hundred hungry ants.* Boston: Houghton Mifflin.

Ross, Catherine S. 1992. *Circles.* Toronto: Kids Can Press.

Salvadori, Mario. 1979. *Building: The fight against gravity.* New York: Atheneum.

Sandburg, Carl. [1933] 1993. *Arithmetic.* San Diego: Harcourt Brace Jovanovich.

Singer, Marilyn. 1991. *Nine o'clock lullaby.* New York: HarperCollins.

van Noorden, Djinn, ed. 1994. *The lifesize animal counting book.* New York: Dorling Kindersley.

Wise, William. 1993. *Ten sly piranhas: A counting story in reverse (A tale of wickedness—and worse!)* New York: Dial.

Three great books for adults

Holmes, Nigel. 1991. *Pictorial maps.* New York: Watson-Guptill.

Murphy, Pat. 1993. *By nature's design.* An Exploratorium Book. San Francisco: Chronicle.

Slocum, Jerry, and Jack Botermans. 1992. *New book of puzzles: 101 classic and modern puzzles to make and solve.* New York: W. H. Freeman.

Part One

Children, Teachers, and Authors

Thinking Mathematically

1

In *Beyond Numeracy* (1991), John Paulos describes a car ride he took into New York City, inviting the reader into a kind of mathematical stream of consciousness. As Paulos looks out his car window, he frames what he sees from a mathematical perspective. For instance, he uses the concepts of equivalence and inequality to determine whether the kindness exhibited by one motorist's helping another is greater than the aggravation caused by their interrupting the flow of traffic for everyone else. He uses the concept of probability to consider the likelihood of his becoming a famous writer or the chances that the cables of the bridge will snap as he drives across it. Thinking about concepts of time and distance, he devises a strategy for nabbing speeding motorists by stamping the time they enter and exit a toll road.

Children's literature, just like John Paulos's book for adults, can be a powerful demonstration of what it means to view the world from a mathematical perspective. Through books, children can appreciate mathematics as a way of thinking; the stories become tools for giving perspective to the observations and wonder they have about their world.

One of the best children's books to demonstrate this kind of mathematical musing is Rod Clement's *Counting on Frank* (1991). In this story a young boy, accompanied by his dog Frank, presents the reader with a series of interesting facts and comparisons. This bespectacled, serious-looking boy and his dog perform most of their calculations around the house: they draw a long line back and forth across a wall, over a lamp, and across Dad's body to show that the average ballpoint pen draws a line twenty-three hundred yards long before the ink runs out; they calculate that twenty-four Franks could fit into the boy's bedroom; they estimate it would take eleven hours and forty-five minutes to fill the entire bathroom with water if both the hot and cold faucets were running in the tub; and because the young boy dislikes peas, he estimates that if he had accidentally knocked fifteen peas off his plate every night for the last eight years, the peas would now be level with the tabletop! He knows that the gum tree in his yard grows about six and a half feet every year and therefore calculates, "If I had grown at that same speed,

I'd now be fifty-three feet tall!" He hypothesizes about the pesky mosquito that keeps him awake at night: "If it were four million times bigger, it wouldn't fit inside my ear, but I guess it would make more noise than a jumbo jet." He even speculates about the family's old toaster, which shoots the toast about three feet into the air: "It makes you think—if our toaster were as big as the house, it could endanger low-flying aircraft." These speculations nicely portray a mathematical view of the world. The young boy uses various mathematical concepts to frame things in his household: length, as he calculates the length of the line of a ballpoint pen; volume, as he calculates the number of dogs in the bedroom and peas in the dining room; capacity and time, as he calculates the amount of water that is needed to fill his bathroom; and ratio, as he calculates his own growth rate based on that of a tree in his backyard. These concepts are the bedrock of what it means to think mathematically. They are not facts, skills, or operations but underlying generalizations that can be realized in many different ways. "Mathematicians are interested more in general concepts than in specific calculations, seeking in fact to formulate rules that can apply to the widest possible range of problems" (Gardner 1983, p. 135). Although the young boy in this story does not travel far nor have the credentials of a college-educated mathematician like John Paulos, he still enjoys the opportunity to view his world from a mathematical perspective. Thinking mathematically is not reserved for a select few; it is a stance we can all take in observing and interpreting our daily living.

Another valuable aspect of *Counting on Frank* is the use of the word *if*. Throughout the story, the young boy asks readers to consider hypothetical situations:

> *"If I had accidentally knocked fifteen peas off my plate every night for the last eight years . . ."*
> *"If I had put on every piece of clothing in my closet . . ."*
> *"If I had grown at [six and a half feet per year] . . ."*
> *"If [a mosquito] were four million times bigger . . ."*
> *"If our toaster were as big as the house . . ."*

If allows us to break the bounds of what is and wonder about what might be. It allows us to change or even abandon the given parameters of a problem and entertain alternative scenarios.

Another book that emphasizes the word *if* is David M. Schwartz's *How Much Is a Million?* (1985). He imagines, "If one million kids climbed onto one another's shoulders, they would be . . ." or "If you wanted to count from one to one million . . ." or "If a goldfish bowl were big enough for a million goldfish . . ." and so on. During an interview (see Chapter 5), Schwartz commented that *if* was an important word for him even as a youngster. This ongoing speculation about the world is at the heart of mathematical thinking.

We now want to examine how teachers have used *Counting on Frank* as a framework to support their students' attempts to view the world from a mathematical perspective. Then, at the end of the chapter, we will explore how children's literature can help learners understand two familiar topics, animals and food, from a mathematical point of view.

that's a lot!
I think that it would take twintythousand pieces of soap to fill my dad's garage. Only when my dad's car and tools are out. Olso when my brother isn't using soap while he is taking a bath.

FIGURE 1–1

Children create their own stories

Second-grade teacher Terri Bingham read *Counting on Frank* to her students and invited them to write and illustrate their own calculations. Their work was later bound into a class book called *Counting on Frank, Part 2.*

Sean created an estimate that involved volume (see Figure 1–1): "I think that it would take twenty thousand pieces of soap to fill my dad's garage. Only when my dad's car and his tools are out. Also when my brother isn't using soap while he is taking a bath." Sean's dad had in fact built a large shed next to their house and had recently come home with four packs of soap. Sean used these two familiar events in his story. Although Sean's actual figure of twenty thousand was "just a guess," he did incorporate the concept of volume into a situation that made sense to him. It was his way of looking at his world from a mathematical perspective.

It is this kind of thinking that is advocated by the new curriculum and evaluation standards promulgated by the National Council of Teachers of Mathematics (1989). NCTM calls for learners "to be active participants in creating knowledge" (p. 15) and to have regular opportunities "to read, write and discuss ideas in which the use of the language of mathematics becomes natural" (p. 6). These second graders' stories underscore the notion that "everybody is a mathematician" and that

I don't like go
ing to bed. I
have to change my
under wear. It
wouldtake 3 books
to fill up my
dad's underwear.

FIGURE 1–2

If I were to take a
big peace of chalk and go
up and down the chalk
boardten times
threre would be no
more chalk left.

FIGURE 1–3

"doing mathematics is a common human activity" (p. 6). Writing these kinds of stories encourages learners "to value the mathematical enterprise, to develop mathematical habits of mind" (p. 5). One such habit is using the strategy of estimation across a variety of mathematical concepts. Sean and his classmates are learning that they can look at their world mathematically. It is this more global realization that underpins the mathematical literacy espoused by the NCTM standards.

Adam wrote an estimation story that also involved volume (see Figure 1–2): "I don't like going to bed. I have to change my underwear. It would take 3 books to fill up my dad's underwear." Just as the young boy in *Counting on Frank* lets us know that he dislikes eating peas, Adam shared one of his own dislikes. He even went home and tested his estimate and found that his dad's underwear held "3 ½ books, and the ½ was a small book." Another student, Sam, tried to describe exactly what volume measurement encompasses when he wrote, "My room is pretty big so I predict it would take 31 beds to fill, top to bottom and side to side in my room."

Anna was intrigued by the part of the story that discussed the length of a line from a ballpoint pen. She wrote her own estimation story using the concept of length (see Figure 1–3): "If I were to take a big piece of chalk and go up and down the chalkboard ten times there would be no more chalk left." Anna's mother is a teacher, and Anna was used to making designs on her mother's chalkboard after

FIGURE 1–4

If I were to whatch onehundred movies
it would take four months. My dad would go
crazybecausehe could not whatch his
favorite show.

school. She figured, "When I color in on my mom's chalkboard I use up about a half of a piece," so she thought her estimate of ten times was fairly close.

Carl used the concept of length to express his estimate about his savings account: "I calculate that if I take all my savings account out of the jar and spread it out it would take fifteen feet to do it." He said afterward, "I have a lot of money in my jar but I don't know how much fifteen feet is." Nevertheless, he created a unique comparison using concepts of money and length that he could test later.

Jennifer incorporated the concept of time in her estimate (see Figure 1–4): "If I were to watch one hundred movies it would take four months. My dad would go crazy because he could not watch his favorite show." Jennifer later explained her reasoning: "Well, I could probably only watch one or two a day 'cause we only have two TVs and dad watches one and my mom and sister watch the other. But when they cook supper I can go watch TV. That means in four months you could only see a hundred movies."

When Lynn Meekins read *Counting on Frank* to nine-year-old Blake, he found several pages particularly intriguing. As Frank and his owner try on all the clothes in the closet, Blake commented, "I wonder how long that would take in my closet. I'd have to start with the things that are almost too little and go on to the ones that are big and stretchy." Blake used the mathematical concept of time as a lens for viewing this story; he also used the strategy of ordering to structure putting on all his clothes.

As Linda read further, Blake responded to the image of dropping peas on the dining room floor: "I'd keep those peas, if I could get rid of brussel sprouts, tomatoes, and fat from beef!" Isn't this the concept of equivalence, trading one relatively appealing food for others that seem more distasteful?

As Linda finished the story, she asked Blake if there were any calculations he would like to make. He answered immediately. "Yeah. If I could tear down Mt. Everest, but keep a picture of it, and have the specs and the exact coordinates, I'd like to see how many cats you would have to stack up to build a mountain the same

FIGURE 1–5

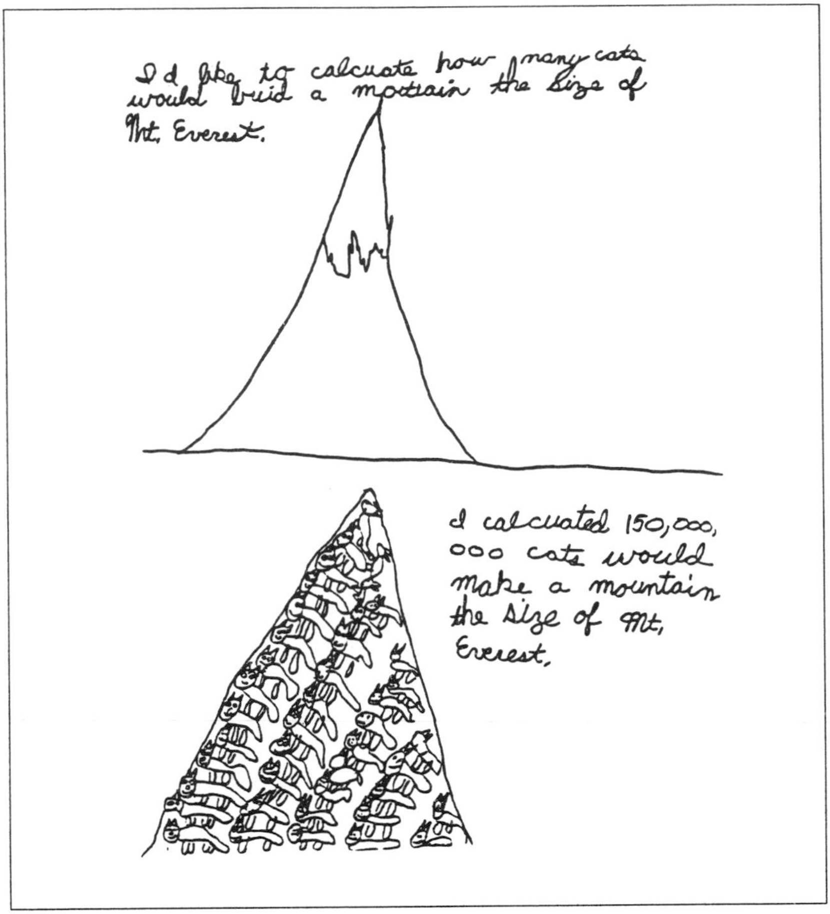

size. Of course, I'd have to think about the size of the cat." His own cat had recently given birth to five kittens, and this may have influenced the creation of this story. He said that if he could ever complete such a project, he would then sell the cats for a "considerable profit," reasoning that cats would make great souvenirs. When he had completed his drawing and written text (see Figure 1–5), he explained that his calculation was only an estimate because he did not have all the information he needed.

Lynn Turner read *Counting on Frank* to Emily, seven, and asked her if she would like to do some of her own calculating. She thought for awhile and then asked if she could use the telephone. She called her dad and asked him how many people could fit in their swimming pool. He said twelve, but Emily argued that twenty was a better estimate. When she hung up the phone she announced, "I'm going to calculate that fifty people can fit in our pool."

"But your dad said only twelve," reminded Lynn.

FIGURE 1–6

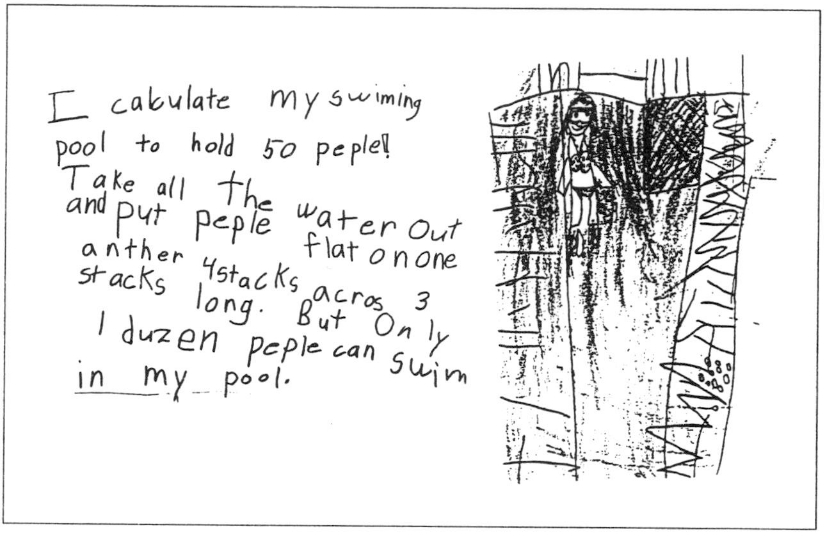
I calulate my swiming
pool to hold 50 peple!
Take all the water out
and put peple flat on one
anther 4stacks acros 3
stacks long. But Only
1 duzen peple can swim
in my pool.

"Oh, he means a dozen to swim, but did I say swim? First we have to take all the water out," she said. Emily wanted to calculate the number of horizontal bodies she could stack up in an empty swimming pool. She tried to calculate the volume by measuring off distances in Lynn's living room. She used paces to measure the width of the pool and said, "We could get about four stacks across." She stepped off the length of the pool by walking from the living room to the porch. Since she knew the pool was six feet deep, she was ready to begin her calculations. She started to stack the families into the pool, naming each one, and asking Lynn to keep track of the total. As she began with the first layer she ran into a problem: "I got a problem here with Uncle Billy's family. They're all too fat, so I'll just have to put Luke and Sissy with you and Mr. Ronald, since you don't have any children." Realizing that the members of Uncle Billy's family would stack up higher than thin people, she compensated by putting two of them with two smaller people. She kept using her hands to demonstrate the height of each stack; she also kept talking about each new person in the stack, visualizing his or her size and making adjustments when necessary to equalize the total height of this growing pile of bodies. Sometimes she left people out but always justified her decision, "I feel bad about leaving out your mother, but she does not live with you." She also justified the placement of other bodies: "The daddy must always go first because he is longer [*her dad is very tall*]. Then the mom is next, except for Aunt Dean. She must be on top because she is pregnant." Eventually Emily stacked up forty-eight bodies in the pool but wanted to reach fifty, since that was her original calculation. She decided to use Lynn's twin nephews "because they're just babies and wouldn't take up a lot of space." Her story (see Figure 1–6) summarizes these calculations.

When Linda Mathis read the book to eight-year-old Austin, he used the concept of equivalence in the context of cartoon characters (see Figure 1–7). He wrote, "I

FIGURE 1–7

FIGURE 1–8

calculate that there are not enough penguins in the world to overcome Batman," using an inequality to represent either the triumph of good over evil or Batman's superior strength.

When Mary Ann Elvington read *Counting on Frank* to nine-year-old William, he became intrigued with filling a room with dogs: "My dog's name is Spike. If I wanted to fill this room with Spikes, I'd get a lot of boxes, all the same size, and stack them all over the floor, all the way up to the ceiling."

"Why did you think of boxes?" asked Mary Ann.

"Well, it would be neater," he said, "and Spike wouldn't be so wiggly. The last box would be at the top, but near the door so I could get out!"

After Sandra Jones read this story, Brandon, ten, wanted to calculate the number of pianos that would fit in his living room. He had received a piano for Christmas and really enjoyed playing it. When Sandra asked him why he drew only forty-eight pianos instead of the fifty that he had actually calculated (see Figure 1–8), he replied, "I didn't want to draw them in front of the window, but two will fit in that place."

The calculations that children perform are often tied to their own personal interests. Brandon enjoyed pianos, Austin watched *Batman,* and Emily's family had a swimming pool. When teachers give children open-ended invitations to create their own stories, they give them the opportunity to connect literature to their own life. In this way children can not only frame a slice of their life in a mathematical perspective, they can also fashion it in a way that makes sense to them. Several other examples help demonstrate this point.

Debbie Franken read *Counting on Frank* to ten-year-old Brent, who was particularly interested in the number of Franks that could fit in the boy's bedroom. When Debbie asked him, "What does this book get you thinking about?" Brent thought for a minute and then responded, "Do you mean, what I would like to estimate? Well, I'd like to calculate how many soccer balls it would take to fill up my bedroom." Brent was thinking about soccer because the following week he was leaving for soccer camp; he was also interested in the concept of volume. He therefore put these two ideas together to create his own story. Since there wasn't a soccer ball at hand, Brent made an imaginary one with his hands and said, "My room is about the size of this one," looking at the den of Debbie's house. He then proceeded to measure the width of the room with the imaginary ball and calculated it to be about fifty soccer balls long. He decided to measure part of the perimeter rather than actually calculate the volume, and created a story to accompany his findings (see Figure 1–9). His familiarity with the size of a soccer ball gave him a handy reference for figuring out the problem he posed for himself.

Debbie Poston's third graders enjoyed hearing about Frank's owner. "He's sort of like a scientist because he was predicting all the time." They claimed that the word *calculate* is like the words *estimate* and *predict* and began to offer their own calculations as the story progressed. They too were intrigued by the number of Franks that would fit into the boy's bedroom and began to relate their own pets to this same situation. Naomi said, "I got a smaller dog than Frank but my bedroom is real big so I would need a lot more dogs to fill up my room." Naomi was noting

FIGURE 1–9

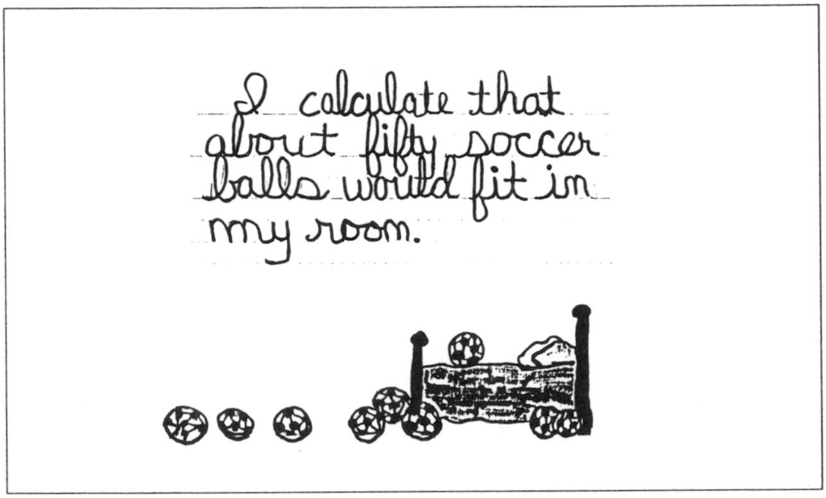

for her classmates the inverse relationship between the size of a measuring unit and the number of units that would cover a particular area. Her comment prompted others to make their own canine comparisons. Laricci said, "It would take only ten of my dogs to fill my room because I got five big dogs."

"You mean two apiece?" asked Josh.

"No, I said ten," replied Laricci.

"I know, but you have five dogs, so that would only be two of each," reasoned Josh.

"I think Josh is dividing," said Dawn. As the conversation continued, it became evident that Laricci really meant ten sets of his five dogs could fill his bedroom, or $10 \times 5 = 50$ dogs altogether. Debbie was impressed with the children's reasoning as they helped each other clarify their own calculations. She later wrote, "By this time I was really amazed because they were actually seeing these operations of division and multiplication that I had been trying to convey for weeks. They were just using them in their conversation like it was nothing!" Stories provide a meaningful context for children to use operations in a way that makes sense to them.

Determining more exact calculations

After listening to *Counting on Frank,* some students are intent on making exact calculations. When Fran Miller read this story to her fifth graders for the third time (on three different days), the children decided to create their own version of the book, *Counting on Fifth Grade.* Many created stories with exact calculations. For instance, John, an aspiring basketball player, was naturally attracted to the part of the story that describes Frank's owner's growing six and a half feet each year, the growth rate of a gum tree. John recognized the advantages of being tall and so created his own story of personal growth (see Figure 1–10): "If I started growing an inch a year and

If I started growing an inch a year and stopped when I was 100 years old I would be
12 feet and 5 inches.
Bulls

FIGURE 1–10

If California moved a half-inch away from the Mainland every year for 79 years it would be approxomately 39 1/2 inchaway from the Mainland.

FIGURE 1–11

FIGURE 1–12

FIGURE 1–13

FIGURE 1–14

stopped when I was 100 years old, I would be 12 feet and 5 inches." John calculated one inch of growth at birth and then one inch per year after that. Through his drawing he tried to show this proportionally.

Another student was interested in the earthquake that shook California and calculated the movement of land (see Figure 1–11): "If California moved a half inch away from the mainland every year for 79 years it would be approximately 39 ½ inches away from the mainland."

Jane Gore read *Counting on Frank* to Keli, twelve, who suggested her own ideas for calculating throughout the story. Keli illustrated three of her ideas and included them in a book entitled *Counting on Keli.* Her first calculation (see Figure 1–12) came from watching her little sister Elizabeth, who was three years old. While Jane and Keli were enjoying the story together, Elizabeth spent a lot of her time spinning around and around in a circle on the rug. Viewing this behavior from a mathematical perspective, Keli predicted that if Elizabeth kept going around in a circle with a circumference of two feet, she would probably get dizzy after twenty-five turns.

Since Keli lives near the sea and often goes to the beach, her second picture (see Figure 1–13) was an ocean scene. She wondered how many waves rolled onto the beach during her average stay at the ocean. She estimated that she spends about seven hours on the beach and decided that about twenty waves rolled in per minute. She used her calculator and found that 8,400 waves would roll in during her seven-hour stay.

Her last story involved clothes (see Figure 1–14). As Jane read the part of the story where Frank and his owner were wearing all the clothes in the closet, Keli pointed to the hat rack in Jane's house and remarked, "That reminds me of our hat rack." She said that her stepfather, Gary, was always bringing home different hats. She calculated that if Gary had brought home a hat every day of her life for the past twelve years, they would now have 4,380 hats.

Ginger Altman read *Counting on Frank* to her two children, Ryan, eleven, and Marianne, eight. When Ginger asked the children to create their own counting books, Marianne had several ideas to get herself started but Ryan didn't know what to do. Ginger suggested the topic of professional wrestling, since Ryan spent a lot of time reading about this "sport" in magazines and watching it on television. Ryan was intrigued, but he admitted, "I'm not very good at drawing wrestlers." However, when Ginger suggested that he use pictures from his wrestling magazines, Ryan eagerly went to work, knowing he could focus on the numbers and the calculations without worrying about his drawing ability. His calculations were a mix of exact answers and general estimates.

Some of the more exact ones ones were: "I know it will take nine wrestling cards to fill up the front cover of W.C.W. [*World Class Wrestling*] magazine." "I calculated that if you put Sting's weight 251 with Big Van Voder 445, you would get a total weight of 696 pounds." "I calculated that if you put an infant on one El Gigante their height would reach my bedroom ceiling. Because El Giganti is 7′ 7″ tall!"

Ryan made other calculations that were estimates: "I predict it will take fifteen wrestling rings to fill up my back yard." "Did you know I calculated that it would take about 70 W.C.W. posters to fill up my room?" "I think by the end of the month Paul E. Dangerously, who is a manager, would have used his telephone in one out of every five matches to knock out one of his wrestler's opponents." Ryan used the concepts of area, weight, length, time, and probability to discuss one of his favorite topics.

His sister Marianne enjoyed creating her own estimates about objects and events in her house (see Figure 1–15). She used the concept of volume to estimate the number of people in a television, dogs in a bedroom, radishes in the kitchen, and apples in the sink. Although some of her estimates may not be close approximations, the important point is that she is speculating about her world from a mathematical perspective; it is this playing around with mathematical scenarios that we as teachers must cherish and nurture.

Generating hypotheses and extending the data

Sometimes *Counting on Frank* has been a springboard for children to generate their own hypotheses about the world. Cheryl Poston read it to ten-year-old twins Erin and Rebecca, who were fascinated with the enlarged mosquito. They had recently visited the Smithsonian and had become very interested in the insect display. Perhaps it was this trip, along with the book, that helped nourish their hypothesis: "Mrs. Cheryl," said Rebecca, "you know insects have lots of eyes. If insects had a tear gland for every single eye, I wonder about that." They continued to wonder together. "If every single insect, you know there are millions and millions of them, had a tear gland for every single eye, you know every insect has lots of eyes, not just the part that we see and call our eyes, and they all started crying at the same time and shedding all those tears, what would happen? Would it be enough [water] to flood the earth?"

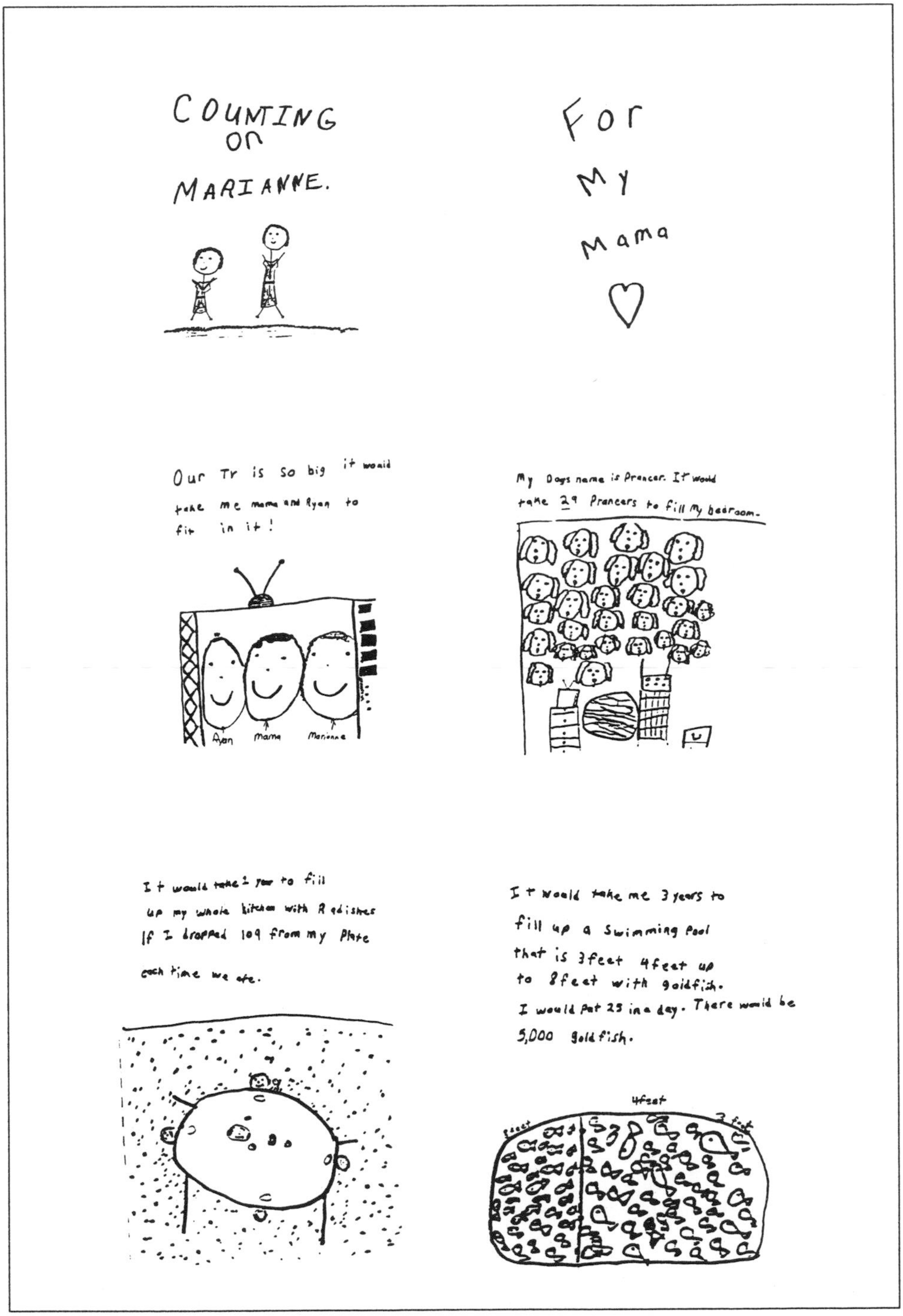
COUNTING on MARIANNE.
For My Mama
Our Tv is so big it would take me mama and Ryan to fit in it!
Ryan
mama
Marianne
My Dogs name is Prancer. It would take 29 Prancers to fill my bedroom.
It would take 1 year to fill up my whole kitchen with Radishes If I dropped 109 from my Plate each time we ate.
It would take me 3 years to fill up a Swimming Pool that is 3feet 4feet up to 8feet with goldfish.
I would Put 25 in a day. There would be 5,000 goldfish.
4feet
3 feet

FIGURE 1–15

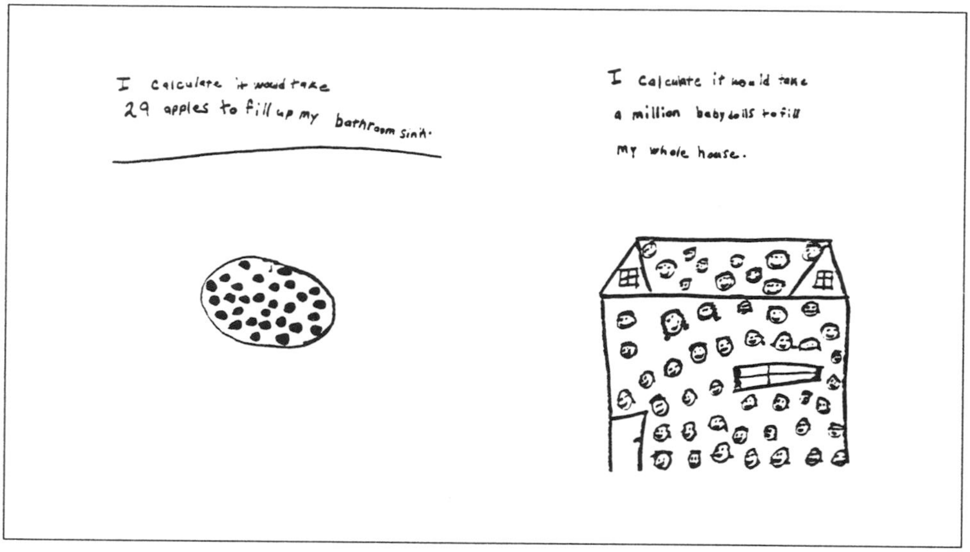
I calculate it woud take
29 apples to fill up my bathroom sink.
I calculate it would take
a million baby dolls to fill
my whole house.

FIGURE 1–15 *(CONTINUED)*

"I don't really know," replied Cheryl. "It probably would depend on several things."

"It would depend on if every eye cried one or lots of tears," they reasoned, "and how big each bug tear is. Do you think bug tears are salty? I guess that wouldn't really matter."

The twins used the important word *if* to hypothesize about a topic that was interesting to them. They used the mathematical concept of capacity to frame their wondering. This kind of ruminating needs to be a continual accompaniment to the rhythm of classroom life.

When Cathy Christman shared *Counting on Frank* with several children, Paul, nine, commented, "That boy was always writing and thinking 'bout facts." Hoping to extend this observation, Cathy responded, "Yes, that boy must have been very curious because he did a lot of writing and thinking about facts. You might want to draw a picture about some fact that you've been wondering about." Paul drew a picture of the earth with a long beard (see Figure 1–16) because he had wondered exactly how old the earth was. He knew the earth was very old, so he drew the beard and created a large number to convey his current thinking on the matter.

Sometimes children want to extend some of the calculations that are mentioned in *Counting on Frank*. For instance, when Angela Brown read the story to some seventh graders, they wanted to manipulate data themselves. Since Frank's owner hypothesized that he would be fifty-three feet tall if he had grown at the same rate as a gum tree (six and a half feet per year), the children wanted to determine his actual age. They divided 53 by 6.5, and found the owner to be about eight years old. They also wondered how many peas would actually accumulate on the floor if fifteen were dropped from the table each night for eight years. They reasoned:

FIGURE 1–16

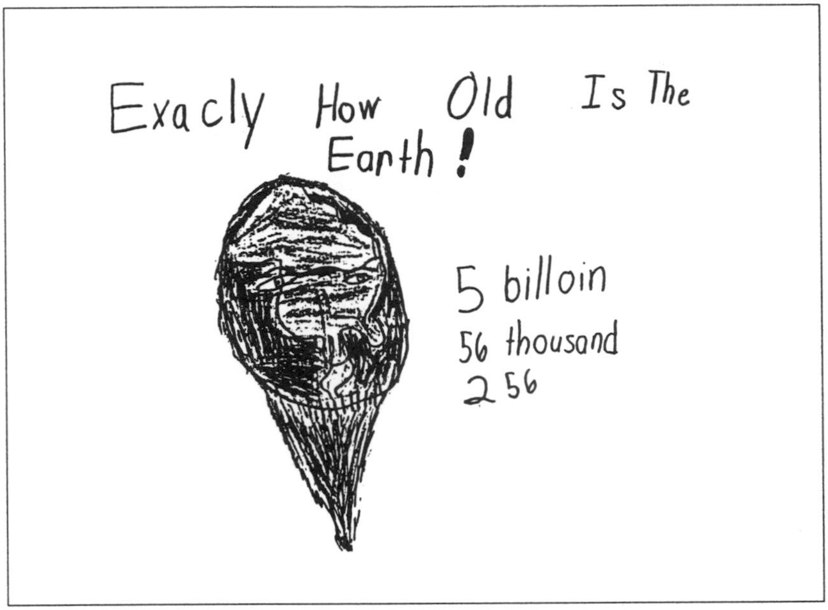

15 peas × 7 days = 105 peas per week
105 peas per week × 52 weeks = 5,460 peas per year
5,460 peas per year × 8 years = 43,680 peas in eight years

The children were intrigued by a line of ink 2,300 yards long and wondered how many inches and miles that would be. They reasoned:

2,300 yards × 36 inches = 82,800 inches long
2,300 yards × 3 feet = 6,900 feet
6,900 feet ÷ 5,280 feet in a mile = 1.3 miles

In these examples the children expressed the calculations of the book in another way and gained a different perspective on the data. They were using the concepts of quantity (the number of peas) and equivalence (other names for 2,300 yards) to extend the given data in new ways.

Children have occasionally challenged some of the data presented in the book. When Mary Ann Elvington read this story to nine-year-old William, he wanted to know how the mother knew that the dad's head was one-tenth of his whole body. He tried to solve his own problem by suggesting, "I'll draw one circle for his head, and I'll try to put that circle down ten times to cover his whole body." Observations like this can lead children to wonder if this same ratio is reflected in their own bodies, as well as the bodies of other children and adults.

When Susan Gray read the story to her daughter, fourteen-year-old Liz wanted to investigate the geometric configuration of 110 cans of dog food. After much figuring she claimed it was impossible to build a pyramid of 110 cans of dog food, and added consecutive numbers to prove her point:

*	1
* *	1 + 2 = 3
* * *	1 + 2 + 3 = 6
* * * *	1 + 2 + 3 + 4 = 10
* * * * *	1 + 2 + 3 + 4 + 5 = 15

Continuing this sequence of numbers, known as triangular numbers, one arrives at the following sums: 15 + 6 = 21, 21 + 7 = 28, 28 + 8 = 36, 36 + 9 = 45, 45 + 10 = 55, 55 + 11 = 66, 66 + 12 = 78, 78 + 13 = 91, 91 + 14 = 105, 105 + 15 = 120. Thus, 105 and 120 cans of dog food would build a pyramid, but not 110.

These kinds of investigations are healthy ones to pursue, because they are initiated by children and because they are built on a lingering skepticism about the validity of numbers. Skepticism is an important aspect of what it means to think mathematically. Mathematical thinkers know that numbers are human constructs that they can manipulate, revise, and debate. There is no human truth inherent in numbers as such; real meaning resides in the stories that surround mathematical calculations.

Mathematics and animals

Although *Counting on Frank* is a particularly good book for viewing the world from a mathematical perspective, there are hundreds of books that give children the opportunity to think about familiar topics from a mathematical point of view. Animals, for example, can be portrayed in various ways.

Bert Kitchen uses the concept of quantity in *Animal Numbers* (1987). In this beautifully illustrated book, readers are shown a typical number of offspring for certain animals: one joey for a kangaroo, two cygnets for swans, three baby squirrels, four woodpeckers, five green lizards, and so on; numbers beyond ten include fifteen piglets, twenty-five garter snakes, fifty sea horses, seventy-five leatherback turtles, and one hundred common frogs (although the female can lay up to 30,000 eggs at a time in clusters of frog spawn). This quantitative perspective on the animal kingdom may prompt readers to ask why there is such a range in the number of babies and lead them into interesting biological research.

Animal Numbers can also be a framework for viewing animals in terms of other mathematical concepts. David Whitin shared this story in Tim O'Keefe's second-grade classroom and invited the children to think of mathematical ways to view animals. The children wanted to keep track of the number of legs various creatures have. Over the course of several days they continued to add names to their list: two—people and birds; four—dogs, cats, horses, mice, elephants, frogs, and many more; five—starfish; six—most insects; eight—octopuses, spiders. The children noticed that there were examples for almost all the even numbers but not for most of the odd numbers, and they wondered why. Their question prompted them to talk about symmetry, balance, and self-protection. A mathematical stance toward animal life provided quantitative data that allowed them to ask new questions and gain new understanding.

Other books help children see animals in still other ways. Lois Ehlert looks at animals from a geometric perspective in *Color Farm* (1990) and *Color Zoo* (1989). In both books, Ehlert introduces three sets of animals through a series of bright colors and cutout shapes that overlap from one animal to the next. The circular head of a dog is transformed into the heart-shaped head of a goose with a turn of the page. This overlapping format encourages flipping back and forth to look at these transformations in more detail. Questions often arise: How did that rooster change into a duck? Which features were changed and which ones remained the same? These questions may encourage readers to do some further research: Is a duck's beak really longer than a rooster's? Ehlert uses basic geometric shapes to depict other parts of animals as well: a triangle for the beak of a chicken and the noses of a cat, a cow, and a pig; a quarter circle for the beak of a rooster; a triangle for the ears of a dog; a teardrop for the ears of a sheep. Again, children might want to do some research on their own to see if they agree with these geometric comparisons. As children look more closely at the shapes of animals, they become aware of the concepts of length, angle, and area. This geometric perspective allows them to pose a different set of questions about animals than the ones prompted by a quantitative perspective and increases their understanding of the animal world.

Two other books that do an excellent job of enlarging this geometric perspective are *What Neat Feet!* (1991) and *Breathtaking Noses* (1992), by Hana Machotka.

In *What Neat Feet!* Machotka uses color photographs and an informative text to describe how the shapes of animals' feet and noses enable them to survive in their environment. Readers learn that feet come in various sizes and shapes, such as flippers, paws, or hooves, and that their shape is specially designed to meet the natural conditions in which the animal lives. The webbed foot of a swan enables it to walk easily over a soft riverbank without getting stuck in the mud, acts as a powerful propeller in the water, and resembles a pair of water skis when the swan lands on water. The large feet and soft pads of a rabbit act like shock absorbers to soften its landing. The split hoof of a goat allows it to grip rocks tightly, so that it can climb the highest, steepest mountains where few predators dare to go. The flat, round foot of an elephant acts like a cushion: it expands under the weight of the elephant and gets smaller again when the elephant lifts its foot, thus preventing the foot from getting stuck in the mud when the elephant goes to the water hole for a drink or a bath.

Machotka takes this same perspective in *Breathtaking Noses*. The hard, flat nose of a pig not only gives the pig an excellent sense of smell but its resemblance to a shovel makes it useful for rooting out tasty morsels in the dirt. The large nose of a dog is a million times more sensitive to smell than human noses; dogs can follow a person or animal over long distances even though the trail may be old or covered. The muscles around a camel's nostrils close to protect it from blowing sand and dust. The camel's upper lip is split so it can collect moisture from its own breath, thereby helping it preserve water and go without drinking for about two weeks.

All these books provide fascinating details about animals and may be good starting places for readers to investigate the shape and size of other animal features. While Ehlert's books provide a more aesthetic comparison of animal shapes, Machotka's books give a more functional look at shape and size.

Another way to look at animals is in terms of how much they weigh. Roald Dahl uses the concepts of weight and equivalence to frame his humorous novel *Esio Trot* (1990). Mr. Hoppy is a shy, lonely man who lives in a tall apartment complex and whose love for his flowers is surpassed only by his love for the woman who lives directly below him, Miss Silver. However, Miss Silver is too busy to give Mr. Hoppy any attention, for she is consumed by her love for Alfie, her pet tortoise. Mr. Hoppy finally devises a plan to win her hand, a plan that involves a mysterious riddle, a large number of tortoises, and a jury-rigged tortoise snatcher. Since Miss Silver is distraught about Alfie's slow growth (three ounces in eleven years), Mr. Hoppy assures her that he can guarantee Alfie's growth if she will only whisper "Esio trot" to the tortoise three times a day (*esio trot* is *tortoise* spelled backward). Mr. Hoppy then visits several pet shops, buying a large collection of tortoises that have the same markings as Alfie but weigh more than he does, ranging from slightly more than Alfie's thirteen ounces to a great deal more. Hastily, Mr. Hoppy combines a long pole with some metal claws and wires to create his most necessary "tortoise catcher." While Miss Silver is at work one afternoon, Mr. Hoppy leans over his balcony and uses his pole catcher to replace Alfie with a slightly larger tortoise. Mr. Hoppy continues this clandestine tortoise exchange every day for eight weeks, each time substituting a tortoise that weighs two ounces more than the previous one. The unsuspecting Miss Silver is delighted with the results; in fact, "Alfie" grows so much that he can no longer fit into his tortoise house. But the clever Mr. Hoppy merely gives Miss Silver another backward message to recite, and within a few weeks "Alfie" has grown just small enough to fit into his house again! As the story ends, Mr. Hoppy and Miss Silver are happily married and the original Alfie finds a nice home with another loving owner.

This story certainly invites children to do some weighing in the classroom. Students might use a balance scale to make some general comparisons between objects, remembering some of the comparisons that were used in the story, such as Alfie's weight of thirteen ounces being close to the weight of a grapefruit, or two ounces being less than the weight of a smallish hen's egg. Teachers might also use this story to suggest that students weigh their own classroom pets—tortoises, guinea pigs, hamsters, and so on. Do the students notice any pattern over time? They might compare their results with the two-ounce increments that Mr. Hoppy devised over the course of eight weeks.

In *Big Old Bones* (1989), Carol Carrick uses proportion to give children another perspective about dinosaurs and help them learn how archaeologists use this concept in their work. Professor Potts discovers some unusual bones on his trip out West and brings them back to his laboratory for further study. He finds no mention of bones like these in any of his textbooks and so tries to put the bones together in various ways. In his first attempt the head looks too big for the body, and besides, there are too many bones left over; in his second attempt the head looks more proportionate but the front legs are too small for the size of the body; in his third attempt the neck is so long he has to build a bigger laboratory (he concludes that "an animal this size could never walk on earth"). In a brief addendum to the book, Carrick describes a few of the many blunders that archaeologists have made in putting together dinosaur bones. It is easy to make mistakes, since sets of bones are often incomplete and bones of many animals are often mixed together. A head was once placed on the wrong end of a dinosaur, and a well-known brontosaurus skeleton contained the skull of another kind of dinosaur (scientists did not correct this mistake until 1979!).

These are just some of the many books that view animals from a mathematical perspective. The concepts they explore are lenses that allow us to think about animals in varied ways. Each concept broadens our understanding and prompts new questions. Multifaceted perspectives are at the center of mathematical thinking. Through them we see that mathematics is not a sea of symbols to memorize or rules to follow but a stance for expressing insights and exploring new meanings. Children's literature can help demonstrate to children that mathematics is a way of thinking. Stories preserve the wholeness of an event; mathematics becomes not a fragmented and disjointed experience on the isolated pages of a workbook but an integrated tool for framing the stories we want to tell.

Mathematics and food

Food is a popular topic of conversation among students, and books can help them view food from a mathematical perspective. Bruce McMillan uses food to explore the concept of equivalence in *Eating Fractions* (1991). In a series of large color photographs, two children are shown preparing and then dividing various foods. They eat halves of bananas and ears of corn; thirds of rolls and a gelatin pear salad; and fourths of a pizza and strawberry pie. (The back of the book includes all the recipes.) An interesting question that students might pursue is how the two children can share three thirds. One of the photographs shows the young girl, with an impish grin on her face, holding two thirds of the roll while her friend holds only one third. Discussing how the extra one third could be shared could lead to exploring odd and even numbers as well as to understanding the multiplication of fractions (i.e., $\frac{1}{2}$ of $\frac{1}{3}$ is $\frac{1}{6}$ of the whole roll).

Elizabeth Spurr uses concepts of quantity, volume, and area in *The Biggest Birthday Cake in the World* (1991). In this story the richest man in the world was also (of course) the fattest man in the world. He lived in the biggest house in the world, all alone except for one hundred cooks and three vice presidents. Four weeks before his fortieth birthday he instructs his cooks and vice presidents to bake him the biggest birthday cake in the world. Large quantities of ingredients are needed for this monumental (it is also described as *colossal, prodigious,* and *gargantuan*) effort: 40,000 eggs, 31,500 pounds of flour, 12,000 pounds of sugar, 7,000 pounds of cocoa, and 2,500 gallons of milk. Readers get a feel for the concept of volume as workers bake parts of the cake in huge ovens; they grasp the magnitude of this cake even better when it is assembled on a huge linen napkin that covers a seven-acre area. Children might enjoy looking up cake records and other interesting food firsts in the *Guinness Book of World Records.* They might also use the concept of proportion to test whether the ingredient amounts listed in the story are feasible.

William Jaspersohn uses the concepts of quantity, volume, average, weight, and rate (quantity/time) to tell the true story of Famous Amos Chocolate Chip Cookies in his book *Cookies* (1993). Through a series of black-and-white photographs, readers watch as the cookies are prepared—from mixing the batter to delivering the finished product to 200,000 stores throughout the nation. Statistics reveal the magnitude of this large operation: on average, Famous Amos uses over fifteen tons of flour a week in its cookies; a factory in Augusta, Georgia, produces one million chocolate chip cookies in a day; two large mixers, capable of stirring one thousand pounds of dough at a time, mix the cookie dough; fifty sealed bags of cookies roll off the assembly line every minute; and each truck carries away over 300,000 cookies, enough to provide dessert and snacks to a small city. Children might explore how long 300,000 cookies would feed the people in their community or how long it would take to produce enough bags of cookies to feed all the students in their school.

The authors of these three books use a variety of concepts to help readers understand the problem of partitioning food (equivalence) and the decisions involved in baking large quantities of food (volume, proportion, quantity).

Fostering mathematical thinking

Stories provide an important avenue for helping children understand that mathematics is a tool for helping us live, learn, and explore. Stories demonstrate what it means to wonder mathematically, whether calculating the distance covered by ink from a pen, speculating about the number of offspring of an Irish setter, or questioning why the a camel's upper lip is split. Mathematics is an integral and natural part of the good stories we've discussed in this chapter, because the story came first, not the mathematics. Sometimes teachers complain that in planning theme units they can integrate everything except mathematics. Somehow mathematics doesn't seem to fit in, as if it were some foreign or artificial substance that doesn't mix well with the others. But if we trust our belief that mathematics is a tool for giving us perspective, then it will arise naturally from the stories we tell and the questions we ask about those stories. In children's literature, children see mathematics operating in an authentic context. They see mathematics not as a contrived experience but as a purposeful tool for writing and understanding their own stories. Embedding mathematical thinking in a meaningful context supports understanding.

References

Carrick, Carol. 1989. *Big old bones: A dinosaur tale.* New York: Clarion.

Clement, Rod. 1991. *Counting on Frank.* Milwaukee: Gareth Stevens.

Dahl, Roald. 1990. *Esio trot.* New York: Viking.

Ehlert, Lois. 1989. *Color zoo.* New York: J. B. Lippincott.

———. 1990. *Color farm.* New York: J. B. Lippincott.

Gardner, Howard. 1983. *Frames of mind.* New York: Basic Books.

Jaspersohn, William. 1993. *Cookies.* New York: Macmillan.

Kitchen, Bert. 1987. *Animal numbers.* New York: Dial.

Machotka, Hana. 1991. *What neat feet!* New York: Morrow.

———. 1992. *Breathtaking noses.* New York: Morrow.

McMillan, Bruce. 1991. *Eating fractions.* New York: Scholastic.

National Council of Teachers of Mathematics. 1989. *Curriculum and evaluation standards for school mathematics.* Reston, VA: National Council of Teachers of Mathematics.

Paulos, John. 1991. *Beyond numeracy.* New York: Knopf.

Schwartz, David M. 1985. *How much is a million?* New York: Lothrop, Lee & Shepard.

Spurr, Elizabeth. 1991. *The biggest birthday cake in the world.* San Diego: Harcourt Brace Jovanovich.

Following Children's Leads 2

Sharing literature books with children often leads to interesting mathematical investigations, especially when the catalyst for these explorations comes from the children; good teachers listen to their students' comments and questions. When teachers follow their students' leads, children develop a sense of ownership of the exploration and a responsibility for and commitment to carrying it out; they learn that the personal connections they make with stories are valued and therefore view themselves as trusted decision makers and problem solvers; and they see that raising questions, running risks, and sharing anomalies are a legitimate and essential part of the learning process. All these benefits contribute to the development of empowered learners who know their voices make a difference in building a collaborative community of mathematical explorers.

Teachers play a key role in fostering the development of these investigations. This chapter discusses some of the strategies that good teachers use to encourage children's personal explorations:

1. They cultivate the art of problem posing.
2. They share books that invite personal investigations.
3. They capitalize on children's skepticism and doubt.
4. They invite personal connections to stories.
5. They share books that relate to children's interests.
6. They offer open-ended choices for responding to stories.
7. They contribute their own personal connections to the stories.
8. They share books that present a mathematical challenge.

We will discuss each of these strategies and then highlight one or more classroom scenarios in which the strategy is used.

The strategies are not, of course, mutually exclusive. It is also important to remember that these particular responses did not necessarily occur after the first reading: in some cases the children said very little after hearing the story for the first time. However, the teachers could often tell by children's expressions or brief comments that the story was intriguing and would read the story several more times, either that day or another day. Just as adults see good movies several times and notice new things in them each time, children frequently make interesting observations and personal connections after a second or third reading. It is difficult to attend to all the features of a story at one time. Multiple readings give children time to hear the rhyme and rhythm of the language, note the relationship between text and illustration, analyze a character's motives, evaluate a major decision, and so on. Fruitful discussions sometimes need time to develop.

All the stories discussed in this chapter are picture books, and teachers provide plenty of wait time between the turning of each page—not so long as to disrupt the flow of the story, but long enough for children to observe more closely and to comment on what they see or expect to happen. These comments are often good starting places for conversation after the story is over.

The teachers featured in this chapter frequently ask open-ended questions to generate discussions: Who would like to say something about this story? What did you think about this story? What did this story make you wonder about? The intent of these kinds of questions is to encourage diverse responses; good teachers know that multiple interpretations enrich and extend everyone's personal interpretations.

It is important to keep these strategies in mind. Otherwise, it may seem that merely reading these kinds of books will automatically generate brilliant and insightful discussions. This is certainly not the case, and the teachers in this chapter would be the first to admit it. In fact, they have all read books they thought their students would really enjoy and been surprised to find very little response. Time, patience, and artful questioning by teachers are useful groundwork for fostering classroom investigations.

Cultivating the art of problem posing

Stephen Brown and Marion Walter (1990) describe the underlying belief that supports the strategy of problem posing:

> *There is an underlying attitude towards "coming to know" something that we would like to encourage. Coming to know something is not a "spectator sport," though standard textbooks, especially in mathematics, and standard modes of instruction may give that impression. To say, rather, that coming to know something is a participant sport is to commit ourselves to a point of view requiring that we operate on and even modify the things we are trying to understand.*

Their strategy consists of describing and modifying characteristics of a given problem or situation. They argue that these modifications open up "new vistas" in the way we think about common situations; data seem to take on a life of their own, since "every particular has a world within it" (p. 23). Let's look at how this strategy is played out in the classroom.

David Whitin and fifth-grade teacher Robin Cox shared *Gator Pie* (Mathews 1979) with Robin's students. Two alligators, Alice and Alvin, intend to share a pie equally. Then other alligators hear about the dessert and clamor for a piece. As each new set of alligators arrives, the size of each potential piece becomes smaller and smaller. Finally, one hundred alligators are each demanding a piece of pie, and an argument erupts over the size of the pieces ("Hey, your piece is bigger than my piece"). A free-for-all ensues, and when the dust finally clears only Alvin and Alice remain. They divide the pie between them as they first intended.

After reading the story to the children, David and Robin asked them to list some attributes of the story. The children said that there was only one pie; all the alligators wanted the same-size piece; the gators never ate before a new gator arrived; they didn't care what kind of pie it was; and so on. David and Robin then asked, "How could you modify or extend some of these attributes to create a different kind of story?" All the attributes and possible variations the students suggested are listed in Figure 2–1.

David and Robin then invited the children to create their own story by modifying whatever characteristics seemed most interesting to them. Tennille and Latoya were particularly interested in the size of the pieces; they felt that people of different ages would eat different-size pieces. So they wrote a story entitled *The Family Pies*. The characters included a grandmother, a grandfather, a mom, a dad, three boys, and four girls. The ages of the children—an important piece of information to know when partitioning the pie—ranged from two to twenty. All these characters must figure out a way to split the two large apple pies and the one tiny pie that Grandmother has baked. Tennille and Latoya used age as the criterion. Grandmother and Grandfather each get one half of one of the large pies. Since the children's parents are the next oldest, they share one half of a large pie (one fourth of a pie for each). Fourths are divided into eighths, and so on, until all the pies are eaten. The full story appears in Figure 2–2.

This story reflects Tennille and Latoya's understanding of the concept of equivalent fractions and of the process of multiplying fractions ($\frac{1}{2}$ of 1 = $\frac{1}{2}$, $\frac{1}{2}$ of $\frac{1}{4}$ = $\frac{1}{8}$). Robin also noted that the girls spent a long time making sure their illustrations were consistent with their written text. These two students decided which variables of the original story were most interesting to modify and then challenged themselves to create their own story. They also coordinated the systems of art and written narrative to make sure their story was consistent.

Third-grade teacher Christie Forrest employed this same strategy with another book, *Dollars and Cents for Harriet* (Maestro & Maestro 1988). Harriet needs five dollars to buy a kite and performs several different jobs to earn the money. Each time she is paid in common one-dollar equivalents: one hundred pennies, twenty nickels, ten dimes, four quarters, and two fifty-cent pieces. After Christie shared this story, she asked the class to list attributes, or "known facts." The children made these observations: 1) Harriet needed five dollars; 2) she was trying to buy a kite; 3) she had four jobs; 4) she started with one hundred pennies; 5) she got twenty nickels; 6) she got ten dimes; 7) she got four quarters; 8) she got two half-dollars.

FIGURE 2–1 ***Problem Posing Attributes and Modifications***

Attributes of Gator Pie	Possible Variations
There were 2 alligators. Their names were Alvin and Alice.	What if there were more than 2?
They used pie as the food.	What if they ate something else?
There was 1 pie.	What if there were lots of pies?
More alligators kept coming.	What if some came, but then went away?
They all liked the pie.	What if some didn't like the pie?
They never cut it before the others arrived.	What if they had already cut it?
They hold off eating the pie, as more kept arriving.	What if they started eating it sooner?
There were 100 alligators at the end.	What if there were a different number?
The fractions always had 1 on the top: $1/2$, $1/4$, $1/8$	What if the fractions were different?
It's like *The Doorbell Rang*. Groups of people kept coming.	What if groups kept leaving?
The alligators keep getting bossier.	
They were greedy and hasty.	What if they tried to share?
They came from the swamp.	
They all seemed to know about the pie as they arrived.	
They all wanted the same size piece.	What if older ones got bigger pieces?
They didn't care what flavor the pie was.	What if there were different kinds of pies?
They didn't guess the pie was chocolate marshmallow.	
They didn't ask for a piece, they just demanded it; they had no manners.	
The pie in the story looked larger than normal.	

Christie and the children then discussed the consequences of changing some of these problem characteristics.

CHRISTIE: What if we were to change this part about Harriet needing five dollars?
SHANNA: We could say that she needed seven dollars.
CHRISTIE: How would that change the rest of the story?

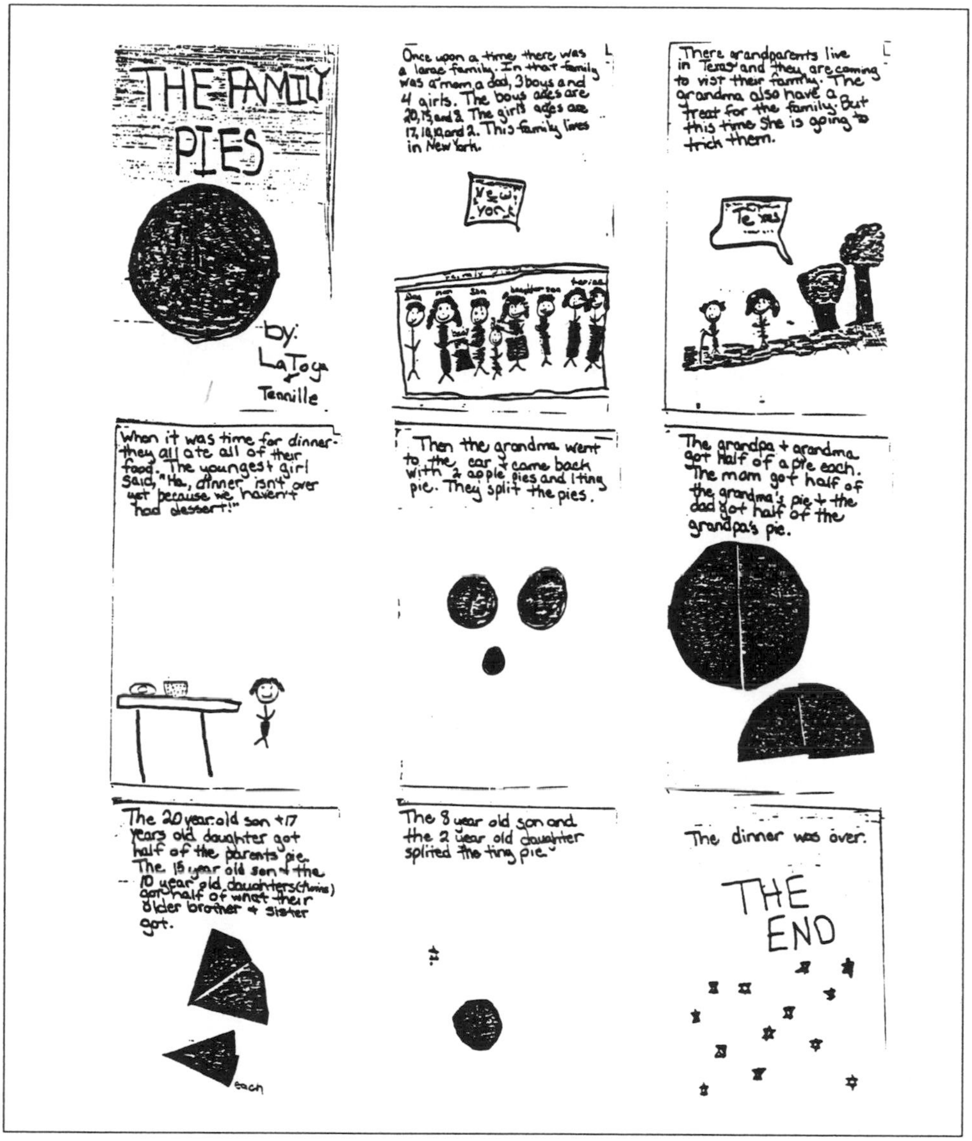

FIGURE 2–2

Cleve: Well, Harriet would have to get more money.
Christie: How could we change the story to do that?
Cleve: Keep all the same jobs and money in the book already, and then she could get another job and get a dollar bill and then get another job and get five dimes and . . . uh . . . ten nickels [*combining two different coins to make one dollar*].
Ben: She could get a dollar bill from the next job, but then get a silver dollar for the last job.
Christie: Let's look at the next attribute, buying a kite. How could we change that?

LIZZY: She could want a bike instead.
CHRISTIE: How might that new attribute change the rest of the story?
CLEVE: It costs more for a bike!
BILL: Yeah, the book would have to be a lot longer too, if it showed her doing all the jobs to get something like fifty dollars instead of only five dollars.
CHRISTIE: How might she earn fifty dollars?
CLEVE: She could work for fifty days and get one dollar a day.
RYAN: Or how about if she cleaned up in the whole inside of the house and the whole outside of the house and the whole yard and everything. I bet she would get fifty dollars for it.
CHRISTIE: Those are all good answers. Let's look at the next characteristic, of Harriet having four jobs. How might we change this?
BILL: Instead of four jobs she could only have two jobs.
CHRISTIE: How might this change the rest of the story?
RYAN: Well, she got a dollar from each job in the story. So that's four dollars for four jobs. If she only had two jobs and needed four dollars, she would have to get two dollars from each job to equal up to four dollars.
CLEVE: Well, she could get two dollars and fifty cents from one job and a dollar fifty from the second job.
SHANNA: Or three dollars from one job and a dollar from the next job.
CHRISTIE: All your answers make good sense. Who would like to change the next attribute?
SHANNA: Let's change that she had a hundred pennies to start with to she had five hundred pennies.
CHRISTIE: How much is five hundred pennies worth?
ALL: Five dollars!
RYAN: It would be done already!
BILL: She could go buy her kite without working! Or she could work anyway and buy something else.
CLEVE: What if she had only fifty pennies in her bank?
CECELIA: Well, she'd need four dollars and fifty cents. She could keep the same jobs she already had in the book and add cleaning one room for fifty cents.
SHANNA: Or she could have just two jobs [*modifying another attribute*] and get two dollars from one job and get two dollars and fifty cents from the second job.

As the discussion continued, the children began to brainstorm more and more changes in the given attributes. When they reached the final attribute of two half-dollars they suggested a whole range of possibilities.

RYAN: Let's change it so she only gets one half-dollar. Then she'd need fifty cents more.
CECELIA: That's easy. Get two more quarters from the giraffe in the story.
CHRISTIE: Can anyone think of another possible solution?
BILL: How about adding five more dimes to the job where she got ten dimes. She'd get fifteen dimes instead of ten.
CLEVE: I know! She could start with one hundred and fifty pennies instead of just one hundred!

BILL: Let's change it from getting two or one half-dollars to not getting any.

SMITH: Then she would only have three dollars instead of four dollars, so she would have to earn an extra dollar somewhere.

SHANNA: Like getting six quarters instead of only four and starting with one hundred and fifty pennies instead of one hundred.

MEAGAN: She could also get twenty dimes instead of ten.

CLEVE: Or how about one dollar more in nickels. That would be twenty more nickels, plus the twenty she already got, so she would get forty nickels!

CLEVE: [*going back to the first attribute, Harriet making five dollars*] Since we changed it and went up to seven dollars, can we change it so that she needs only two dollars?

CHRISTIE: Sure. How would she earn only two dollars?

BILL: By going to two jobs and getting one dollar for each job.

CLEVE: One job could give her two half-dollars and another job could give her twenty nickels.

SHANNA: [*doing some figuring on paper before sharing her answer*] How about three dimes, two quarters, and four nickels from a job and three quarters, two dimes, and a nickel from another job.

SMITH: She could also just do one big job and get all the two dollars at one time. Like someone could give her eight quarters.

CLEVE: What if someone gave her all the two dollars in pennies! That would be two hundred pennies!

This conversation captures the spirit of problem posing. Children were having fun playing around with these variables. Since Christie kept the conversation open by encouraging multiple solutions, everyone was challenged and willing to contribute ideas. As the conversation developed, children changed the variables on their own and then pursued together the consequences of those changes. They were not afraid to hypothesize, use the all-important *if* word, and imagine alternative scenarios. As Christie reflected on this experience she saw the benefits of promoting this problem-posing strategy:

> *I was glad that they observed the potential of continually changing the story and posing new problems to solve. I was quite impressed with my students' abilities to engage in problem posing. They seemed to enjoy changing the story and producing their own "new story" based on their changes. It gave them a chance to feel in control, as if they were the writers. It also gave them an opportunity to share and practice their concept of money. Throughout their revisions, I saw a great many calculations, figuring and counting, on paper as well as mentally. I feel it was a wonderful creative learning experience. Students were their own problem producers as well as problem solvers.*

Sharing books that invite personal investigations

Some books seem to invite hands-on investigations. For instance, when teachers read either *The Button Box* (Reid 1990) or "The Lost Button" (Lobel 1970), they need to have a jar of buttons handy because children invariably clamor for their own set of buttons to classify. Or if teachers read *Ed Emberley's Picture Pie: A Circle Drawing Book* (Emberley 1984), they need to have a ready supply of circles, scissors, and glue so children can do their own exploring with circular areas. And they will need mirrors after reading Marion Walter's books—*The Magic Mirror Book* (1971) or *The Mirror Puzzle Book* (1978)—so that children can conduct symmetry investigations.

Only Six More Days (Russo 1988b) also invites an immediate response from children. As the story begins, Ben looks at a calendar and sees there are only six more days until his fifth birthday. When he announces there are only five more days, he finds out all his friends can come to his party. He assembles all his party favors when there are only four more days, and so on. All the while his older sister Milly is being very disagreeable. She finally celebrates Ben's birthday without any more derogatory remarks when she realizes that there are only forty-seven more days until her birthday!

When second-grade teacher Betty Dixon read this story to her children, one of her students asked (as they always do!), "How long is it till *my* birthday?" The other children were also interested in their birthdays, so Betty distributed calendars to each group of four children and had them calculate the number of days. Their results were:

Shantanna	215
Tiffany	312
Antonio	158
Shawn	349
Keionda	352
Tarvan	56
Dadrin	110
Cassandra	162
Stephanie	175
Lakenya	233
Trevoris	190
Sherea	184
Stacey	190
Terance	180
Rasheeda	223
James	180

Each group then figured out which student had the next birthday, and which one had the longest wait. Even though James and Terance had the same birthday, when they counted the days on the calendar they were amazed to find that their answers were the same. Stacey and Trevoris found their answers to be the same, and then realized why. After the class had examined the data from all the groups, they found that Tarvan had the next birthday and poor Keionda had the longest wait—352 days! Although she was not thrilled about the long wait, she said she was still enjoying the new bike she had received for her last birthday, only thirteen days before. Toward the end of the discussion, Betty asked the children if there were other questions they wanted to pursue. Many were eager to suggest other problems:

> "How long is it until our parents' birthdays?"
> "How long is it until my dog's birthday?"
> "How many more days until Father's Day?"
> "How many more days until Mother's Day?"
> "How many more days until Earth Day?"

Antonio was particularly interested in this last question because the class had been making special shirts to wear for Earth Day. Another child asked, "How long until summer vacation?" Rasheeda wanted to figure out that answer but asked, "Do you mean Saturday and Sunday too?" Betty let the children decide; they agreed not to count Saturday and Sunday because otherwise summer would seem too far away! Another group decided to calculate the number of days until May Day, a favorite school celebration, and figured the answer both ways, counting weekends and not counting weekends. Betty wrote afterward, "I was very excited when they came up with this idea. The cooperative effort of all the students really helped a great deal. Once we got started it seemed to just keep on going."

Second-grade teacher Dori Gilbert discusses the calendar with her students every morning. One morning in September one of her students commented, "Hey, in nine more days it's my birthday!" Dori capitalized on this comment by reading *Only Six More Days* to her students the next day. As she finished the story, she found that her students too wanted to figure out the number of days until their birthdays. She asked them to go home that night and work with their parents to find the answer. Some of their results are shown in Figure 2–3. The children each wrote down their number on a class graph, along with a picture of a birthday celebration. Examining the graph, they made a variety of interpretations:

> "You can tell the month somebody's birthday is in."
> "You can tell how many birthdays in December."
> "You can see if someone's birthday has passed."
> "You can see how many people have birthdays in each month."
> "You can count the other way and see how many days ago was your birthday."
> "You can tell whose birthday is next."

Another story about time that invites immediate exploration is *The Stopwatch* (Lloyd 1986). Tom receives a stopwatch as a present from his grandmother and he runs off to time all kinds of activities: holding his breath, taking a bath, eating his

FIGURE 2–3

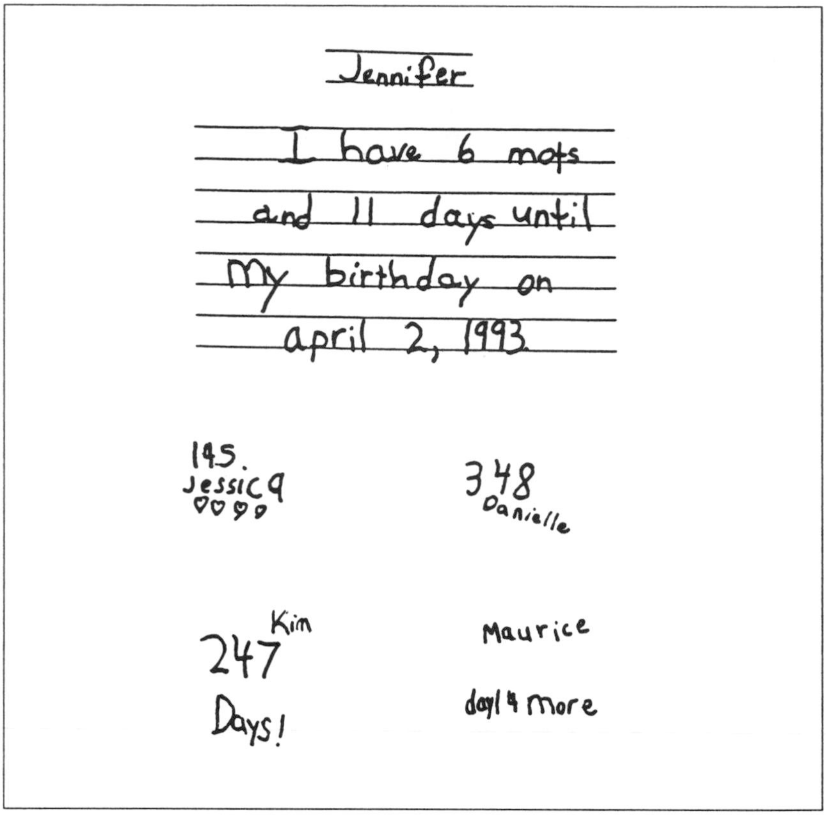

lunch, and so on. When third-grade teacher Christie Forrest was reading this story aloud, her students were already making comments: "I can hold my breath for sixty seconds." "I can hold mine about a minute and ten seconds." "He must have not really taken a bath if he did it in only one minute and forty-three seconds!" As Christie finished the story, one of her students asked, "Mrs. Forrest, do you have a stopwatch here?" Christie had anticipated the question, because this story really begs readers to find a stopwatch and do some timing themselves.

Christie pulled out a stopwatch from her desk drawer and let the children set the direction for what was to follow. They brainstormed a long list of things to time, from putting the chairs on top of the tables (as they are required to do at the end of each day) to sharpening pencils. They finally narrowed their list to six activities:

1. Clapping your hands five times over your head and then writing "Mrs. Forrest" on paper.
2. Spinning the globe five times.
3. Tying a shoe.
4. Looking up the word *spring* in the dictionary.

GOING TO THE BATHROOM. Running outside around the portable classroom.

Robbie then suggested, "Let's guess how long we think it will take to do the activities before we do them and then time them."

Adam agreed. "All right, let's start with the first one. I think it will take twenty-five seconds to clap your hands and then write Mrs. Forrest's name."

"No, less than that. More like eight seconds," said Lacy. After everyone had made a prediction, the group decided that fifteen seconds was about the average and recorded that figure on their chart.

Next they made predictions on spinning the globe. Adam wanted to know how fast it was going to be spun, "normal" or "superfast"? They decided to spin it as fast as possible.

"If we spin it really, really fast, it should take about five seconds, one second per turnaround," said Nicholas.

"I think it will be more like twelve seconds because it does have to go all the way around five times," Cassidy cautioned.

The children finally recorded an average of ten seconds on their chart. Then they chose Cassidy to enter the shoe-tying event, estimating a time of six seconds. Robbie boasted of his dictionary skills so he was chosen to find the word *spring.* His classmates predicted thirty-seven seconds. Going to the bathroom was going to take longer, since the children were in a portable classroom and had to enter the main building to find a restroom.

"Is this person going to run or walk into the building?" asked Adam.

"She has to go like she regularly would, and walk," said Lacey. The children chose Melissa, since she said she really had to use the restroom anyway, and they predicted a time of one minute and thirty-two seconds.

Everyone wanted to run around the portable classroom, so each student made a prediction before the event took place.

CLAPPING HANDS AND WRITING "MRS. FORREST"

LACY: You did it in eleven seconds!
ADAM: Hey, we were real close.
LACY: Yeah, we said fifteen seconds. That's only four seconds more.

SPINNING THE GLOBE FIVE TIMES

NICHOLAS: Wow, that was real fast. Only three seconds!
ROBBIE: I thought it would take longer than that. Adam must have a real fast hand!
ADAM: We didn't do as good this time. We were seven seconds off.
MELISSA: That's still pretty close.

TYING A SHOE

Cassidy completed the task in five seconds, only one second off from their prediction.

LOOKING UP THE WORD *SPRING* IN THE DICTIONARY

CASSIDY: Stop! That was thirty-one seconds.
JOHNNY: We're getting closer again. It was thirty-one and we said thirty-seven.
ADAM: That was pretty fast, Robbie. I don't think I could have found it that fast.
ROBBIE: That's why I told y'all to let me do it.

GOING TO THE BATHROOM

Compared to the other tasks this activity took the longest. At first there was silence as Melissa left, everyone anticipating an early return. However, as the seconds ticked away, small conversations began; after awhile it seemed as if Melissa had been forgotten. Finally, after what seemed forever, Melissa returned.

JOHNNY: Man, it took you a long time.
ROBBIE: Yeah, I bet she was gone for about five minutes.
MELISSA: I told you I had to really go, but I had to tuck in this shirt and everything. How long did it take me, Johnny?
JOHNNY: A long two minutes and fifty-one seconds.
LACY: Well, we messed up on this one.
CASSIDY: How much different is that?
ADAM [*after several seconds of calculating*]: We're off by one minute and nineteen seconds.

RUNNING AROUND THE PORTABLE

Almost all the children predicted it would take longer to complete this activity than it actually did.

MELISSA: It seems like it should have taken longer.
LACY: Maybe it seemed that way because the room seems so big and running around seemed like it would take longer.
ADAM: Nobody was real close to their prediction except Robbie. Everyone was way over.
JOHNNY: I guess we don't know how fast we can really run!

When Christie asked the children what they had learned from this experience, Robbie said, "I think that we are pretty good time guessers!" She then asked them, "Why do you think your predictions were so close to the actual times?"

The children commented that the book gave them a basis for comparison. "I think that after you read that book we had some examples to kind of go by," said Adam.

"Yeah," added Lacy. "Like we knew that you could probably stand on your head for eleven seconds, like they said in that book, and then we could think of what we were guessing about, and think if it would take longer or shorter than standing on your head."

Timing to go to the lunch room

→ How long will it take me and the class to walk to the lunch room? I put 2 min for the class to walk to the lunch room and it took us 2 min and 39 sec.. It took us a short time and we took all mose the right time and if 39 sec was off I wold hide it.

FIGURE 2–4

How long will it take me to walk to the pencil store. I predicted 10 sec. but I divcoved it took me a long time I may not be the fasted walker in the world but I did not run in the hall way.

FIGURE 2–5

→ I thought it would take me noly 1 min. run a around the playground but it took me 1 min. 11 sec. I learned that the playground is very very big.

FIGURE 2–6

One day after recess we came in and had three sips of water and I predict it would most take 15 minutes it toke 2 minutes and 50 seconds But I thouht it would take the hole class 15 minutes to get water because most of the time they get more then 3 sips. That is why I said 15 minutes.

FIGURE 2–7

The Stopwatch

I didn't know how long it would take me to put Mr. Potato Head together and to take him apart. I predicted it would take me two minutes to do that. But it took me only one minute and 18 seconds to put him together and take him apart. I only did the daddy potato head. I was a lot faster than I thought I was. To be putting Mr. Potato Head. I would like to time me packing my book bag and un pack it again. I would like to time me washing and Erasing the boards with the stopwatch.

FIGURE 2–8

When Christie reflected on the benefits of this experience she was particularly impressed by the initiative the children took in setting the direction for this investigation. She wrote: "This was a wonderful exploration created by the students. They predicted, observed, recorded, and compared—all a vital part of understanding mathematics. Their curiosity and exploratory nature carried them on a great mathematical adventure!"

Elaine Cope also shared *The Stopwatch* with her third-grade students. They too become involved in predicting and timing a range of activities, such as going to the lunchroom, walking to the pencil store, running around the playground, taking three sips at the water fountain, and putting together Mr. Potato Head. Their written descriptions of these events are represented in Figures 2–4 through 2–8.

Capitalizing on children's skepticism and doubt

Skepticism and doubt are the hallmarks of an inquiring mind and are precious assets for students living in a democratic society. In his book *Innumeracy* (1988), John Paulos argues that one of the root causes of mathematical illiteracy is the belief that numbers don't lie. If three out of four doctors recommend product X, that's good enough for most people. However, it's not good enough for critical thinkers and well-informed consumers. Students must be perennially skeptical of numerical information (Whitin, Mills & O'Keefe 1990); they must debate it, challenge it, ask questions about it, test it out. Good teachers look for this skepticism as they read stories to their classes and encourage students to investigate that doubt in some way.

A well-known book that often raises questions is *How Much Is a Million?* (Schwartz 1985). When teacher Lynne Wells read this story to a group of Girl Scouts (who can now earn a mathematics badge), the girls questioned whether or not it would really take twenty-three days to count to one million. Six of the girls thought it would probably take that long, but the other twelve girls disagreed. When Lynne asked, "Why do so many of you disagree?" they claimed that the story had to be make-believe, especially since a magician appeared throughout the story. Even when they looked at the back of the book and read about how the author calculated this figure of twenty-three days (an average of two seconds per number) they still were skeptical about the answer. Shelly argued that "reasonable people" would have to eat and take short breaks. Tabitha reiterated the importance of breaks by describing a contest that her mother had entered. A local radio station held a contest in a nearby mall and the prize was a brand new car. Each contestant began by placing his or her hand on the car; the last person with that hand still on the car was declared the winner. Although Tabitha's mother did not win the car, Tabitha knew that during that contest all participants were given a break every so often in order to stretch, eat, or use the restroom. After hearing Tabitha's story, the rest of the Girl Scouts decided to recalculate this answer of twenty-three days by figuring in a fifteen-minute break every two hours. They would use the same rate of two seconds per number and would not stop counting to sleep. Using a calculator they made the following revisions:

8 breaks @ 15 minutes each = 120 extra minutes per day
120 minutes × 23 days = 2,760 extra minutes
2,760 ÷ 60 minutes in an hour = 46 hours
46 hours = 1 day and 22 hours, or about 2 days

These revised calculations showed them that it would take almost twenty-five days to count to one million if fifteen-minute breaks were taken every two hours. Although this new figure seemed more realistic, the girls still were not satisfied. They doubted that any one person could perform such a feat; they even began to speculate how long someone could go without sleep. They decided to recalculate the figure once again, based on their group of twenty (eighteen Girl Scouts and two leaders):

23 days × 24 hours × 60 minutes = 33,120 minutes
33,120 minutes ÷ 20 people = 1,656 minutes each
1,656 minutes ÷ 60 minutes = 27.6 hours

Thus, if each person in the troop counted one number every two seconds and continued counting for 27.6 hours, and then let the next person take over the counting for 27.6 hours, and so on, they could complete the task in twenty-three days. These latest calculations did not involve any fifteen-minute breaks, but the girls reasoned that although the task seemed difficult, it would be at least conceivable, since each person would have to count for only a little bit longer than a day.

Both revised calculations were based on the girls' initial skepticism about counting nonstop for twenty-three consecutive days; they claimed no one would want to do it, or could do it. They refused to accept the conditions on which this figure was based, and revised them to be more plausible. Their skeptical attitude toward the original figure of twenty-three days was the impetus for some good exploration; they were willing to question the author's estimate, challenge his assumptions, revise the underlying conditions, and create a more plausible explanation for themselves. Good teachers encourage this skeptical attitude toward numerical information because they know it develops learners who are more critical consumers of information.

The following example from Patricia Black's third-grade classroom also demonstrates the importance of capitalizing on children's initial skepticism. She read *A Million Fish . . . More or Less* (McKissack 1992), a tall tale about a boy named Hugh Thomas who goes fishing in the bayou and learns how exaggeration can lead to some pretty interesting storytelling. The children began to express doubt early on; when Hugh Thomas claimed he had caught a million fish, more or less, April said, "No one can catch a million fish," and Tiffany added, "Even a cat couldn't eat that many fish." At a later point in the story, Donny doubted that a turkey could weigh five hundred pounds. When Patricia asked the children how much they thought a turkey might weigh, the children estimated between ten and two hundred pounds. Patricia suggested that they ask their parents about the weight of the last turkey cooked at home, and the next day everyone reported between ten- and sixteen-pound turkeys. Eric wondered what ten pounds really felt like, so Patricia asked cafeteria workers to show the children different cans and packages weighing about ten pounds.

During the next part of the story, Malcolm doubted that a crocodile could be 150 feet long. After the story was over he used an encyclopedia to find more accurate measurements and reported these to the class. He found that crocodile babies are about nine inches long and that females may reach nine feet in length and rarely weigh more than 160 pounds. However, males may be eleven or twelve feet long and weigh as much as 550 pounds. Malcolm also discovered that crocodiles grow at the rate of one foot per year. When Brandi wondered what twelve feet would look like, Patricia encouraged the children to use some rulers and tape to mark off the lengths of the female and male crocodiles on the classroom floor. Several children stretched out alongside these measurements to see how many of their own body lengths would fit into a twelve-foot length. When Malcolm later reported to the class that crocodiles used to reach a length of eighteen feet, the class had an interesting discussion about the possible reasons they no longer did, including poachers, pollution, and other environmental factors.

The children's next doubt concerned the number of jumps in a rope-jumping contest between Mosley the raccoon and Hugh Thomas. April said, "I'm a good

FIGURE 2–9

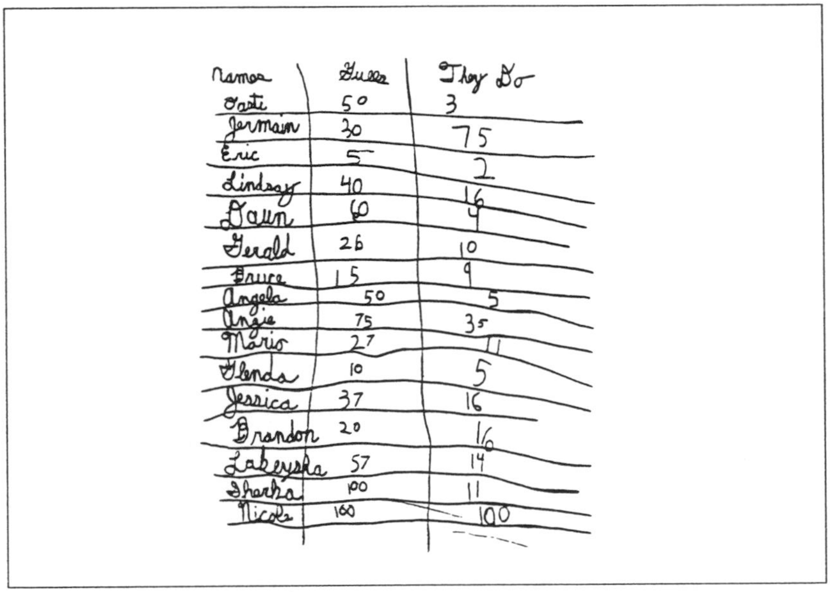

Names	Guess	They Do
[illegible]	50	3
Jermain	30	75
Eric	5	2
Lindsay	40	16
Dawn	60	4
Gerald	26	10
Bruce	15	9
Angela	50	5
Angie	75	35
Mario	27	11
Glenda	10	5
Jessica	37	16
Brandon	20	16
Lakeysha	57	14
[illegible]	100	11
Nicole	100	100

jumper, and I've never jumped more than a hundred times. There is no way a raccoon or a boy could jump 5,553 times!" Patricia then asked, "Well, how many times do you think each of you could jump?" Kristen suggested, "Let's have a contest and find out." After recording their predictions and actual results they decided to include the other third-grade classes in the event. They chose recorders and rope turners for each class and spent four recesses gathering their data. One of their charts is shown in Figure 2–9. They eventually made one large chart to display all their information.

Inviting personal connections to stories

The personal connections that children make with stories can often be the impetus for further explorations. Before Elizabeth Toole read *Millions of Cats* (Gág 1928) to her fourth graders, she decided to bring her own cat, Sebastian, to school so the class could meet him. After Elizabeth introduced Sebastian and answered the children's questions, she began the story, while Sebastian settled into a beanbag chair to take a nap. As the story ended, Tyneesha commented, "I liked the book very much because I like cats a lot." Ann wondered, "Why didn't that couple want to keep all those cats that came to their house? Those old people would never be lonely again if they kept all the cats with them." Eddie replied, "But their house wasn't big enough for a million cats." Children then began to discuss their own cats and discovered that eight of them owned cats. Paul said, "But we have to count Mrs. Toole's cat, so that makes nine." Carey then remembered, "You know, Mrs. Douglas [another teacher at the school] has a cat too. She talks about it a lot in class."

FIGURE 2–10

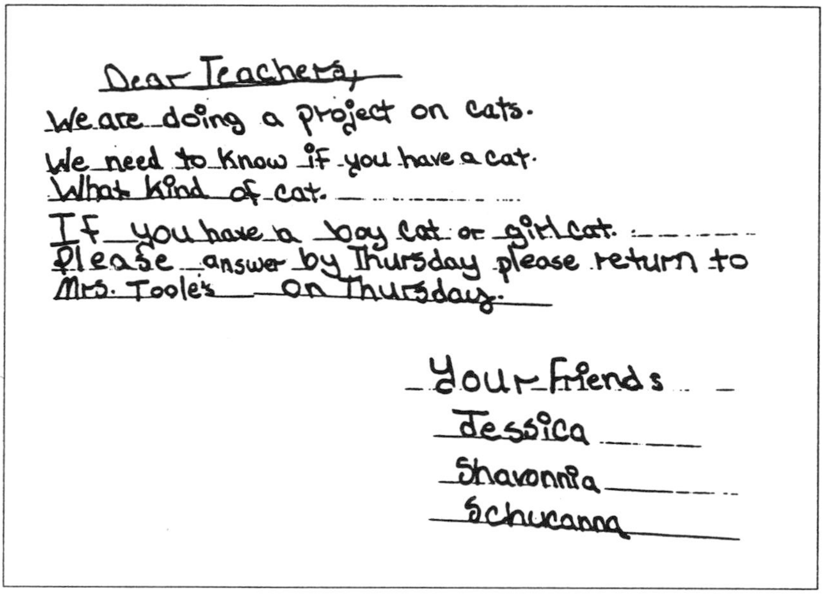
Dear Teachers,
We are doing a project on cats.
We need to know if you have a cat.
What kind of cat.
If you have a boy cat or girl cat.
Please answer by Thursday please return to Mrs. Toole's on Thursday.

Your friends
Jessica
Shavonnia
Schucanna

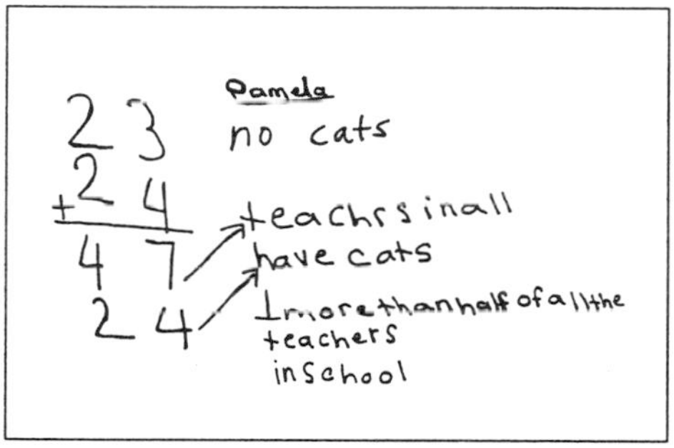

Pamela
no cats
23
+24
47
24
teachrs in all
have cats
1 more than half of all the teachers in School

FIGURE 2–11

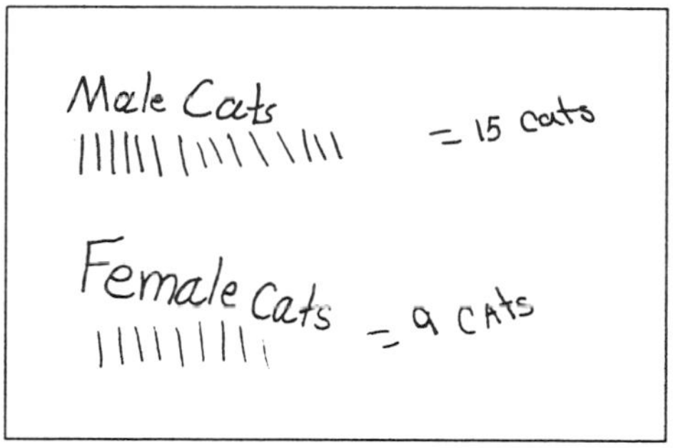

FIGURE 2–12

Schucanna prompted a class exploration when she asked, "I would like to know what other teachers in our school have cats." Octavia and Shavonnia wanted to go right then and ask each teacher if they owned a cat, but the class decided that writing a letter might be a more appropriate strategy—that way the teachers wouldn't be interrupted in class. Three of the students wrote the letter shown in Figure 2–10. When the replies came in, they recorded some of their findings (see Figures 2–11 and 2–12). The children also noticed that the replies contained a lot of good descriptive information:

> *Yes I have a cat. He is a tabby. Big and fat. Gray in color. His name is Chester, so he is a boy.*
>
> *I have a female cat named Queenie. She is a mixed breed which her veterinarian calls a domestic short hair. She is a striped cat (gray, white, and light brown).*

Puddy—"all boy," 18 lbs, Siamese; Pepper—boy, "lucky black" cat; Tiger—boy, striped; Lucky—girl, striped; all cats are immunized and neutered/spayed and LOVED!

I have 2 cats. Twinkletoes, "Winkie" for short, is the momma. She is mostly black, but her feet, her tummy, and a little stripe on her face are all white. She is a fat cat. Her tummy almost drags the ground and it wiggles when she runs! Twinkletoes' daughter, Lightening Bug ("Bug" for short), also lives with us. She is also black and white, but she is much thinner than her mother and she runs a lot faster. Twinkletoes' favorite hobby is sleeping. Bug's favorite hobby is chasing squirrels up the trees—or sometimes other cats!

About 6 years ago, I had an orange tabby cat. He was a boy and his name was "Boo-Boo." I have pictures if you need them. Just let me know.

The children were impressed with the details of these descriptions as well as the affection that these owners displayed toward their pets. They decided to draw each of these pets, based on the written descriptions, photographs, or follow-up interviews they conducted. They taped all the drawings together to create one long horizontal mural. Paul was impressed by the total length: "Wow, that's a lot of cats!" However, Jessica reminded him, "Yeah, but there are still more teachers that do not have cats than do have cats." Laron then reasoned, "This graph would be twice as long if all those teachers had cats."

Another data-collection activity was triggered when Kimball Baker read *How Many Teeth*? (Showers 1991) to second-grade student Ryan. Losing teeth was familiar to Ryan, who told of his recent losses and his reimbursement by the tooth fairy. When the book described children with twenty-two teeth, Ryan immediately responded, "I don't have twenty-two teeth because I've already lost four." "So how many do you have?" asked Kimball. At first Ryan tried counting his own teeth but found that to be a difficult task. He solved his problem by drawing a picture of twenty-two teeth and crossing off four. "There, I have eighteen teeth," he exclaimed proudly. Near the end of the book, Ryan noticed the illustration of a tooth chart hanging on a wall that showed the number of teeth that the children in the story had lost. "We had one of those in my classroom," he said. "It tells you how many teeth are lost."

The personal connections that Ryan made throughout the story probably provided the impetus for the investigation he wanted to pursue, recording the number of teeth each person in his family had lost. The results of his survey are shown in Figure 2–13. He included his mom (Julie), his dad (Ansel), and his older brother (Brent), as well as himself and a friend, Paul. He decided to use a colored circle to represent "no teeth" for Julie, since he thought a zero might look like a tooth.

Sometimes stories related to measurement invite personal connections. When teacher Jackie Bankert read the poem "One Inch Tall" (Silverstein 1974) to third grader Jennie, there was much discussion about this unit of measure. Jennie said her thumb was about one inch long and compared her thumb to Jackie's. She also said the poem reminded her of *Thumbelina,* which features a small character of only a thumb's height. Jennie enjoyed making these comparisons and decided she wanted

FIGURE 2–13

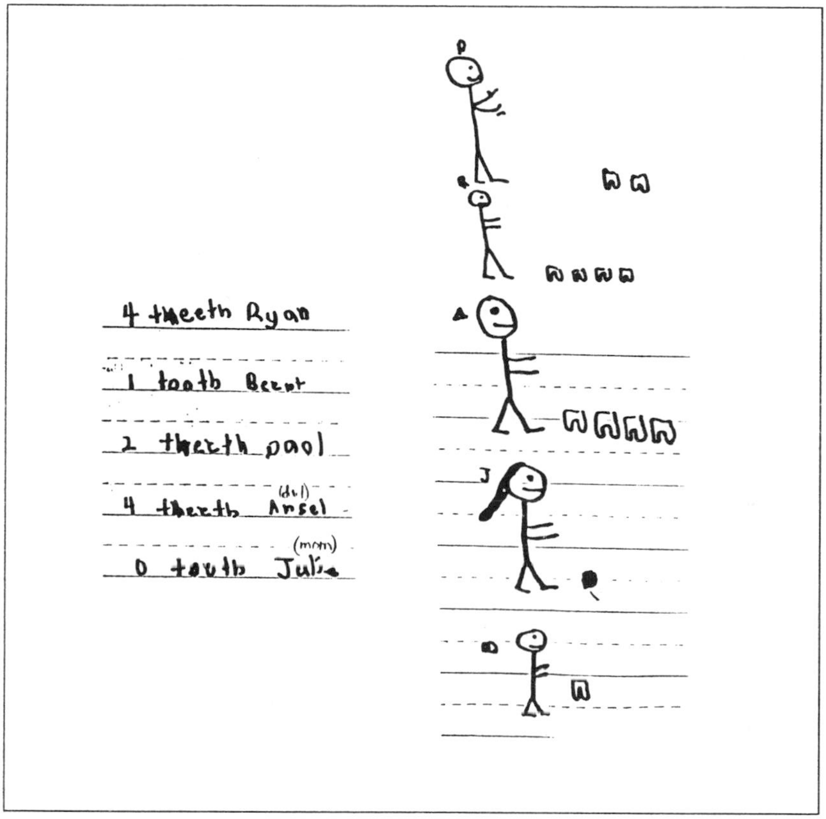

to create her own poem based on the length of four inches. She liked four inches because she imagined "that was about as big as a rat." She used the structures of Shel Silverstein's poem to create her own:

Four Inches Tall

If you were only four inches tall like a rat, you'd ride on a robot horse to school.
A teardrop from a crying mole would be your swimming pool.
A whole apple would be an enormous feast
And would last you three weeks at least,
A frog would be a frightening beast
If you were four inches tall.

If you were only four inches tall, you could walk under a chair,
And it would take a whole day to get to the store.
You could sleep in a doll baby's bed,
You could play with a little mole,
And wear a baby doll's hat on your head
If you were four inches tall.

You'd surf across the bathtub upon a bar of soap.
You couldn't hug your mama, you'd just have to hug her hand.
You'd run from chickens' feet in fright,
To move a pen would take all afternoon,
(This poem took ten years to write—
Cause I'm just four inches tall).

Discussing her poem, she reasoned, "Since four inches is just a little bit bigger than one inch, I had to think just a little bit bigger than in the poem." In the original poem the last stanza states it took fourteen years to write the whole piece, but Jennie changed hers to ten years: "I backtracked four times from the original fourteen because mine is four inches tall." Jennie enjoyed describing objects in her own life from the perspective of only four inches; she liked "thinking about math in stories," as well as "creating math more than just doing math" (as in a textbook).

Sharing books that relate to children's interests

Becky Brunson decided to read fifth grader Jennifer the story *Six-Dinner Sid* (Moore 1991) because she knew Jennifer owned a cat. The story is a delightful one about a cat named Sid who loves to eat and devises a plan to reward his appetite. He pretends to be owned by six different owners who feed him, play with him, and give him a cozy place to sleep. Since none of the neighbors talk to each other, they do not realize the trick that Sid is playing on them. Life continues to go well for Sid until the day he catches a cold. Each owner brings poor Sid to the vet, adding up to six different occasions where he is forced to swallow nasty-tasting medicine! Finally the veterinarian uncovers the ruse, but Sid quickly moves to another street and begins his shenanigans all over again. At the end of the story Becky asked Jennifer, "Is there anything else you'd like to know about Sid, or anything else about Sid that you could figure out?"

Since Jennifer was familiar with the feeding schedule of her own cat, she was intrigued by Sid's eating schedule and wanted to figure out how many times Sid would eat in a week. She multiplied 6 dinners times 7 days a week to find a total of 42 dinners per week. This discovery led her to try to determine the number of dinners Sid would eat in a month. She realized the answer would depend on which month she was using. So she calculated the possible solutions. First she multiplied 6 dinners times 30 days to get 180 dinners in a 30-day month; she then added 6 to 180 to arrive at 186 dinners in a 31-day month; lastly, she subtracted 12 from 180 to arrive at 168 dinners for the 28-day month of February.

Jennifer was also interested in calculating how many times Sid had to take his medicine. Becky thought Sid only had to take it six times, the day of the six vet visits. However, Jennifer interpreted the story to mean that Sid took the medicine six times every day until the owners found out what was happening. She said these people did not discover the trick until six days later, because the veterinarian had to think about the problem for a while, look back at his records, and finally contact all six families. So Jennifer multiplied 6 doses of medicine per day times 6 days and calculated 36 doses of medicine. She was surprised he was still alive after all that medicine!

Finally, Jennifer wanted to know how much weight Sid would have gained in a week. This question surprised Becky, because the book neither mentioned Sid's weight nor showed him getting fatter as the story proceeded. However, it was an interesting question for Jennifer, and she chose to use her own cat's weight as a basis for comparison. She estimated her own cat's weight to be three pounds but decided from looking at the book's illustrations that Sid probably weighed a bit more, so she settled on five pounds as his starting weight. She estimated that he would gain five pounds a day eating all that food, thereby gaining thirty-five pounds in a week. "Do you suppose he might work off some of that weight by walking from one house to the next?" Becky asked. "I don't think so," said Jennifer, after taking a close look at the illustrations. "Those houses are pretty close together in the book, so I don't think he'd get much exercise."

Becky, amazed at the various questions Jennifer decided to pursue, wrote the following reflection:

> *Jennifer's investigations were much more in-depth than anything I had expected. She explored topics, such as Sid's weight, that were not even mentioned in the story. Once she began thinking mathematically, one idea led to another. I was also fascinated with her methods for solving multiplication and subtraction problems.*

When Becky drove Jennifer home later that afternoon, Jennifer was still viewing the world from a mathematical perspective:

> *While I was taking Jennifer home, a truck loaded with watermelons passed us. She asked if I knew how many watermelons fit on one truck, and I said I had no idea. She went on to tell me that each truck holds about a thousand watermelons, and Mr. Randy Cockrell has seven truckloads a day leaving his farm. She said, "Think about how many watermelons that is in a day!" She talked about how much land he must have needed to plant all those watermelons. Although neither one of us ventured a guess on the exact number of acres, we agreed that it must be a lot!*

Offering open-ended choices for responding to stories

Sometimes children venture off into an interesting mathematical enterprise when teachers offer an open-ended invitation. Sandra Erwin used this strategy after sharing *The Doorbell Rang* (Hutchins 1986) with second graders Ellen and Valerie. She suggested that one way the children could respond to the story was by making a game board. They accepted the invitation enthusiastically and began working right away. Sandra had available a variety of markers, pencils, tagboard, glue, and scissors, and she let the children decide how the process was to proceed. Their three-way conversation as the girls set to work highlights a number of problems the girls had to resolve as they created their own unique game board.

ELLEN: I think that there should be a plate of cookies in the top right corner and that will be the final square.
VALERIE: The winner will be the first to reach the cookies.
ELLEN: You have to get a color to move along the board.
VALERIE: We'll need a spinner.
ELLEN: We need colors like red, green, purple.
VALERIE: We start at Go.
ELLEN: What should Go look like? A door with a doorbell.
VALERIE: Little people to move along the board. The people start at the door.
ELLEN: What are the rules? You spin and move to that color and if you land on the line you spin again. The one who reaches the cookies first, gets the cookies, wins.
SANDRA: What else about the book can you include in your game?
VALERIE: You have to think of ways to split the cookies. There are eight cookies and you have to figure out how to split the cookie six ways.
ELLEN: Maybe we could collect cookie parts as you go from the door to the plate of cookies?
VALERIE: The kids would be bringing the cookies instead of Grandma—would that be all right?
ELLEN: Or one player could be Ma and the other Grandma and you could travel from a plate of cookies to the door and ring the doorbell. And they collect cookies along the board. The one who collects the most cookies along the board—like one half a cookie, one fourth a cookie . . . yeah! And we have different color squares and you would spin to see which color you would land on.
VALERIE: When you land on a special square you would get a part of a cookie.
ELLEN: What sizes do you want? One half, one third, one fourth, one fifth, and whole cookies.
VALERIE: What size is one fifth?
SANDRA: Let's compare—this is one half; this is one third; this is one fourth—so do you think one fifth would be smaller or larger than one half?
ELLEN AND VALERIE: Smaller.
ELLEN: Let's not use one fifth because we already have one half, one third, and one fourth. We don't need a fraction at every square.
VALERIE: Let's pick up cookies on the way and put them on the plate.
ELLEN: The person who has the most cookies on the cookie plate wins. You don't have to be the first one there.
VALERIE: Let's make the path zig-zaggy and not straight.
ELLEN: Let's name our game "The Doorbell Rang" or "The Dude with the Cookies."
VALERIE: What's your plan?
ELLEN: I was thinking that we could go back and forth across the board to use up all the space.

VALERIE: We need a welcome mat by the door.

ELLEN: We need to place the colors.

VALERIE: This will be a fun game. We'll take it to our school and share in our class. We can share it with first graders and teach them about fractions. First graders don't know about fractions.

ELLEN: We can write all the characters' names so we can decide who we want to be.

VALERIE: Where will we put the cookie pieces?

ELLEN: Let's make a pocket and put the pieces in it. We need separate pockets for each size.

VALERIE: Let's put dots in some of the squares, and you would be stuck on that spot until you spin that color.

ELLEN: Let's have cookie steps between two squares so you can take a shortcut, because our story is mostly about cookies and we have been taking shortcuts.

VALERIE: Let's make the pockets out of yellow. I like colorful stuff.

ELLEN: You start coloring the squares and I'll cut the pockets. I don't need to make these pockets the same size, do I?

VALERIE: We need to decide which squares you'll land on to get a cookie part.

ELLEN: I'll make a door. The name is "When the Doorbell Rings," no, "The Doorbell Rings." Let's put it on the cookie plate.

VALERIE: We need to write "Start" at the door, and the characters' names, but not four cousins.

ELLEN: We don't want any more rules.

At this point the girls tested out their game and encountered a problem. Ellen got stuck on a square with a dot and could not spin the right color to move on. They therefore eliminated the spinning feature, instead requiring that a player landing on a square with a dot miss only one turn before moving on. They felt good about the revisions they made, because the changes were a natural part of improving the game. Figure 2–14 is their final game board. Their conversation shows how inventive they were as problem solvers: they incorporated their knowledge of how game boards work as they discussed the object of the game, how the pieces were to move, and how the game was to be organized, and they included elements of the story in the game (the partial cookies, the name of the game, and the final cookie tally). Sandra's invitation to create a game board provided a wonderful opportunity for the children to respond to this story in an open-ended way.

Mary Ogburn gave her kindergarten class an open-ended invitation when she read *Farmer Mack Measures His Pig* (Johnston 1986). The children had been studying life on a farm and Mary thought the book would be a funny addition to the unit. In this story, two farmers argue over whose pig is the biggest and the best. At the end they discover that both pigs are pretty clever, and are pretty big indeed—their bellies are a hundred inches around. When Mary asked the children if they could think of anything that was approximately one hundred inches, their responses ranged from a dog, a snake, and a crocodile to the school, a church, and the universe.

Later that morning Mary cut several pieces of string that were a hundred inches long and invited her students to find objects that were approximately that same

FIGURE 2–14

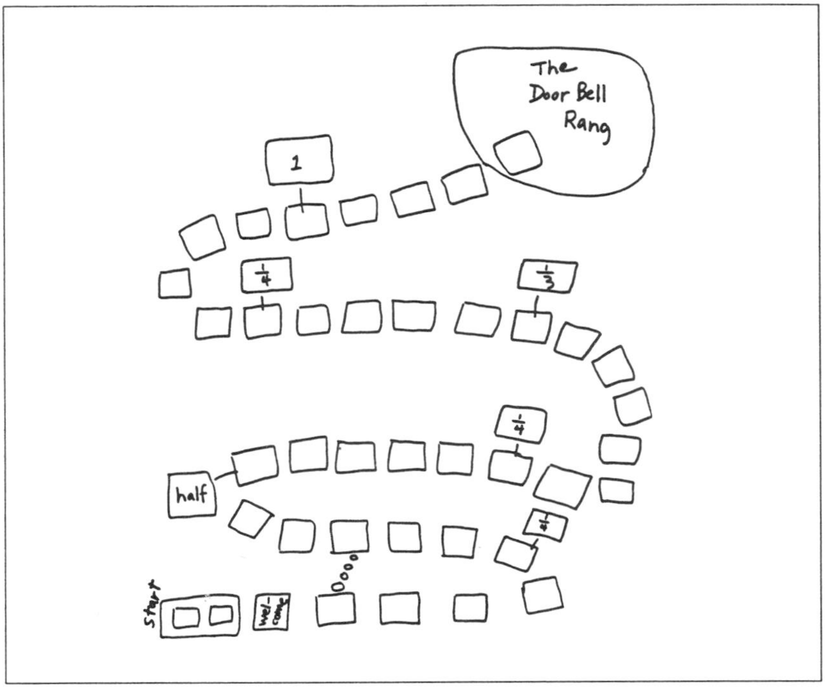

length. Christian and Curtis were particularly interested in this investigation. At first they measured the bulletin board and announced, "Not one hundred," and then the side of the wall, "Not one hundred." Christian wondered how many floor tiles it would take to make one hundred inches; they stretched out their length of string on the floor and then counted tiles to find their answer, ten. Each discovery seemed to generate new enthusiasm for the next exploration. "Hey, let's measure the sand table," suggested Curtis. They measured and then loudly announced, "It's half of one hundred," seeing that a large portion of their string was still unused.

At this point Steven joined them and wanted to figure out how many children it would take, standing side by side, to line up and make a length of one hundred inches. As he rounded up twelve students to find out, others were making various predictions—one hundred, ten, twelve. Steven measured and found it took ten students. Justin then wondered how many students it would take to measure one hundred inches if they were in a standing in a circle. They were amazed to find it took ten students again, that it didn't matter whether the ten students stood in one long line or in a circle.

The children went outside during recess and found that the slide was longer than a hundred inches but the distance around the sliding tube was less than a hundred inches. Justin tied this measurement to the story and logically concluded, "I guess Goldie [*one of the pigs in the story*] is too fat to slide through our tube!"

Christian then measured the height of another teacher and inferred, "Well, I know now there are no kids in here that are one hundred inches." Justin and Steven measured the outside width of one of the portable classrooms using both their strings and announced, "It's two times as long as one hundred inches."

Brenda Strickland shared *Farmer Mack Measures His Pig* with fourth grader Dustin, and they became involved in some different kinds of investigations. At the end of the story Dustin said he couldn't quite picture in his mind what one hundred inches was like, so Brenda invited him to cut a length of string that was one hundred inches. He then placed his string in a circle to see what a hundred inches would look like. "That picture in the book made Goldie look like a pig, but if she were a hundred inches around then Goldie would definitely be a hog," he reasoned. Dustin was working with Brenda in his house and wanted to find some round objects that had a circumference of one hundred inches but could not find anything close. He then began to look for squares and rectangles and noticed the washing machine. "I'd like to measure that washing machine but I can't get behind it," he said.

"Is there a way you could figure out the measurements without getting behind it?" asked Brenda.

Dustin thought for a few seconds and then exclaimed, "Yes, I can measure the sides. . . . Oh yeah, it's a rectangle, that means the front and the back are the same. This is perimeter. We did this at school." He used his string and a ruler to find the perimeter of the washing machine to be 106 inches, the clothes dryer 108 inches, and a chest of drawers 98 inches. For each item he measured the length and width only once, then doubled each one and found the total. These few measurement experiences made him wonder, "Can a square and a rectangle have the same area if they have the same perimeter?" Brenda gave him some graph paper and invited him to see what he could find out about the relationship between perimeter and area. After several trial-and-error attempts he found a square and a rectangle with the same perimeter:

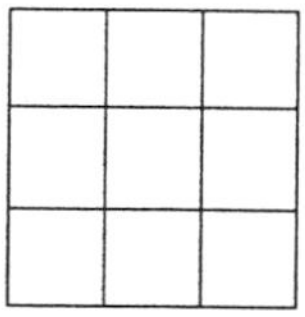

square
P = 12 units
A = 9 square units

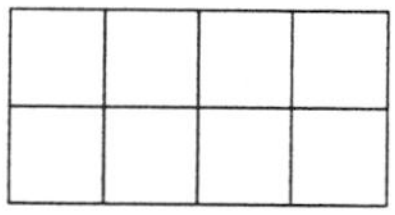

rectangle
P = 12 units
A = 8 square units

Dustin commented, "The square is taller and narrower than the rectangle. That's why it has more room inside." He then created some other examples:

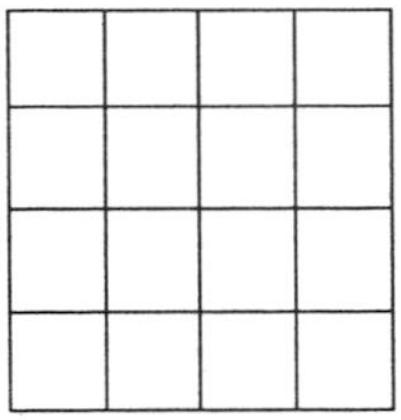

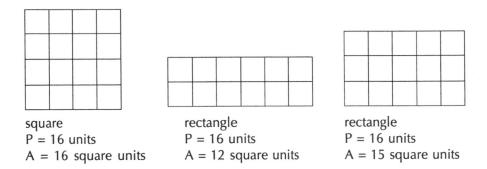

square
P = 16 units
A = 16 square units

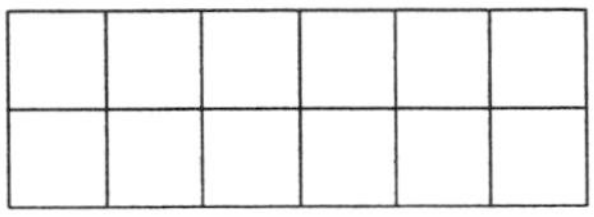

rectangle
P = 16 units
A = 12 square units

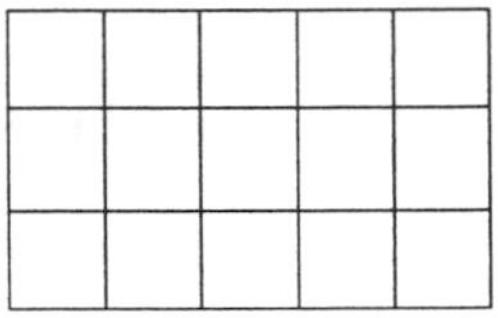

rectangle
P = 16 units
A = 15 square units

Dustin concluded, "A square has more area than a rectangle. The skinnier the rectangle, the less area there is to cover. A long narrow room would be cheaper to cover with new floors than a square room." This investigation had gone off in a direction that Brenda had not anticipated, but she saw the value in it: "I had planned on talking about the diameter and the radius of circles. But this was more interesting to Dustin, and children learn more when it's something they are wondering about."

The (frequently conflicting) opinions that children have about some aspects of stories can also be used as a basis for exploration. Our last example of an open-ended invitation by a teacher involves data gathering. Carolyn Webber shared *Animal Numbers* (Kitchen 1987) with a group of children at a day-care center (the children's ages ranged from five to nine). This is an unusual counting book that features animals and their offspring: a mother kangaroo has a single joey, a swan swims with two baby cygnets, an Irish Setter sits beside her litter of ten puppies. Except for a brief introduction there are no words. Instead, each page contains a large numeral, with the mother and her babies crawling or swimming around it. A short text at the back of the book describes why these particular animals were chosen.

The children noticed by the third page that the numeral represented not the total number of animals per page but only the number of babies. Throughout the story the children chimed in with their knowledge and opinions about each animal that appeared:

> "Squirrels live in holes and eat nuts."
> "Lizards are ugly and carry their babies on their backs."
> "Woodpeckers peck holes in things."
> "Shrews bite each other's tails and play follow the leader."
> "Opossums give their babies free rides."
> "Goldfish are pretty but are not good mothers."
> "Salamanders are pretty but mean."
> "Dogs are nice."
> "Pigs are gross and lazy."
> "Snakes are mean and can kill you."
> "Sea horses are funny."
> "Turtles are big and ugly."
> "Frogs have bunches of babies."

FIGURE 2–15

FIGURE 2–16

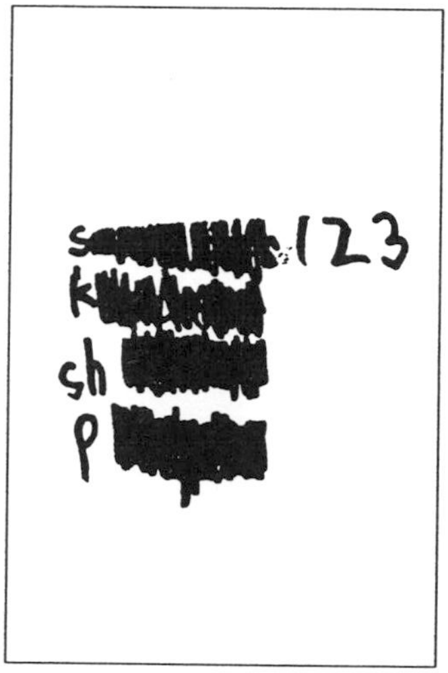

FIGURE 2–17

Since much of this was opinion, Carolyn discussed with the children what opinions were. They realized they did not all share the same opinion about many of the animals mentioned in the book. At this point Carolyn suggested they might want to gather some data on these differences of opinion. The children liked this invitation, particularly because so many interesting opinions about animals had been raised.

Kirk, nine, decided to ask the group, "What animal is the meanest?" Since he did not know how to spell *salamander,* he colored a brown rectangle to represent that response (see Figure 2–15). Noel, six, asked, "What animal is the nicest?" and marked brown areas for those who agreed with his choice, kangaroo (see Figure 2–16). Mathew, six, asked, "What animal is ugly?" He used letters to signify each animal—S for salamander, K for kangaroo, SN for snakes, and P for possum (see Figure 2–17)—with each horizontal band representing one response. Since several people voted for salamander, he decided to write numbers next to that band to show the three responses. Seven-year-old Hodges asked, "What is the best animal to hunt?" Almost every child he asked responded "dog," meaning that was the best animal to hunt *with.* Hodges tried to clarify the misunderstanding by asking his friends, "Do you want to shoot, kill, and eat a *dog*?" Children soon changed their responses. Brandon wanted to know, "Who is the furriest?" He was convinced the right answer was a squirrel and so drew a large squirrel on his paper (see Figure 2–18) and campaigned on its behalf. Those who disagreed were persuaded otherwise and the squirrel was thus chosen unanimously.

Encouraging the children to share their knowledge and opinions about animals throughout this story led them to gather their own data. Carolyn supported the children's right to pose their own questions and represent their data in their own way, and they used various combinations of pictures, letters, numbers, and symbols to record their responses.

FIGURE 2–18

Contributing personal connections to stories

Teachers' observations about their personal connections to stories will sometimes prompt further investigation. Barbara Creighton used this strategy with some fourth graders when she shared *Two Ways to Count to Ten* (Dee 1988). In this Liberian folktale, a hyena becomes the new king of the jungle because he is the only animal that can count to ten before a javelin hits the ground (the hyena counts by twos). After hearing the story, the children tried to skip count by twos to one hundred and then tried by multiples of five and ten. Barbara asked the children what objects in the world came in sets of two, three, four, and so on. Children suggested shoes, eyes, and ears for two; tricycles and tennis balls for three; and the tires on cars and go-carts for four.

At this point Barbara shared her own example, the presidential election every four years. Dana figured that since we just had an election in 1992, then we would have another one in 1996 and "maybe someone different would be president." Others suggested that it would still be possible to have the same one. This led the children to wonder how many different presidents the United States could have had since we started having a president. They made predictions of nineteen, forty-three, and a hundred.

"How can we figure out the answer?" asked Barbara. One child suggested multiplying the number of possible presidents by two to include the vice presidents in the count as well. However, the class decided they wanted to limit it to the presidents. They decided to record the year of the most recent election and chose 1993, since they wanted to keep track of the inauguration year rather than the year of the actual election. Barbara said they could be time travelers who kept leaping back into the past until they reached the inaugural year of the first president, George

FIGURE 2–19

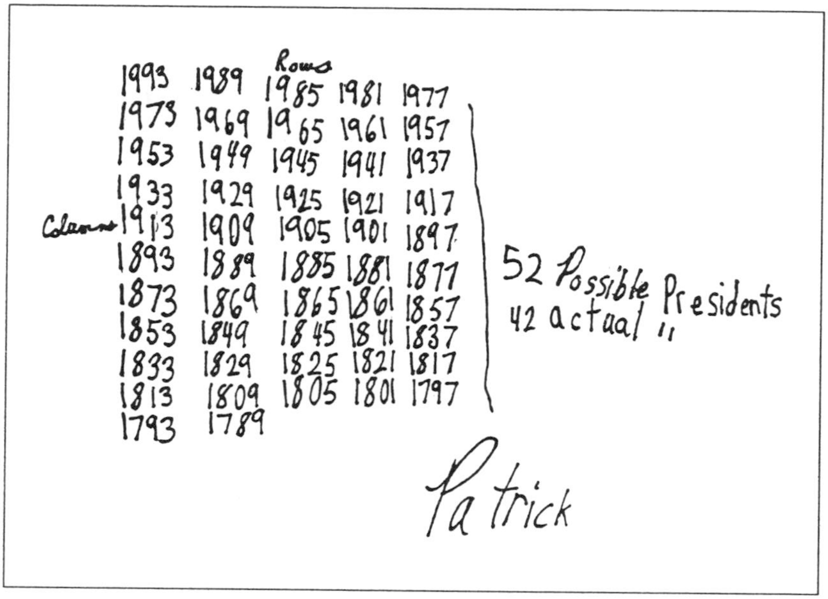

Washington. The children knew they had to subtract four each time and began to record their answers horizontally in an array format (Patrick's chart is shown in Figure 2–19). Some used pencil and paper, others used calculators, and still others performed the computations mentally. When one child reached 1877, she decided to calculate the number of possible presidents at this point by multiplying the six rows in the chart by the five columns, nicely using an area model to find her answer efficiently.

As the children looked at their charts they noticed some interesting number patterns:

"If you look down, the numbers go down by twenty each time."

"I see all threes [*in the ones place of the first column*]."

"I see a column of nines too [*in the second column*], then fives, ones, and sevens."

Others noticed that the tens place had a pattern of either odd or even numbers. The patterns helped children check their subtraction. At one point Marlin had written 1888 instead of 1889; he noticed that the number did not fit his pattern of nines and then checked his subtraction and found his error. Patrick used his completed chart to count the number of possible presidents and then used an encyclopedia to count the number of actual presidents.

Barbara's contribution about the presidential election proved to be an intriguing point of departure for these students. Good teachers are contributing members of the classroom community and their voice is one of many that enrich the conversation.

Sharing books that present a mathematical challenge

Books that contain a mathematical puzzle or challenge can sometimes provide children with a good starting point for further investigations. Tammy Woodley found this to be true when she shared *Socrates and the Three Little Pigs* (Anno 1986) with her sister Amanda, who had just completed the eighth grade. In this story the author uses diagrams of three pigs and five houses to explore permutations and combinations. Socrates the wolf in trying to figure out where the three little pigs are sleeping in order to catch one for his supper, stays up all night trying to figure out all the different possibilities. As Tammy began the story, Amanda wondered about the name Pythagoras that was given to a frog. She asked, "Is Pythagoras the guy who did the Pythagorean theorem? I bet that's what this story is about."

"Let's find out," said Tammy as she continued to read. Amanda was fascinated by the way the wolf was trying to figure out all the possibilities for three pigs in five houses and she frequently asked, "Please read that page again. I didn't quite get that. Read it again and let me concentrate on that." As Tammy wrote afterward, "I was thrilled to see this much interest generated by this book. I wish I could describe adequately the look of concentration on her face. She was really getting into this book, and I was so excited to see this."

When the story was over Amanda was still wondering about the connection between the story and the name Pythagoras: "There has to be some reason that they used the name Pythagoras; there has to be some reason that this story is like the Pythagorean theorem." She drew upon her recent experience in algebra and tried to connect that experience to the intentions of the author. Tammy asked Amanda to talk about what she was thinking. "Well, I know the Pythagorean theorem is when you have the measure of two angles of a triangle and you need to figure out the third angle or side, I can't remember exactly. The only thing that's alike [*between the story and the theorem*] is that we know about two things and need to figure out one. We know how many pigs and how many houses but we need to know which house or houses the pigs are in."

"Is there anything else you'd like to say about this story?" asked Tammy.

"I thought it was a kiddie book, but little kids couldn't understand it. It takes a lot of concentration," said Amanda.

"Is there anything else you wondered about after hearing this story?"

"Yeah, I wondered why they decided not to eat those pigs after all that trouble."

"Why do you think?"

"Well, it was morning, but they could have waited and caught the pigs the next night. I wanted to see them catch the pigs and see if it worked. They were really smart to figure out how to do it first, and then try to get the pigs, instead of rushing into it. I would like to take this book home and figure out how they did this." The next day she showed some of her calculations (see Figure 2–20) to Tammy.

"What is the difference between possibilities and arrangements?" Tammy asked.

"Possibilities are the different choices the pigs have and arrangement deals with where in a house they could be, like closer to the door."

"Why don't you have any arrangements in your first two situations?"

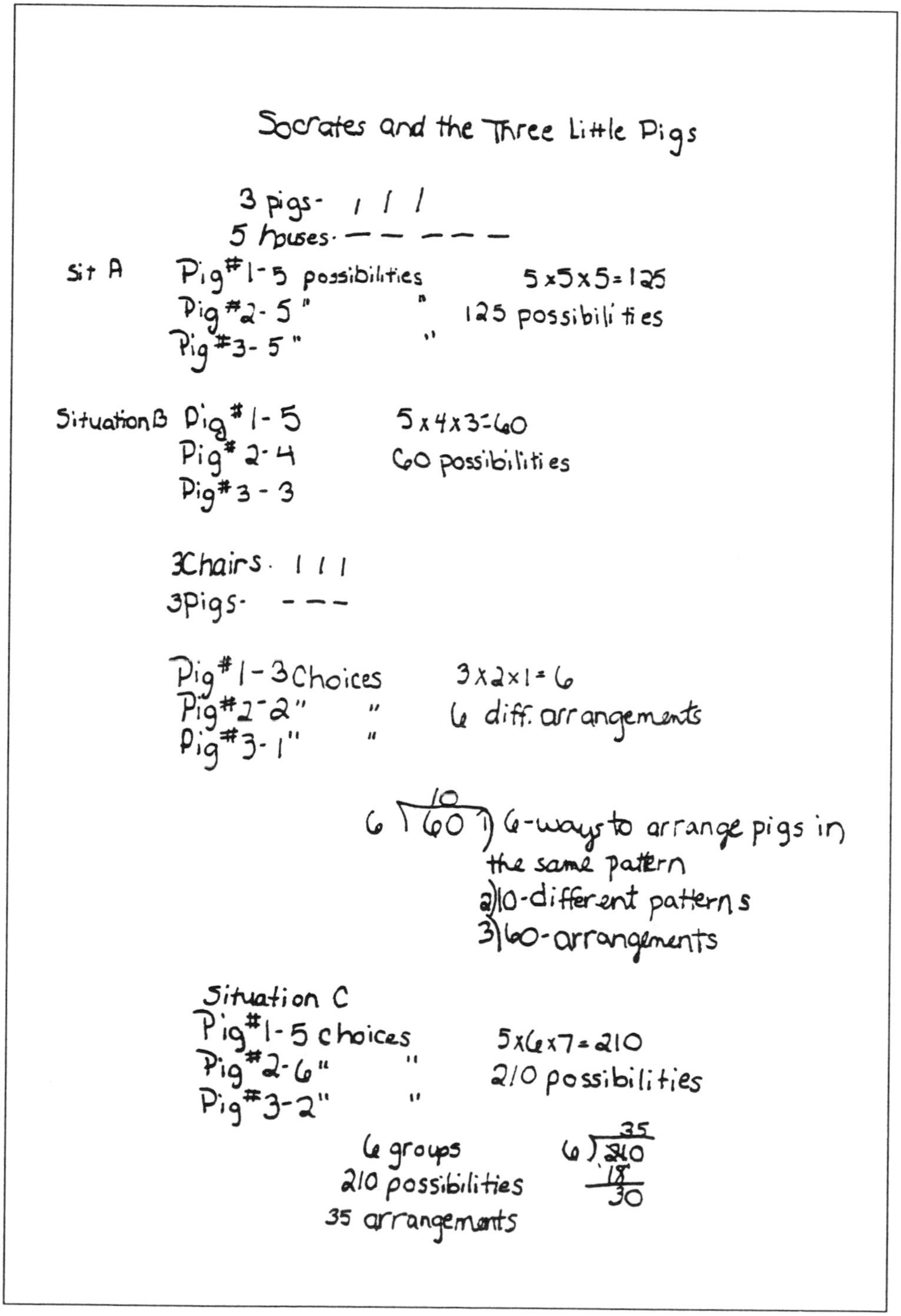

Socrates and the Three Little Pigs

3 pigs - / / /
5 houses - — — — — —

sit A Pig#1-5 possibilities $5 \times 5 \times 5 = 125$
Pig#2-5 " " 125 possibilities
Pig#3-5 " "

Situation B Pig#1-5 $5 \times 4 \times 3 = 60$
Pig#2-4 60 possibilities
Pig#3-3

3Chairs - / / /
3Pigs - — — —

Pig#1-3 Choices $3 \times 2 \times 1 = 6$
Pig#2-2" " 6 diff. arrangements
Pig#3-1" "

6) 60 (10
1) 6-ways to arrange pigs in the same pattern
2) 10-different patterns
3) 60-arrangements

Situation C
Pig#1-5 choices $5 \times 6 \times 7 = 210$
Pig#2-6" " 210 possibilities
Pig#3-2" "

6 groups
210 possibilities
35 arrangements

6) 210 (35
18
30

FIGURE 2–20

A related problem 2 Socrates and the Three little pigs.

problem- If I get up in the middle of the night on a camping trip and had to find an adult, what is the possibility that I would go into the right tent.

There are 18 people going camping. 4 of them are adults.

4 tents have an adult in them, 3 do not. There are 7 in all.

6 tents 

4 adults

Adult # 1 - 6 possibilities 6x5x4x3=360

Adult # 2 - 5 possibilities

Adult # 3 - 4 possibilities

Adult # 4 - 3 possibilities

There are 24 possible arrangements because 4x3x2x1=24

There are 15 combinations because 360÷24=15

Therefore if only one adult is in each of those 4 tents and I got up and needed any one of them there are 24 possible arrangements 24 ways for 4 adults to live in 6 tents. That is of course unless there were 2 in one them, but that's a different story.

FIGURE 2–21

"Because in those there is only one pig in each house but in the others I was thinking that some pigs could share a house."

"Does this story make you think of anything else?"

"Yes. I was thinking about other things you could do and figure out. Like the camping trip we're going on. I was thinking, if there are eighteen people going on our trip, and four are adults, and I have to get up in the middle of the night and need an adult, what are the possibilities of finding an adult in the first tent I go to?" (She was assuming there was no adult in her own tent.) She drew a picture and wrote a narrative to explain her reasoning (see Figure 2–21). She decided to use seven tents, but based her calculations on only six because she would be in the seventh. She found twenty-four possible ways for four adults (singly) to be in six tents. She was sensitive to the conditions that surrounded her problem, because she warned the reader at the end that if she had considered the possibility of two adults in one tent, then "that's a different story."

A final reflection on following children's leads

The strategies described in this chapter are ones that teachers have identified. Although good teachers know that the most interesting explorations come from kids, this is not to say that teachers do not play a key role in developing these leads. Good teachers look for books that invite hands-on investigations, that present an intriguing puzzle or mathematical challenge. They encourage children to play around with the variables of a given problem or story, knowing that these kinds of changes deepen a learner's understanding of the process. They offer open-ended invitations for responding to the story and support their students' collaborating with others and interpreting the text through different representational forms, such as art, drama, or written narrative. They value differences of opinion and encourage skepticism and doubt, because they know these can be the driving force behind further mathematical journeys. Most of all, these teachers value children, and respect their background and experience as assets for learning. They listen intently to children because they know all learners have stories to tell. They view children as curricular informants (Harste, Woodward & Burke 1984). They look to children to help set the direction of where to go. And they know that the best journeys are the ones that teachers and children plan together.

References

Anno, Mitsumasa. 1986. *Socrates and the three little pigs.* New York: Philomel.

Brown, Stephen, and Marion Walter. 1990. *The art of problem posing.* Hillsdale, NJ: Lawrence Erlbaum.

Dee, Ruby. 1988. *Two ways to count to ten.* New York: Holt.

Emberley, Ed. 1984. *Ed Emberley's picture pie: A circle drawing book.* Boston: Little, Brown.

Gág, Wanda. 1928. *Millions of cats.* New York: Coward, McCann and Geoghegan.

Harste, Jerome, Virginia Woodward, and Carolyn Burke. 1984. *Language stories and literacy lessons.* Portsmouth, NH: Heinemann.

Hutchins, Pat. 1986. *The doorbell rang.* New York: Greenwillow.

Johnston, Tony. 1986. *Farmer Mack measures his pig.* New York: Harper and Row.

Kitchen, Bert. 1987. *Animal numbers.* New York: Dial.

Lloyd, David. 1986. *The stopwatch.* New York: Lippincott.

Lobel, Arnold. 1970. The lost button. In *Frog and toad are friends.* New York: Harper and Row.

Maestro, Betsy, and Giulio Maestro. 1988. *Dollars and cents for Harriet: A money concept book.* New York: Crown.

Mathews, Louise. 1979. *Gator pie.* New York: Dodd, Mead.

McKissack, Patricia. 1992. *A million fish . . . more or less.* New York: Knopf.

Moore, Inga. 1991. *Six-dinner Sid.* New York: Simon and Schuster.

Paulos, John. 1988. *Innumeracy: Mathematical illiteracy and its consequences.* New York: Hill and Wang.

Reid, Margarette. 1990. *The button box.* New York: Dutton.

Russo, Marisabina. 1988a. *The line up book.* New York: Greenwillow.

———. 1988b. *Only six more days.* NY: Greenwillow.

Schwartz, David M. 1985. *How much is a million?* New York: Lothrop, Lee & Shepard.

Showers, Paul. 1991. *How many teeth?* New York: HarperCollins.

Silverstein, Shel. 1974. One inch tall. In *Where the sidewalk ends.* New York: HarperCollins.

Walter, Marion. 1971. *The magic mirror book.* New York: Scholastic.

———. 1978. *The mirror puzzle book.* Norfolk, England: Tarquin.

Whitin, David, Heidi Mills, and Timothy O'Keefe. 1990. *Living and learning mathematics.* Portsmouth, NH: Heinemann.

Fostering Mathematical Conversations 3

For many years mathematics classrooms were silent places. The focus of instruction was computational proficiency, achieved by memorizing rules and performing hours of mechanical practice. The teacher dispensed lockstep procedures and corrected problems, the answers to which were either right or wrong. An astute eighth grader describes the role of her past mathematics teachers this way:

All of my teachers in elementary school
always used math class
as their resting time.
Teachers got tired
or they needed to grade papers
and so they needed math class
to rest.
They didn't show you anything
like you do.
They just told you to study the examples
from the book
and get to work.
Then they sat down to rest.

When mathematics class is "resting time," there is no need for conversations. As a fifth-grade teacher recently reminded her students, in a rather stern voice, "You can't talk and do math at the same time." Math class is number-crunching time, and there's nothing else to talk about. We can discuss novels in literature class, and political issues in social studies class, but how do we discuss an algorithm in math class?

The little talk that has occurred in mathematics classrooms has been based on "the tyranny of the short, right answer" (Karp 1985, p. 69). Summarizing the current state of American education, and drawing upon the research of John Goodlad, who conducted research in over one thousand classrooms, critic Walter Karp concludes, "From the first grade to the twelfth grade, from one coast to the other, instruction in America's classrooms is almost entirely dogmatic. Answers are 'right' and answers are 'wrong,' but mostly answers are short" (p. 69).

However, times are changing. The NCTM's *Standards* documents have set a new direction for what really matters in mathematics education. The NCTM standards emphasize the need for students to be active constructors, not passive recipients, of their knowledge; they also highlight the importance of talk as an integral part of this constructing process. Learning to communicate mathematically is one of the NCTM goals, and it can be best accomplished when "students have the opportunity to read, write and discuss ideas in which the use of the language of mathematics becomes natural. As students communicate their ideas, they learn to clarify, refine and consolidate their thinking" (NCTM 1989, p. 6). Many of the other verbs used in the standards emphasize the importance of talk: conjecture, reason, test, estimate, build a logical argument. Talking allows learners not only to reflect on what they know but also to generate new insights into their current understanding. It is this generative aspect of talk that has been highlighted by so many people in the field of language education (Barnes 1987; Harste, Woodward & Burke 1984).

Children's literature can play a powerful role in restoring talk to mathematical concepts and ideas. Stories naturally embed mathematical concepts in a meaningful context; they provide a common base at which all learners can connect and from which they can extend their understanding and generate new stories; they describe situations that contain mathematical language operating in an authentic and purposeful manner; and they demonstrate that mathematics is not a subject unto itself but a tool for helping learners understand issues in social studies, science, health, and so on. Books can help restore the story (and thus the talk) to the teaching and learning of mathematics.

This chapter shows the kinds of conversations that are possible when teachers share mathematical books with their students. The first part of the chapter looks at how mathematical understanding can be extended by using good literature: understanding factorial numbers, understanding large numbers, understanding measurement concepts, and understanding fractions. The latter part of the chapter discusses three strategies that teachers have used to generate mathematical conversations: sharing a text set, engaging in written conversations, and conversing with parents. The chapter concludes with a look at the teacher's role in fostering mathematical discussions in his or her classroom.

Understanding factorial numbers

When asked what they learned about factorials in school, most people remember a rote process: 5! means $5 \times 4 \times 3 \times 2 \times 1 = 120$. And many people even got the right answers by learning in that way. However, if they had been asked, "Could you tell me a story that illustrates what 5! means?" most would have been at a loss. They had learned to be symbol pushers, not storytellers.

If we are to restore understanding to the teaching and learning of mathematics, we must first return the stories, since stories breathe life into abstract symbols and provide a basis for holding mathematical discussions. Christie Forrest explored the meaning of factorials with her third graders using *Anno's Mysterious Multiplying Jar*

(Anno 1983). (We described this book in our introduction.) Her experience is best described by Christie herself.

CHRISTIE'S STORY

Getting my class of third graders to talk had always been relatively easy, so I knew that *Anno's Mysterious Multiplying Jar* would definitely generate some mathematical talk. While I read the book, none of them said a word, as if they were soaking in all the words and pictures. This was not unusual. They are always intent about looking at and listening to any book I read. Their conversations and comments usually waited until after the last word. I finished the last sentence in the book.

"How did it get to be that many jars?!" Cassidy asked.

"Because there were lots of villages and then lots of houses in those villages and then lots of rooms in the house and so on," said Lacy.

"It was like everything was multiplying!" Melissa added.

Cassidy looked a little less confused, but was still not convinced there could have been 3,628,800 jars.

I then read the story again using the version in the second half of the book, where dots represent the items. I could see Cassidy nodding her head as if she was beginning to understand how such a large number was obtained. The question she asked was, "Well, what are those numbers with exclamation points after them at the top?" I explained that they were called factorials and that the exclamation point was the mathematical symbol designating the process for figuring out the number of items in each section of the book. The exclamation point meant that the number in front was to be multiplied by the next smallest number by the next smallest number, and so on, down to one.

"Oh, like five times four times three times two times one?" asked Adam. I told Adam that he was correct and then asked if this made sense to the class. I saw a lot of shaking heads.

I drew a large circle on the board and said, "This is our island." I then drew two circles inside the larger one and said, "These are our two countries." I put three squares in each country. "These are our states. How many states do we have in all?" The answer was yelled out, "Six!!" I then explained that we could get the same answer by representing it as $3 \times 2 \times 1$, showing the three states in each of two countries, which were both on one island. I then turned to the page in the book where it said, "On each mountain there were four walled kingdoms." I asked, "How could we figure out how many walled kingdoms there were in all?"

Lacy immediately responded, "So you could figure it out by saying four times three times two times one, right?"

"Well, let's see what answer we get."

Lacy's hand was up first. "You get twenty-four."

I acknowledged Lacy's correct answer, wrote 6! on the board, and said, "This is how many villages there were. How many is that?" I saw pencils flying across paper as they wrote $6 \times 5 \times 4 \times 3 \times 2 \times 1$ and multiplied.

Melissa was the first with an answer. "Seven hundred and twenty!!" she cried out.

I next wrote 7! on the board and asked what the answer to this would be. Almost immediately Lacy shouted, "That's 5,040!" Robbie looked at Lacy. "How did you do that so fast?"

"I just multiplied 7 times 720, which was 6!'s answer," Lacy said. Obviously, Lacy had caught on that she did not have to start over, multiplying 7 × 6 × 5 × 4 × 3 × 2 × 1. All she had to do was multiply 7 by the 6! answer.

I then asked the class, "Does everyone see what Lacy has discovered? She's found that if she knows the previous factorial answer, like 720 for 6!, if she wanted to find out 7! she would just have to multiply 7 times 6!. If I write out 6! and 7!, what is the difference?"

Adam piped up, "The 7! is the same as the 6! It just has seven times at the beginning. So you can just multiply seven more than the 6!" They all seemed to understand the new shortcut to finding the answers to factorials.

Since we had written out on the board the factorials and their answers for the numbers up to 10, I asked, "Why do the numbers get so large so fast?"

All the children tried to speak at once, but Lacy finally got the floor. "Because you are multiplying the answer before to the next biggest number. You are taking a pretty big number like 720 and then you have to multiply seven times that, because that's the next sequence number, and that gives you a much bigger number and soon it gets really big because the number you are multiplying by is getting so much bigger."

Robbie added, "Yeah, the numbers get so big that I bet if you found out 100! your answer would be so big that you couldn't fit it on your paper!"

Then Nicholas made an interesting observation: "Hey, look at 9! and 10! Their answers look almost the same."

Adam explained to Nicholas, "That's because with 10! it is like multiplying by ten and that's just like adding a zero."

"Oh, that's pretty neat!" said Nicholas.

Lacy's next comment was also very interesting. "Can you also do it backwards like say, I have three puppies and each puppy has two bones and each bone has one spot?"

"Well let's try and figure that out." I drew a picture of three puppies on the board. "What did each puppy have, Lacy?"

"Two bones."

I drew two bones per puppy. "What did each bone have?"

"One spot."

I drew the spot on each bone. "How many spots are there?"

"Six!"

"Just like three times two times one equals six," said Adam.

"I guess you can do the story backwards!" said Lacy.

I could tell that they were really starting to get into these factorials. Robbie commented, "You know, before you explained this book and the factorial thing, if you had read that book and asked me how many jars there were on that island, I would have probably said ten. I would have never thought that the real answer could have been a number that big!"

"You mean the answer 3,682,800," said Lacy.

"Yeah, 3,682,800," said Robbie.

"When you multiply stuff it sure can get big!" said Melissa.

Through their conversation, the students began to grasp the concept of the power of multiplying. Having only recently been introduced to multiplication, the students had not experimented enough to see the power that multiplication can have. They had been used to doing simple one- and two-digit multiplication and had not experienced such large numbers as answers in multiplication. Cassidy put it pretty well when she said, "Well, if you multiply so many numbers together, you are going to get a big answer."

I think my students learned a lot from this experience. Several of them created their own multiplying stories (see Figures 3–1 and 3–2). It was amusing to observe Cassidy as she wrote her story (Figure 3–1). She suddenly changed her picture drawings when she came to 5!. In the previous entry, she had included a picture representation of four towns per three states on the two continents, showing all twenty-four towns. However, when she got to 5! she realized that she couldn't draw 120 schools. "No wonder they didn't put all those numbers of pictures of things in that book. It would take forever and you wouldn't have enough room! Well, at least I got to the 4! page, showing *all* the objects."

Reading *Anno's Mysterious Multiplying Jar* made for a great math-learning morning. The students had a wonderful time learning about factorials. I heard one of them comment, "I think we're learning stuff that you do in high school. I bet my mom doesn't even know how to do this. I am going to read her my book and see if she can guess how many balls there were in all at the end. I bet she'll never guess that there were 3,628,800!!!"

WHAT CHRISTIE DID

This classroom conversation is interesting for a number of reasons. First, it is a child who initiates the discussion by asking, "How did it get to be that many jars?" Christie does not answer the question herself, but lets the other children explain it, thereby involving more people in the conversation right away. Second, when Christie sees that the children still do not understand the mathematics of the story, she creates her own example to talk about. Third, Christie keeps encouraging children to explain their thinking. For instance, she prompts Lacy to describe her shortcut method for finding her answers. Focusing on this process demonstrates to these children that Christie values not just right answers but also the strategies they use to frame and understand the problem. When children sense that teachers respect their thinking they will contribute their ideas to classroom discussions consistently throughout the year. Fourth, Christie asks questions herself ("Why do the numbers get so large so fast?") and accepts the different answers that children give. Lacy, Robbie, Nicholas, and Adam all offered their own unique explanation of the process. Fifth, Christie

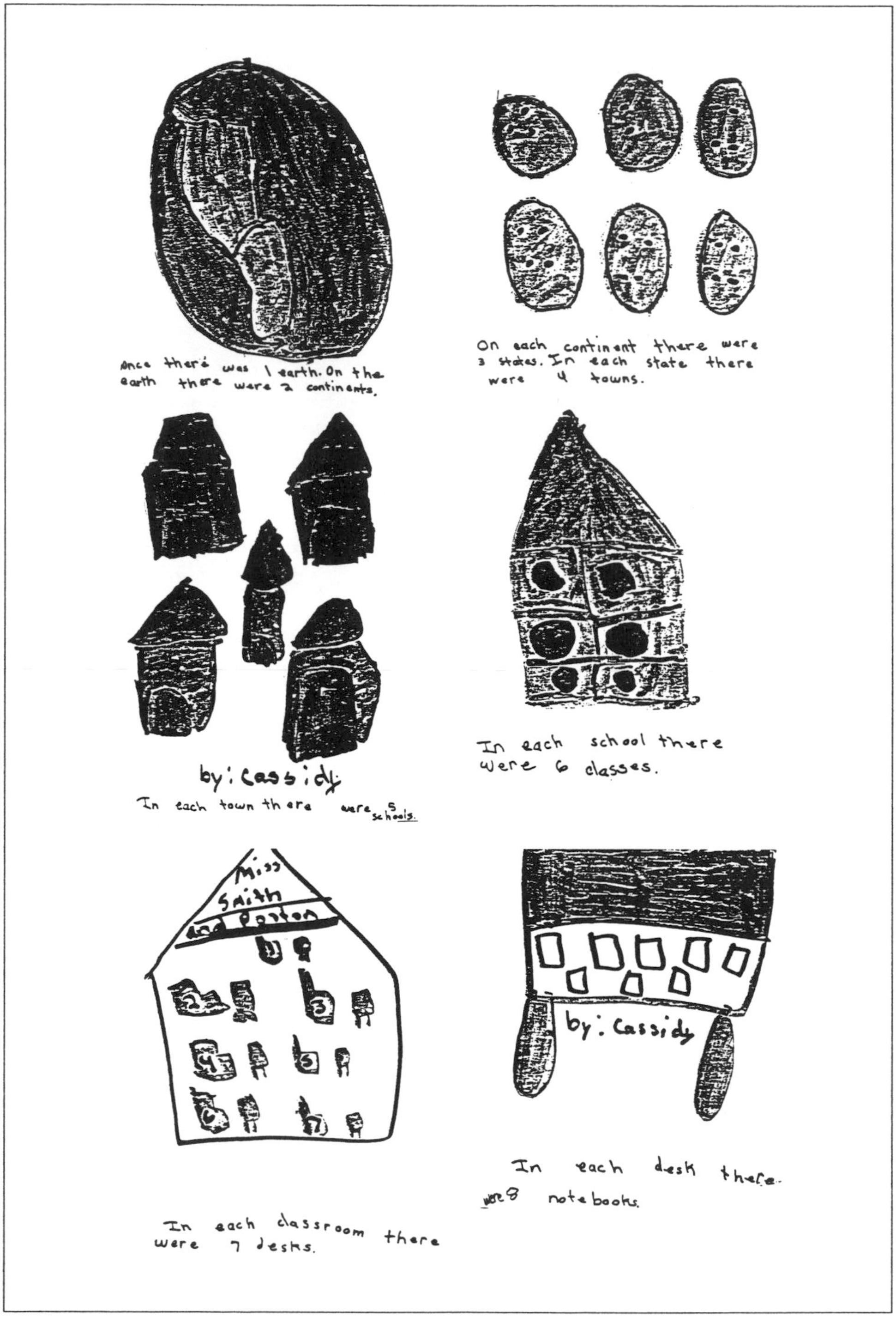
Once there was 1 earth. On the earth there were 2 continents.
On each continent there were 3 states. In each state there were 4 towns.
by: Cassidy
In each town there were 5 schools.
In each school there were 6 classes.
Miss Smith and Paxton
In each classroom there were 7 desks.
by: Cassidy
In each desk there were 8 notebooks.

FIGURE 3–1

In each notebook there were 9 pieces of paper.
On each piece of paper there were 10 lines.
How many lines were there in all?
10! = 10 × 9 × 8 × 7 × 6 × 5 × 4 × 3 × 2 × 1 =
3,628,800

FIGURE 3–1 (*CONTINUED*)

encourages hypothesizing. When Lacy asks whether it's possible to create a factorial story in reverse, Christie supports the problem-posing stance and helps Lacy pursue it. Christie plays a very active role in generating and extending this mathematical conversation.

Understanding large numbers

How Much Is a Million? (Schwartz 1985) often sparks interesting discussions about the magnitude of numbers. In this story a magician conducts a delightful exploration of the size of one million, one billion, and one trillion. We see a million children climbing onto one another's shoulders and stretching up farther than airplanes can fly; we see a billion goldfish swimming in a bowl the size of football stadium; and we discover that it would take twenty-three days to count to one million, ninety-five years to count to one billion, and over two hundred thousand years to count to one trillion. The vastness of these large numbers and the imaginative scenarios that the author describes provide the basis for engaging mathematical discussions.

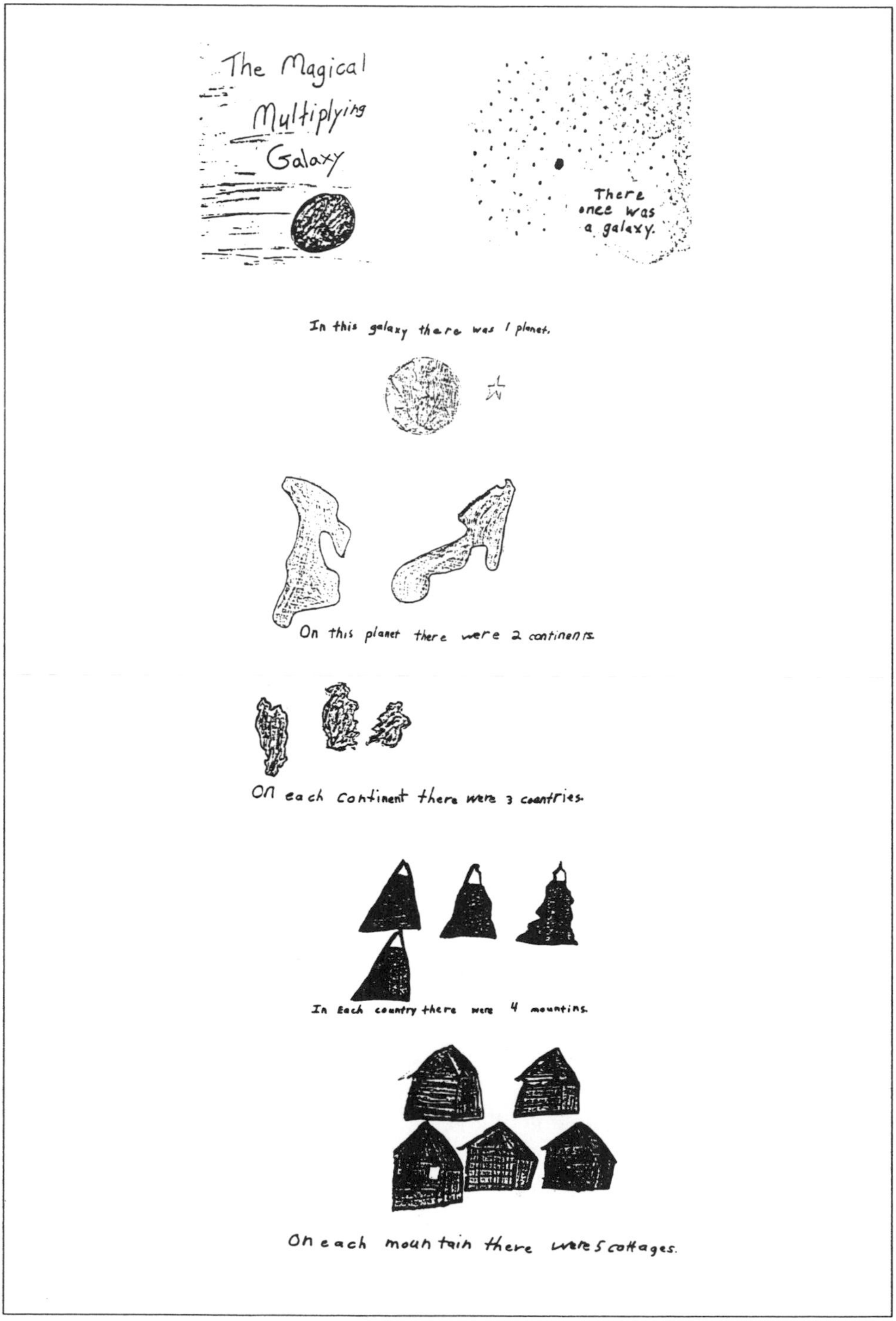
The Magical
Multiplying
Galaxy
There once was a galaxy.
In this galaxy there was 1 planet.
On this planet there were 2 continents
On each continent there were 3 countries.
In Each country there were 4 mountins.
On each mountain there were 5 cottages.

FIGURE 3–2

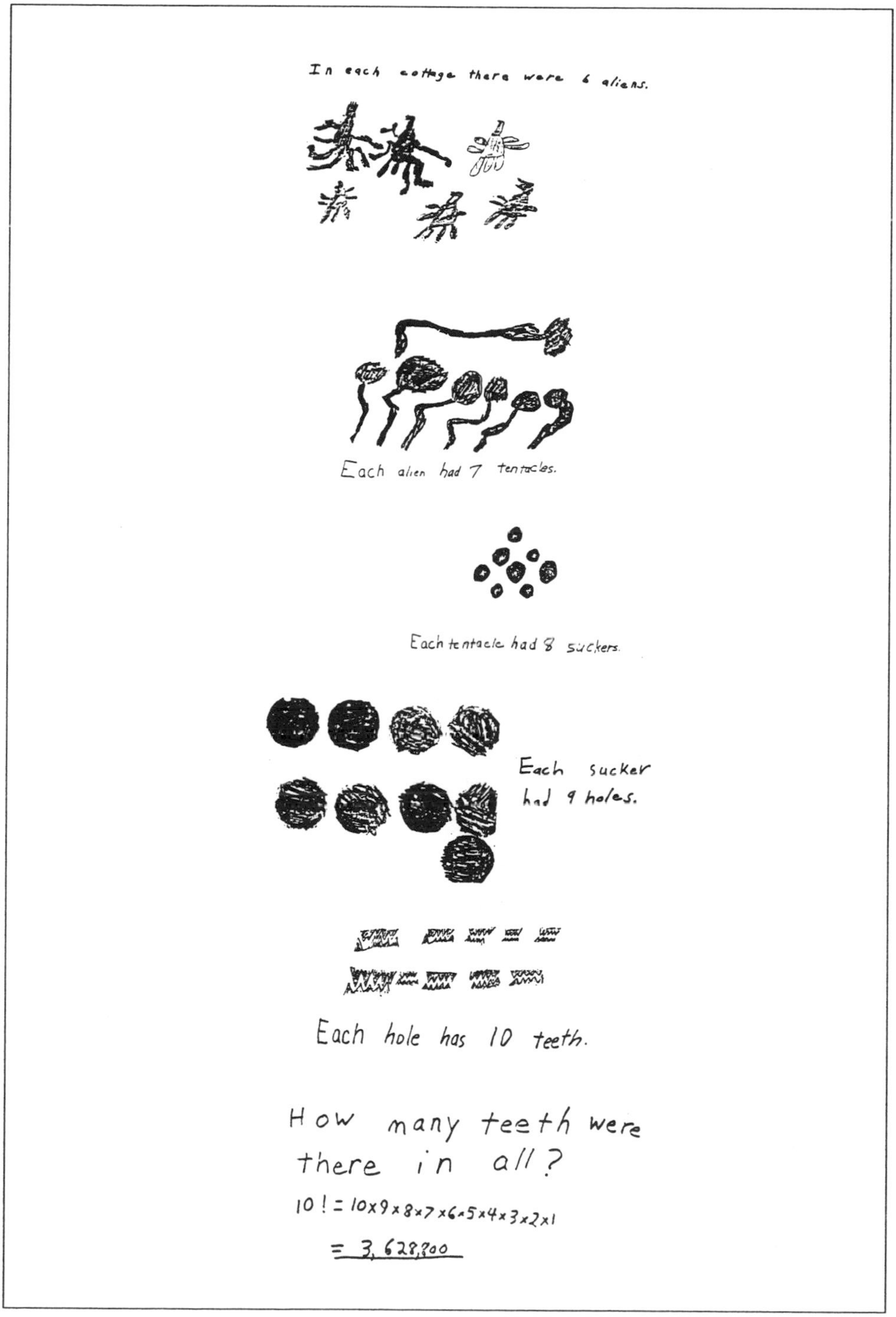
In each cottage there were 6 aliens.
Each alien had 7 tentacles.
Each tentacle had 8 suckers.
Each sucker had 9 holes.
Each hole has 10 teeth.
How many teeth were there in all?
10! = 10x9x8x7x6x5x4x3x2x1
= 3,628,800

FIGURE 3–2 (*CONTINUED*)

Before reading *How Much Is a Million?* aloud, teachers often ask their students to describe how much they think a million is:

HEATHER (*eight*): A million means lots of money.
GINGER (*thirteen*): It means lots; there's a million children in the world; there's nothing more than a million besides God.
RITA (*nine*): A million is like when you go to heaven and there's lots of gold for you to walk on.
LACIE (*four*): It's lots of times.
BRIDGETTE (*six*): I know it's more than a hundred. I think it's a lot. I believe it's more than a lot. Maybe my grandmother has a million strawberries in her freezer.
ADAM (*eight*): I think I saw a million stars, but I couldn't have seen them all at one time.
SHELYNN (*ten*): A million would be like counting all the leaves on a tree that is eight to ten feet around, that is found in Sacramento, California.
MEGAN (*eight*): There's a million people. I heard that on the news.

At first glance one might be tempted to view these responses as cute, naive, or unsophisticated. However, a closer look reveals that these children have made some insightful connections between their lives and the language of mathematics. They are able to place the term *million* in various contexts: money, religion, population, astronomy. They are also aware of its colloquial use by adults to mean "a lot." Think of these commonly used phrases:

Thanks a million.
Once in a million years.
I must have done that a million times.
If I've told you once, I've told you a million times.
I have a million things to do.
You act like your mind is a million miles away.

When children hear Schwartz's story read aloud they are sometimes intrigued by the sound of the mathematical words. For instance, when nine-year-old Paige saw the words million, billion, and trillion written in the text she remarked, "Hey, these look like the months of the year." She connected the repetitive ending of these words to the repetitive ending of some of the months of the year—September, October, November, December. Other children hypothesize about the names of other large numbers: "Is a zillion coming next?" "Is there such a thing as a zillion?" "After a billion you just make up your own." Some children enjoy learning about the names of large numbers beyond one trillion (see Figure 3–3) and even try representing them on an extra-long abacus (which they can construct using beads, coat-hanger wire, and a wooden base).

Children try to compare these large numbers in still other ways. When twelve-year-old Anthony heard his mother read the part in the story that asks, "How big is a billion?" he wanted to find out for himself. He grabbed some paper and a pencil and figured out how much greater a billion was than a million. He announced his discovery, "One billion is 999 million more than one million," and kept referring

FIGURE 3–3
Large Numbers

Million	10^6	Undecillion	10^{36}
Billion	10^9	Duodecillion	10^{39}
Trillion	10^{12}	Tredecillion	10^{42}
Quadrillion	10^{15}	Quattuordecillion	10^{45}
Quintillion	10^{18}	Quindecillion	10^{48}
Sextillion	10^{21}	Sexdecillion	10^{51}
Septillion	10^{24}	Septendecillion	10^{54}
Octillion	10^{27}	Octodecillion	10^{57}
Nonillion	10^{30}	Novemdecillion	10^{60}
Decillion	10^{33}	Vigintillion	10^{63}

Other large numbers

Googol is 10^{100}, or 1 followed by 100 zeroes. A googol is more than the number of grains of sand in the entire world. In fact, it has been estimated that all the grains of sand needed to fill a sphere the size of the earth would be only 10^{32}.

Googolplex is 1 followed by a googol of zeroes.

to this comparison as his mother read him the rest of the examples for one billion. When his mother read, "If a billion kids made a human tower . . .," Anthony completed the sentence with his own comparison: ". . . they would be 999 million higher than one million kids." Later on in the story, when his mom read, "How tremendous is a trillion?" Anthony used the same pattern he had discovered before, responding, "It's 999 billion more than one billion."

The comparisons in the story also prompt children to make some of their own estimations. When ten-year-old Eugene heard the part of the story that described a trillion goldfish, he remarked, "It would take five or six whales to make a trillion goldfish." He'd learned from an earlier part of the book that a million goldfish could occupy a fishbowl large enough to hold a whale, and he used that comparison to help him predict (even though inaccurately) the relative size of a trillion goldfish.

Suzanne Eaddy read this story aloud to her twin eight-year-old daughters, Rebecca and Erin, and was amazed to hear the personal connections they made between the story and their own knowledge of the universe. When Suzanne read about one billion kids standing on one another's shoulders, Rebecca predicted, "Oh Mamma, that would be out of our solar system. You know how heaven is up in the air; I'll bet a billion would reach up to heaven." When Suzanne read about a trillion kids standing on one another's shoulders, Erin began to predict farther into outer space:

ERIN: That would be in another galaxy.
REBECCA: Just imagine all the stars they could touch. They could take a jar and put stars in it.

SUZANNE: Like you do with lightning bugs.
ERIN: Yes, that would be fun, wouldn't it. They would all light up.

Children are also often intrigued by the concept of time in the story and make observations about particular spans of time that occur throughout the book. When the book states that it would take ninety-five years to count to a billion, these children made their own personal connection:

ERIN (*eight*): Ninety-five years is old for someone to live.
LAURA (*six*): That's almost a hundred years.
RACHEL (*seven*): Ninety-five. Holy cow! Some people don't even live that long.
ROBERT (*seven*): My grandma is ninety-one.
KATRINA (*seven*): Ninety-five years is older than my Aunt Edie. She's seventy-two.
ROBERTA (*eight*): [If I counted for ninety-five years] I would be older than my mother is now.
SEAN (*nine*): My great grandpa isn't even that old.
TERRELL (*seven*): You'd be dead.
SARAH (*eight*): Would you be old if you counted that much?
JAY (*ten*): If you add five more years to ninety-five you'd have a century.
GINGER (*thirteen*): When you count to a billion you couldn't because you would be dead. Your ancestors [*sic*] would have to continue counting after you died.
MAURICE (*six*): Nobody could live long enough to count to one billion.
CALEB (*six*): Jesus could do it.

These children are using some important strategies: comparing this span of time to the ages of people they know; hypothesizing about the longevity of human beings; predicting how old they would be; and identifying *century* as a term that describes a specific period of time.

Children also make personal connections with the twenty-three-day period required to count to one million. When seven-year-old Steven heard this span of time mentioned in the story, he jumped up, marched over to the class calendar, and counted backward twenty-three days to determine what the date was twenty-three days ago. As he compared this date with the current date he got a better understanding of the duration of this particular period of time. Eight-year-old Rebecca remarked to her mother, "Twenty-three days is almost a month," making an appropriate comparison to another unit of time.

When Carol Pierce commented to her students, "Twenty-three days is a little bit longer than three weeks," she was informed by seven-year-old Connie, "It's two days longer, because a week is seven days, and seven plus seven is fourteen, and seven more is twenty-one, and twenty-one plus two is twenty-three." Here Connie uses her knowledge of the unit of a week to refine her teacher's initial estimate.

The mathematical comparisons that are made in this story also invite children to explore ideas in the area of social studies. One of the important goals of the NCTM standards is for learners to investigate the relationship between mathematics and the other disciplines it serves, such as the physical and life sciences, the social sciences, and the humanities (NCTM 1989, p. 5). Children's literature provides an important avenue for learners to explore this important connection.

When eight-year-old Richard heard about a trillion kids standing on one another's shoulders, he raised a question about relative populations: "I couldn't find a trillion kids. I wonder if there is a trillion kids in Columbia [South Carolina]?" thus prompting him and his classmates to investigate the populations of other cities and towns of the state. Other children have been intrigued by the distance of ten miles. The story mentions that if the book pages necessary to contain a billion tiny stars were stretched out end to end, they would cover a distance of ten miles. When one student in a fourth-grade class asked, "How far is ten miles anyway?" his classmates offered their own personal comparisons:

"Would it be ten miles to Seven Oaks Parks [*a recreation center*]?"

"I think it's ten miles to Dutch Square [*a local shopping center*]."

"Or maybe even to [downtown] Columbia."

"I think it's about how far my house is from the school." The children investigated this idea with their teacher by taking a map of the city and drawing a circle with a ten-mile radius around the school, thus connecting this distance to familiar landmarks in their community.

When author David M. Schwartz estimates that pages containing a trillion stars would stretch from New York to New Zealand, he invites some other possible explorations. Seven-year-old Michelle admitted, "I don't know where New Zealand is." After she and her classmates located it on a globe she exclaimed, "Gosh, that's a long way. It's farther than Hawaii." Michelle was able to make her own personal comparison between countries and gain a deeper understanding of relative distances. When eight-year-old Andrea heard about paper stretching to New Zealand she wondered, "Would that go from here to China? How about from here to Russia?" She worked with her classmates to determine the relative distances of these different locations. When eight-year-old Adam heard about New Zealand he was already predicting it was a long distance away, because he'd noticed the book's pattern of revealing larger and larger numbers. Since he had just returned to South Carolina from a family trip to Florida and was tired of traveling in the car, he responded (logically): "I don't know how far away New Zealand is, but I know it's a long way. If it's longer than going to Florida I don't want to go!" After he'd located both Florida and New Zealand on the globe, he was adamant about not going to New Zealand!

A fourth-grade class first wanted to estimate the number of miles around the equator. They knew that the distance across the United States was approximately 3,000 miles and used this information to calculate the distance around the equator to be about 25,000 miles. Then they looked again at the distance from New York to New Zealand and figured that distance to be about half of the distance around the globe, or about 12,500 miles. One student even related this distance of 25,000 miles to a personal experience: "Well, if it's 25,000 miles around the world, then my mom would have gone around the world four times, 'cause she has over 100,000 miles on her car."

Another social studies term that intrigues children as they hear this story is the concept of a harbor. Schwartz calculates that the amount of water needed to support a trillion goldfish would be enough to fill a city harbor. When six-year-old Travis saw the illustration of the harbor he remarked, "A harbor is a big place to fish. It's bigger than a pond." Eight-year-old Richard asked, "Is a harbor as big as Lake Murray?" the largest body of water he was familiar with. Seven-year-old Sarah made some other comparisons: "That harbor looks like an ocean. How big is a city harbor? Does Columbia have a city harbor?" Since Sarah had been to Charleston, South Carolina, her teacher helped her make a comparison by explaining, "The water by Charleston is a harbor," to which Sarah replied, "Is it like a bay?" These children were connecting the less familiar concept of a harbor to ones they were more familiar with, such as ponds, lakes, oceans, and bays.

Understanding measurement concepts

Wonderful examples of books with the potential for leading children into a variety of measurement experiences are Joanna Cole's *Large as Life* books (1985a, 1985b). These large-format books, also available as a single volume (Cole 1990), contain beautiful life-size paintings of a variety of animals, such as a red squirrel, a giant toad, a wood mouse, and a fennec fox. The brief text accompanying the illustrations discusses characteristics of each animal. Children find the life-size illustrations particularly intriguing: almost all other storybooks and textbooks about animals have scaled-down representations. Many teachers introduce these books by saying something like this:

> *The animals you see in this book are exactly this same size in real life. It is as if I'm bringing these animals to you alive. If they could crawl, hop, or fly out of the pages of this book and enter our classroom, they would be just as big as you see them here.*

Let's look at some of the conversations teachers and children have had about these books. Pet Harper read the single-book version of Cole's work to a group of children of various ages one summer. Partway though the story, when Pet showed the illustration of the large brown hare, Leslie, six, reached out to pet the rabbit, then looked at Pet with a disappointed expression: "Why is it not soft?" Mary, twelve, was intrigued by the pictures of little blue penguins, the smallest penguins in the world, who actually never see any ice or snow but live on the beaches of Australia. Mary asked, "I wonder if the fact that they are so small has anything to do with why they can live in a warm climate?" Mary also found it interesting that the female Queen Alexandra's birdwing butterfly was so much larger than the male: "Usually the male of something gets to be the largest, and I like it that just the female gets to be called the largest in the world." Mary made other comparisons throughout, noting that the woodpecker was the same size as a pear in the illustration and that the baby monkey was the same size as a banana.

When Pet finished reading the story she asked, "Did you notice anything else about the size of the animals?" Jamie, twelve, offered the following comparison and hypothesis: "I think it is neat that the frog [*giant toad*] is in the book because it is the biggest frog and the antelope is in the book because it is so small for an antelope [*the royal antelope is the smallest antelope in the world, often no bigger than a hare*]. I wonder why the antelope is so tiny and doesn't get bigger and I wonder what makes the toad so big for a toad. Maybe since the toad lives in a hot place it eats things that make it big." The sharp contrasts in size encourage learners to venture hypotheses for further investigation.

JoAnn Smith read the book to her three children, Ewell (twelve), Seth (ten), and Leah (six), because they loved wildlife and enjoyed learning interesting facts about animals. When she showed them the little blue penguins on the opening page, Leah exclaimed, "I wish I could touch that penguin and hold him in my arms." The text helped Leah understand the size of this penguin by stating that it could be held in the reader's two hands. She "lifted" the baby penguin out of the book and pretended to hold it. When the children read about the Queen Alexandra's birdwing butterfly they were again struck by its size. Leah used her hands as measuring devices and was amazed to discover that a butterfly could grow wings as long as three of her hands. Ewell and Seth questioned the size of the illustration: "That wingspan doesn't look like twelve inches to me," said Ewell. The boys went to get a ruler and found the span to be eleven inches. Since the notes at the back of the book state the female could have a wingspan of "up to twelve inches," they were satisfied with the illustration's authenticity. All three children were particularly interested in the picture of the common tree frog, because it was an animal they found in their yard fairly often.

Later on that day the boys were able to catch one of those frogs, and Leah captured a ladybug, an insect depicted on a tree limb in one of the illustrations. The children got out the book and placed the creatures on top of their representations as a way to test their size. To check the proportionality of the frog painting even further, they brought in some leaves and used them to cover the live frog and the illustrated frog. They were struck with the consistency and were satisfied that the illustrations were accurate. They continued to test other pages as well, collecting twigs, leaves, and even an apple to place on the appropriate pages. Their recurring skepticism was the driving force behind all this conjecturing and testing.

The size of a bee hummingbird, the smallest bird in the world, also fascinated the children. They discovered from the book that this little creature, whose nest is the size of a thimble, is lighter than half a teaspoon of sugar. They all wanted to feel the weight of that bird. Ewell went to the kitchen and measured a half teaspoon of sugar and poured it in Seth's hand, and then Leah's hand, so they could really experience the weight of that smallest bird.

The description of the royal antelope, with "legs as thin as pencils" and hooves so small that all four could leave hoofprints on a fifty-cent piece, prompted additional measuring. The children just had to test out these assertions. Ewell placed a pencil on the picture of the antelope's leg to show it was the size of a pencil and then placed his thumb on the hoof to show it was a fairly close approximation. Next he traced a fifty-cent piece on a piece of paper and the children placed four of their thumbs on it at the same time to see how they would fit. Using a part of their own bodies as a comparison helped them understand the size of this antelope in another way.

Seth was most interested in the fennec fox, a desert animal with exceptionally big ears. He measured the illustration and found the ears to be four inches tall and the tail to be eight inches long. All the children were amazed at this unique proportion, ears that were half as long as a tail. JoAnn related, "This sparked Seth's curiosity to go out and measure our own dog's ears and tail. He discovered first that Jessie's ears are not exactly the same size. Secondly, Jessie's chosen ear was about six inches tall and his tail about two feet long. The kids had a great laugh visualizing Jessie with one-foot ears to go with his two-foot tail if his ear-tail proportion were the same as that of the fennec fox. Seth also measured his own bottom so he could imagine how he would look with ears half the size of his backside. This certainly helped us all see how unusual the fennec fox's large ears are."

Other measurement explorations followed. "Leah became interested in measuring with the ruler at this point. The boys demonstrated for her how to measure properly with a ruler. She practiced by measuring an apple and the wood mouse. She was so excited she began to measure everything. Since Seth measured parts of our dog, Leah wanted to measure our pet miniature rabbit. She discovered he didn't like being measured, but he would be small enough to fit on the pages of the book. This opened up a whole new investigation. The boys decided to come up with a list of animals that could appear in the book. They decided they needed the measurements of the length and width of the book. They discovered it was about thirteen inches tall and about ten inches wide and concluded that the animals could not be any larger than eleven inches by eight inches or eleven inches by eighteen inches. When I asked about their conclusion they explained: 'We allowed two inches all around for the plants [appearing in the illustrations]. Plus we figured the animal could cover one page and only be about nine inches long or cover two pages and be about eighteen inches long.' Their list included animals such as snakes, worms, starfish, and hamsters. This became a nightlong game. One would say 'cow' and the other would say 'not' and so forth. Leah was even able to play this game with her big brothers."

Elaine Cope's third graders raised some good questions and made interesting comparisons in using Cole's book. When Elaine read about the Queen Alexandra's birdwing butterfly, Tim was intrigued with butterflies tasting with their feet. His comment led the class into a discussion about the words *foot* and *feet.* They realized that these words had two meanings, a part of the body and a specific unit of measurement, a connection that many of them had not previously made. The illustration of the lesser spotted woodpeckers, one going into its nest and the other lighting on the trunk of a tree, generated several questions related to measurement.

SHEREKA: How big is that woodpecker's beak?
BRUCE: That sure is a small bird.
MATT: How big are the babies?
DAWN: How big are the eggs?
GLENDA: How big is that hole for the woodpecker's home?

When the children read about an eastern chipmunk that could carry seventeen nuts at once they wondered, "How can he do that?" and they tried to work out the logistics. Jermaine suggested, "Well, he could put eight nuts in one pouch and nine in the other one." "Yeah, seventeen is an odd number," said Dawn, explaining

FIGURE 3–4

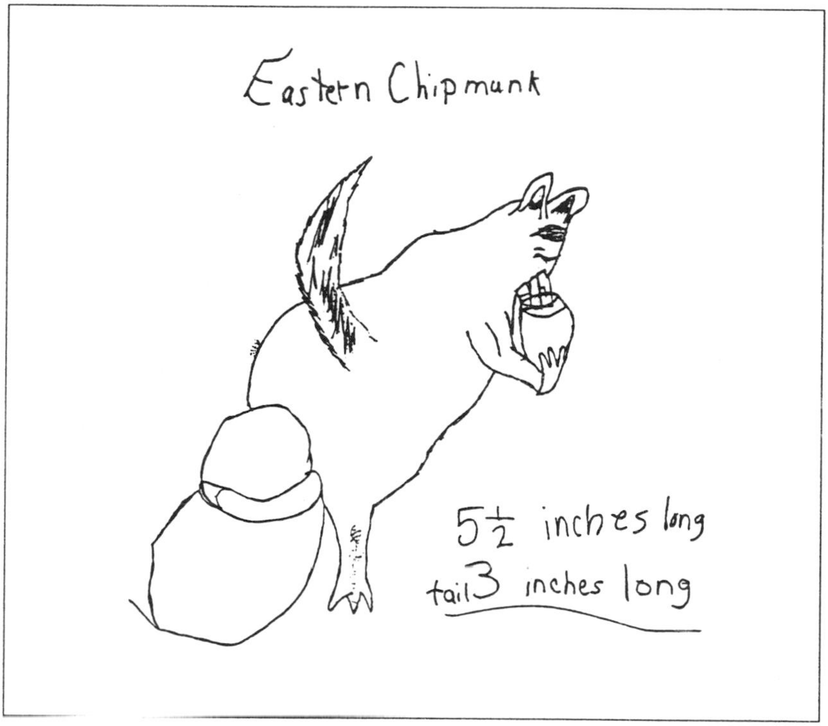

why one pouch has more nuts than the other. "But he could put eight in each pouch and have one left over for later," said Lindsay.

It was the size of the eastern chipmunk that fascinated Brandon. Later on he drew his own chipmunk (see Figure 3–4) and recorded some of his own measurements.

The weight of the hummingbird also intrigued Elaine's students. Elaine measured half a teaspoon of sugar into everyone's hand so they could actually feel the weight, and the children began to identify objects in the room that had a comparable weight, such as a piece of paper, a feather, an empty crayon box, an eraser, a paper clip, and a pencil. These personal comparisons became benchmarks for understanding this particular weight.

Cole's description of the squirrel monkey compares its size to that of a banana and notes that a mother squirrel monkey would fit inside a book bag and her baby would fit into a child's pocket. Taures asked, "Is he called a squirrel monkey 'cause he looks like a squirrel or 'cause he acts like a squirrel?" It was a good question for further research. Brandon asked, "Where does this monkey live anyway?" The children used the world map to find South America; they noticed the equator went through the northern part of the continent and concluded these monkeys must live in a warm climate. The next day Elaine brought a banana to school; students placed the banana on top of the picture of the monkey and found the lengths to be equivalent. Mario was fascinated by the monkey's long tail and traced the tail and the banana on a piece of paper so he could compare the two (see Figure 3–5). Several

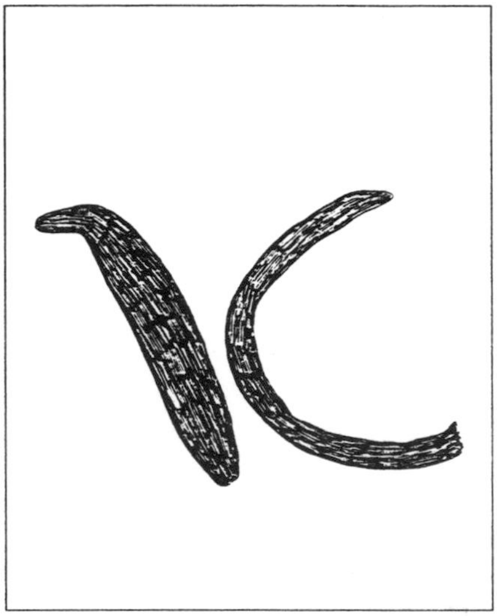

FIGURE 3–5

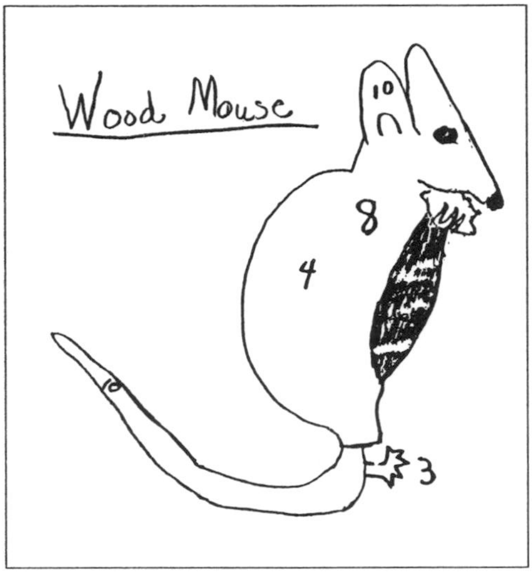

FIGURE 3–6

other children shared their book bags so everyone could visualize the mother monkey fitting inside a pouch that size; others pushed their fists into their pockets to give them a feel for the size of the baby.

The wood mouse was particularly appealing to Bruce. "How long is its body? And its tail is pretty long. How long is that?" Later on, Bruce traced an outline of the wood mouse (see Figure 3–6) and measured various parts of its body using a centimeter ruler.

While sharing *Large as Life Animals* with their students, these teachers were instrumental in fostering rich mathematical discussions. They encouraged children to keep sharing their observations, as Pet Harper did when she asked, "Did you notice anything else about the size of the animals?" When children seemed skeptical about information in the text, such as the wingspan of the butterfly or the size of the frog, their teachers challenged them to find a way to test their doubts. JoAnn Smith supported other explorations by letting her children conduct empirical investigations such as holding a half teaspoon of sugar to feel the weight of a hummingbird, thus supplying more information and extending the conversation in new ways. The teachers also encouraged children to ask questions throughout the story, questions that led other children to offer their own explanations of the size, location, or behavior of animals.

Understanding fractions

Deborah Cotherman shared *The Half-Birthday Party* (Pomerantz 1984) with a group of six-, seven-, and eight-year-old children who were attending local day-care. In this lovely story, Daniel becomes so excited when his six-month-old sister Katie stands for the first time that he decides to organize a half-birthday party for her. He invites Mom, Dad, Grandma, and some neighbors, instructing each one to bring only half a present. A neighbor brings one slipper (half a pair), since her dog had chewed apart the other one. Mom brings one gold earring, having lost the other one many years ago. She shows it to Katie but puts it aside for her to enjoy when she is older. Grandma brings half a birthday cake lit by half a candle. Daniel is so busy organizing the party that he forgets to bring a present himself. However, as the night arrives, Daniel asks everyone to look outside, for his gift is a half-moon. The story uses both a set model for fractions (the slippers and earrings) and a region model (the cake, candle, and moon).

After reading the title of the book, Deborah asked, "What do you think a half-birthday is?"

"Where everybody gets half of something."

"Get half a piece of cake."

"Before your whole birthday."

"Like six and a half."

"Share a birthday with others, like there are three girls in my class that have the same birthday."

"A half a year until your next birthday."

When Deborah read about the invitation asking each person to bring half a present, one child asked "How do you do that?"

"Chop it in half," suggested one.

"No. It's like a friendship bracelet," said another.

"How is a friendship bracelet half a present?" Deborah asked.

"You have part, and you give a friend part, and when you put them together they make something."

Another child suggested that half a present might be "if you like have two cups, give one of the cups."

When Deborah read the part of the story where everyone said "Happy Half-Birthday to you," Jamie, eight, said, "They could have sung 'Happy Half-Birth' 'cause that would be half." The others in the group were amused and tried singing the traditional birthday song, using the words "Happy Half-Birth," followed by some humming each time. However, one of the children complained afterward, "That's not good—you don't know who you're singing to!"

The children had fun predicting what Daniel was going to bring as a present. When he asked everyone to step out on the fire escape so he could show them his present, one child predicted, "I know, it's the stars." Another child extended that prediction: "Yeah, maybe he's going to make half a wish on those stars." At the end of the story, Ashley tried to explain Daniel's answer to his mother when he said it was only "half true" that he knew all along what he was going to give Katie: "He kind of made it up because he forgot to get Katie a present. So he really didn't tell a whole lie."

Since the children still seemed interested in discussing the idea of half, Deborah asked them, "What would you bring to a half-birthday?" The children responded enthusiastically.

"A half stuffed animal."

"A half piece of paper—I mean a half birthday card. The half that says 'happy' on it."

"A half Barbie doll—the top half."

"A half of a teddy bear."

"Half of a puzzle because that person may not be big enough to do a whole one. Then I would give him the whole, or the other part, when he's about six or something."

"I'd give a TV."

"A whole TV?"

"Yeah, cause on the next half I'd give the VCR. Then on another birthday I'd give the tapes."

"How much is one half?" asked Deborah, extending the conversation. Jason walked to the bulletin board and pointed to each part of an equally striped red-and-white flag that was displayed there: "The red and white one right here, that's a half." Another child pointed to a flag with three stripes. "This flag right here has three halfs," he said.

"No, that's three thirds," said Jamie.

"What do you mean by thirds?" asked Deborah.

"Because there's not three halves cause there can only be one half or two in a whole, then it has to go the next . . . three."

"Hey look, you can split this other flag in half again," said Matt, pointing to a flag with four stripes, a green one at the top, followed by a white, a red, and a blue. "Right here," he said, touching the line between the white and red sections of the flag.

"What does that show?" Deborah asked.

"Two halves," said Jason. "See one, the two on top, and one, the two on the bottom. Two halves. That's four. Four fourths."

This particular flag helped demonstrate the equivalence of one half and two fourths. Deborah wanted to encourage them to keep looking around the room, so she asked, "Is there anything else in the room we could put into halves?"

"Yes, these books could be halves."

"How could we do that?" asked Deborah.

"Easy. Put some on this side and some on that side," said Laura Beth. "Like this . . . take one and put it here and then put another one here." She began to separate a pile of books into two piles.

"Keep doing it until you've used them up," said Matt.

"But that's not half," said one of Laura Beth's helpers.

"How do you know?" asked Deborah.

"Because this pile over here is taller. See, it goes up higher than this one," comparing the height of the two stacks with her hand.

"That's because they are fatter books," responded Laura Beth. "It can be half if they both have the same number. See, one side is even with the other side—both are six. It doesn't matter that some are fat. The numbers have to be even for half."

The discussion continued, as some children argued that half could be represented by half a set of discrete objects, such as six books in each pile, while others claimed that half could be shown as a continuous measure, such as the height of each stack of books. Their conversation helped highlight both of these models for fractional parts.

An important aspect of this conversation is the key role Deborah played in fostering and extending it. She encouraged children to share their own thoughts about fractional parts: "What would you bring to a half-birthday party?" She invited children to make predictions: "What do you think a half-birthday party is?" She allowed the children to pose their own alternative scenarios, like Jamie's revised birthday song. Deborah also kept encouraging the children to explain their reasoning: "How is a friendship bracelet half a present?" "What do you mean by three thirds?" "How could we do that?" These open-ended, nonjudgmental comments fostered a spirit of continuous sharing.

Zach and Michael, two students who had just finished the fourth grade, had an interesting fractions discussion after Donna Caprell read them *The Doorbell Rang* (Hutchins 1986). As the story begins, two children are eager to share a dozen cookies, six each. But before they have a chance to eat a single cookie, the doorbell rings and two friends come in, and the four of them now have only three cookies each.

Then the doorbell rings again. Zach spontaneously predicted, "Now it's probably going to be one and a half each."

"Why do you think that?" asked Donna.

"Because it's half. It used to be six each, and now it's three each, and now it's going to be one and a half each. It went from six to three to one and a half. It's going to keep halving." Zach then counted the chairs around the kitchen table. "Two, four, six, eight, ten, twelve. Hey, I guess it's two each."

"So maybe the next would be one half each," suggested Michael.

"No, it's going to be either one, or one and a half, or half," insisted Zach.

Since the boys had been intrigued by the pattern in the number of cookies each child received, Donna read the story again and asked them to think about that pattern.

Zach: "Well, they halved it, six to three, it went down to three, so they halved it and then that made it . . ." He looked at the book. "It says right here 'six each,' then it says right here 'three each,' then it says right here 'two each.'" He paused a moment. "I don't get that. And then it says right here, 'that's one each.' It halved it except for—it should—you see, it went from six to three and then from three to two. Why did it to that? It didn't half it. But then it went from two to one."

When Donna analyzed the conversation later she wrote, "I thought the investigation he was doing was terrific, and I just let him carry on with it."

Zach drew a platter of cookies (see Figure 3–7) to help him understand this anomaly. "Twelve cookies. There's two people. That means you have to divide [the cookies] in half." Zach drew two faces and drew six cookies under each face. "Then when there's four people, you have to divide them into fourths." He made a line through each column of six cookies, creating four groups of three each, and drew two more faces and gave them each three by drawing lines with arrows from the bottom group of three in each column. "Then it says Peter and his little brother came," said Zach.

FIGURE 3–7

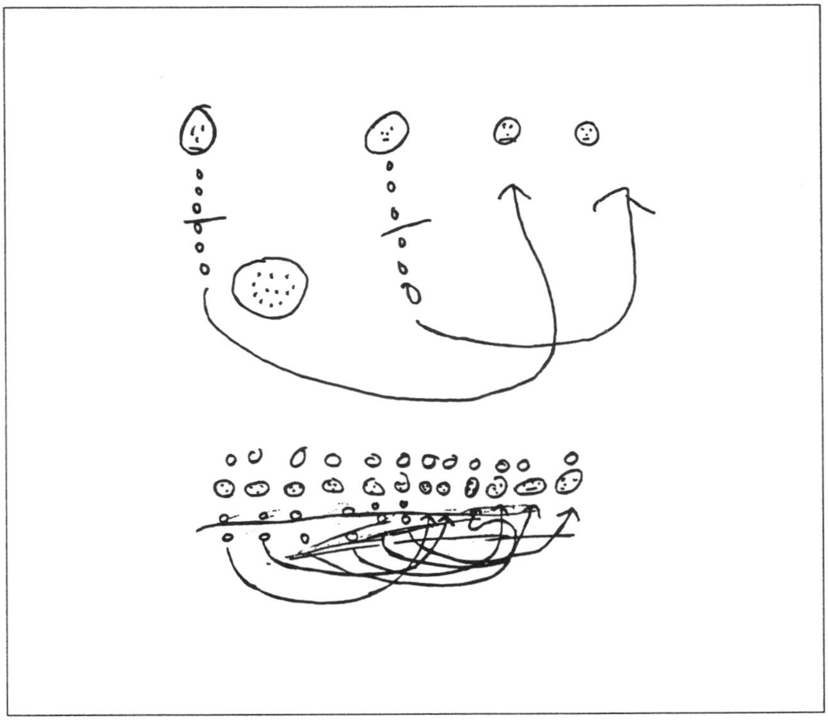

Michael and Zach both agreed, "Yeah, that's six," as they looked at the picture. However, Zach still questioned the next partitioning. "But look, I don't get that. 'Cause then look, if they gave them, oh . . . then each person would have to give one, so that would be . . . no."

At this point Michael pointed to the drawing and explained, "Yeah, wait Zach. Look. One, two, cut right here. Each person would have to get one."

Zach then drew six faces at the bottom of the paper and placed a cookie above and below each face so he could better understand the process: "If each person gave one, you would have two, and he would have two, and then everybody else would have two, 'cause each person gave one and they had three. Then six more people came in." At this point Zach drew six more faces next to his first line of six. He then used arrows to show how each of the first set of six children would give one cookie to each of the second set of six, leaving one cookie for each person.

Notice Donna's role here. She encourages the boys to answer their own questions by saying, "What do you think?" when Zach poses his initial query. She encourages the children to predict, and to explain their reasoning behind these predictions: "Why do you think that?" She rereads the story so Zach can pursue what seemed to be an anomaly in the numerical pattern of divided cookies. Anomalies are the driving force behind many wonderful investigations; Donna recognizes their importance and uses it to extend the discussion.

Sharing a text set

A text set is a collection of books (and often other artifacts as well) associated with a particular concept or topic (Harste, Short & Burke 1988). When learners have the opportunity to see and experience a range of texts, they have more opportunities to make connections and to view that concept in a wide variety of contexts. Let's look at what happened when David Whitin used this strategy with Robin Cox's fifth-grade class.

The children had had an earlier discussion about large numbers and were particularly interested in the concept of infinity. Some argued that infinity represented the largest number while others claimed it was not really a number. Seeing their interest in the topic, David read four books to them—*Owly* (Thaler 1982), *What Is Beyond the Hill?* (Ekker 1985), *Hot Pursuit* (Moerbeek & Dijs 1987), and *The Yellow Button* (Mazer 1990)—and invited the children to respond.

TANYA: They all keep going on and on like infinity.

CHARLIE: The book *Owly* is like *How Much Is a Million?* because it keeps going up and up and up.

BRANDON: That *Hot Pursuit* reminds me of *The Never-ending Story*; it just keeps going on and on and never ends. So if you read that book it never ends. Also, a number isn't infinity because a number always stays the same, and infinity doesn't stay the same, it just keeps going on and on.

BRENT: Well, trees are like infinity because they keep on going; they have seeds that grow into new trees, and so on.

ROBERT: Animals are like infinity, because they have babies, and they grow up and have babies, and it just keeps going on and on.

BRENT: A circle is like infinity because it keeps going around and around. Like a square, you have to stop, and go around a corner, and then start again, but a circle you can just keep going.

NIGEL: But some animals don't go on forever. They're extinct.

DAVID: So what happens to break that cycle?

NIGEL: We kill them, and they can't keep going.

DAVID: Yes, sometimes we break that circle of life.

ROBERT: A line goes on forever. Like a radius, I think, has a beginning and an end, but a line can keep stretching out and go on forever.

TENNILLE: A road can go on forever.

BRENT: No, there are some roads that are dead ends.

ROBERT: Yeah, but on cul-de-sacs there are places to turn around so you could just keep going.

JASON: [*Going up to the globe*] Is the ocean like infinity?

ROBERT: [*Joining him*] Yes, the ocean just keeps going. It just goes around these continents, and up and around, and you could just keep going.

LEE: The roller coaster ride at the fair: that's like infinity. You could just keep going around and around.

JASON: Yeah, like a figure-eight racetrack.

ADAM: There's a ride at Carowinds that's in a circle. You go around in a circle; you could keep going around like that forever.

TENNIELLE: Reading is like infinity. Like if you read a book that you really like, it makes you want to read more. And so you read another good book, and you just keep reading and reading.

TANYA: Holidays. You know, there's Christmas and Easter, and the holidays keep coming every year.

BRANDON: Like weeks—weeks just keep coming.

BRENT: Yeah, and hours and minutes and seconds.

DAVID: Are there any subjects you've studied this year that are connected to infinity?

ADAM: Wars. It seems like we just keep having war. Like we just had Desert Storm.

TENNIELLE: The bomb we dropped on Japan, because they're still feeling the effects of that.

JASON: Heat and cold, because if we didn't have cold, the heat would go on forever.

CATHY: Folktales, because stories are something you keep telling over and over again.

TANYA: We've been studying recycling, and that's infinity. You take a piece of paper, and that's recycled into newspaper, and the newspaper can be recycled, and so on.

ADAM: Well, there's another book that's sort of like infinity, *The Doorbell Rang.* Because the kids could keep coming and coming, and they could keep bringing more and more cookies.

AMANDA: I was wondering if the ocean had a depth.

ADAM: I think it has a bottom. Because if it didn't it would have a hole, and the water would go through the hole and push out into the atmosphere.

This conversation has a number of interesting facets. First, the children connect the books that David read to still other pieces of literature, such as *How Much Is a Million?* and *The Doorbell Rang*; in this way they extend the text set and see new relationships among a larger set of books. Second, the children connect the concept of infinity to a variety of contexts: amusement park rides, a racetrack, war, folktales, and recycling. The concept provides a lens to review other subjects they have studied during the year. Third, the children connect the concept of infinity to other mathematical concepts, such as time (holidays, weeks, minutes, seconds), length (depth of the ocean), temperature (heat and cold), and geometric shapes (circles, squares, and lines). They see the interrelationship of numerous mathematical concepts in a variety of real-life contexts.

Engaging in written conversations

Written conversation is a strategy developed by Carolyn Burke of Indiana University (Harste, Short & Burke 1988). It is a way for learners to continue a conversation by writing their comments rather than talking. Talk is ephemeral; writing provides a permanent record that learners can reconsider and reflect on later. Cassandra Gary used this strategy with several of her first-grade children after reading *The Line Up Book* (Russo 1986).

In this story a young boy named Sam begins to make a long line of objects from his bedroom to the kitchen. He begins the line with some wooden blocks but when he uses them all up he looks for other objects. He finds a pile of books and includes these in his lineup, then incorporates some bath toys. At this point Adrienne noticed that in the book's illustration there was a large vase with two umbrellas. "He could use those umbrellas," Adrienne suggested.

Austin, evaluating this suggestion, said, "Yeah, but there's only two of them," to which Adrienne replied, "I know there's two but they're really long."

This brief impromptu discussion shows Adrienne predicting like a reader and estimating like a mathematician simultaneously. She was predicting like a reader because she had latched on to the repetitive structure of the story and knew that Sam was going to be looking for another object with which to extend his line. She was estimating like a mathematician because she knew that if Sam used longer units in his line he would not need as many units to cover the same distance. She was exploring this inverse relationship between the length of an object and the number of objects required as she explained her reasoning to Austin. Her suggestion was quite inventive, since at this point Sam had only used smaller objects, such as blocks, boots, and bath toys. Although Sam did not use the umbrellas next, Adrienne's suggestion helped demonstrate to her classmates that learners have choices in the devices they choose to employ.

After Cassandra finished reading the story to her students she invited them to do some measuring. "Find some things in the room that you would like to measure. Figure out a way to measure them using something other than a ruler and then record what you find out."

Since the task was left open-ended the children could record their findings in their own way. James wrote (see Figure 3–8): "I measured the inside of my folder and it is ? 3 and a half! I'm going to measure my desk. It is ? 5 and a half! I measured Ms. Gary's desk and it is ? 13 hands! I measured my pencil and it is ? 1 and a half! I measured my chair and it is ? 2 hands!" When he was asked to explain his punctuation marks he replied, "I put a question mark because maybe people didn't know how much. I put an exclamation mark so I can say the answer a little bit louder." James created his own unique mathematical equation, using a question mark instead of the traditional empty square to designate the unknown quantity, thus taking what was familiar to him in the area of language and applying it to this new context of mathematics. He used the exclamation point to help him convey the thrill and joy of his discovery; saying his answer "a little bit louder" was a way for James to announce his results to the world. James is thinking like a mathematician, trying to convey all the significant features of this experience in symbolic form.

Cassandra extended James's original investigation by using the strategy of written conversation. She wrote on his paper, "If I used my hands to measure my desk, would I need more hands or less hands than you?" Cassandra believes that if she poses such questions, children will focus on the process rather than the product of their problem-solving efforts. The original problem does not become an end in itself but a seed for generating additional possibilities. The more opportunities learners have to change the variables of a given problem, the deeper their understanding becomes (Brown & Walter 1983).

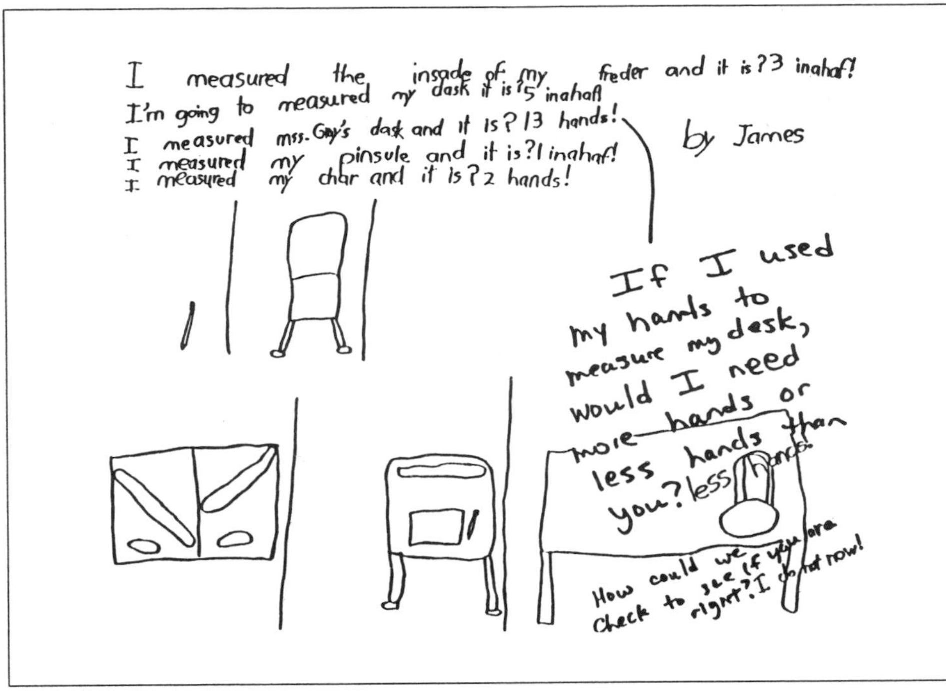

FIGURE 3–8

James read Cassandra's question and wrote his reply of "less hands." "How do you know it will be less hands?" asked Cassandra. "'Cause my hand is small and your hand is bigger, so I think you should have less hands," he reasoned. When Cassandra then wrote, "How could we check to see if you are right?" James wrote back, "I do not know." James had been doing all the measuring himself and wasn't sure how he could do any further measuring to answer that question. However, when Cassandra asked if she could measure the desk, he nodded his head enthusiastically. As she was partway through her measuring, James was already estimating the outcome: "Oh, it's going to be less." Cassandra's extension question helped James see the important inverse relationship between the length of a measuring unit and the number of units required. James was coming to understand not only the concept of length but also the concept of function; that is, how the number of units is a function of the length of that unit. Concepts like these are at the heart of mathematical thinking.

As the children measured a variety of objects in the room they came to learn more about the concepts of equivalence and inequality. Sometimes they noticed that the measuring tool they used matched the length of the object exactly. For instance, Christie wrote, "I measured a popsicle stick and it was one hand," and Casey wrote, "I measured my glue stick and it took my eraser." However, most often the length of the measuring unit and the length of the object to be measured were unequal and, like Sam in the story, the children used a variety of measuring tools to determine the desired length:

WILLIAM: I measured my desk with 22 hands and 1 half eraser. I measured the calendar with 29 hands and 1 pencil. I measured a dictionary. It took 1 hand and 1 pencil.

CHRISTIE: I measured my pencil and it was 1 hand and a sticker. I measured the coat closet and it was 12 hands and a sticker.

AUSTIN: I measured my desk and it took 3 hands and 2 arms.

Cole used some pencils and his fingers to measure the fish tank (see Figure 3–9): "I measured the fish tank with 3 pencils. I used 2 fingers for an inch." He knew that the width of his two fingers was approximately an inch and explained this equivalence in his findings. Cassandra extended his investigation by writing, "If you used fingers to measure the tank, how many would you need?" Cole predicted there would be "a lot," because his pencils were long and his fingers were short. Cassandra's question helped Cole express his answer in two different ways; he saw that both answers were equal to the length of the fish tank, even though he used different measuring units.

In all of these examples, the children demonstrated logical and systematic thinking in trying to address the problem of measuring the remaining length. They always tried to find a smaller unit, such as a sticker, some fingers, or a short pencil. Adrienne even used three different objects to measure the length of her paper (see Figure 3–10): "Big, big, medium, small. I measured [with] my hands, eraser, and a pencil shaving."

Although Adrienne's investigation did not involve the written-conversation strategy, the discussion she had with David Whitin (who was working with Cassandra that day) demonstrated some excellent mathematical thinking. After using both her hands to measure most of the paper she came to David and asked, "What do I do about this [*pointing to the remaining length*]? My hand is too big. Look." She then laid her hand on the paper to show how a third hand extended well beyond the edge of the paper.

"I could say a half," she suggested.

"Yes, you could say one half, because you used about one half more of a hand," replied David. "Or you could use another tool for measuring."

Adrienne paused for a few seconds and then said, "I know. I got my eraser." She rummaged through her pencil box and found a rectangular eraser, which she placed next to the outline of her two hands. After drawing the outline of the eraser she looked at her findings again and still seemed disturbed. "There's still a little bit right here," she said, pointing to a small length of the paper that she still had not measured.

"What else could you use?" asked David.

She glanced at the contents of her pencil box and saw her pencil sharpener. "I can make a tiny pencil shaving," she suggested. She sharpened one of her pencils ever so slightly and glued that sliver of pencil shaving on her paper. Even then she noticed that there was still a very small length of paper that was not measured. However, she was satisfied that the measurements were close enough.

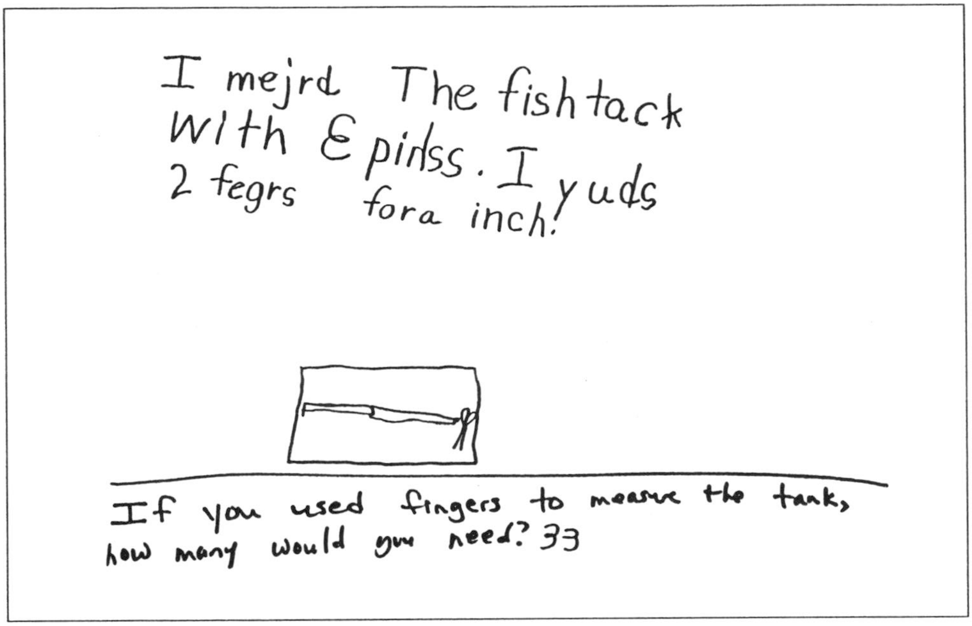

I mejrd The fishtack
With 8 pirlss. I yuds
2 fegrs fora inch!
If you used fingers to measure the tank,
how many would you need? 33

FIGURE 3–9

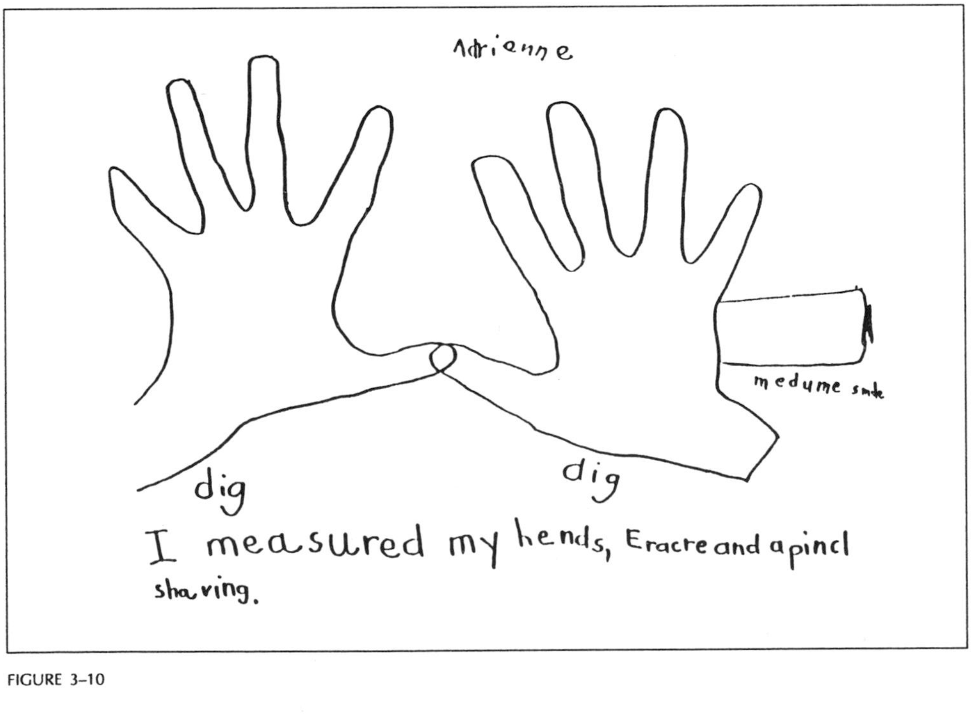

FIGURE 3–10

As she talked with David later, Adrienne noticed that the length of her measuring tools decreased in size and so she wrote "big," "medium" and "small" to describe this relationship. They also looked at a standard ruler together to see how an inch was divided into "medium" and "small" parts to help people measure smaller distances. Adrienne was coming to understand that there was an appropriate use for all measuring tools; as more precise measurement is necessary, people create more exact tools or subdivide an existing tool.

Conversing with parents

The discussion prompted by books often carries over to home, something that happened when John Gorman read *The King's Chessboard* (Birch 1988) to his fifth graders. In this story the king wants to reward the grand vizier, his principal counselor, for his helpfulness. Although the king offers jewels, palaces, and many other wonderful prizes, the grand vizier refuses them all, saying that serving the king is reward enough. However, when the angry king insists that he choose a prize, the grand vizier notices a chessboard hanging on the wall of the king's palace and decides to ask for a seemingly humble reward: one grain of rice for the first day, twice that on the second day (two grains), twice this amount on the third day (four grains), doubling the amount daily sixty-four times, once for each of the sixty-four squares on the chessboard. The king thinks the request is a bit strange but agrees. But the king is in for a rude surprise. Although the number of grains of rice starts out rather small (1, 2, 4, 8, 16, 32, 64, 128, 256, 512, 1,024), by the time the scheme is about half completed the amount of rice is astronomical.

John's students were intrigued with how fast the numbers increased. John related this geometric progression of doubling to the concept of money: "How much money do you think you would have if, instead of receiving your weekly allowance, you received one cent for the first day of the month, two cents the second day, four cents the third day, and so on, for thirty days?"

The children were eager to find out. Before they set to work, John asked them to predict the amount of money they thought they would accumulate; even after hearing the story, their answers were quite conservative, ranging from $20 to $300. They knew the numbers kept getting larger but they also knew the small value of a penny. However, as they began to tabulate the total, some using calculators and others using pencil and paper, they soon realized the amount was going to be much larger and revised their estimates to be in the thousands and millions of dollars.

Afterward, some of the children wanted to see how much money they could have accumulated if they had started with a nickel, a dime, or a quarter. John helped them use a computer program to find the results (Figure 3–11).

John then invited the children to play this mathematical game with their parents. "Would your parents agree to such a mathematical proposal in place of your allowance, or some work you might perform around the house? Try it out, and then discuss with them the results that we found." Several children even drew up a contract for their parents to sign (see Figure 3–12). John also asked the children to write

FIGURE 3–11

Doubling Allowances: Nickels, Dimes, and Quarters

Days	Nickel	Dime	Quarter
1	$0.05	$0.10	$0.25
2	$0.10	$0.20	$0.50
3	$0.20	$0.40	$1.00
4	$0.40	$0.80	$2.00
5	$0.80	$1.60	$4.00
6	$1.60	$3.20	$8.00
7	$3.20	$6.40	$16.00
8	$6.40	$12.80	$32.00
9	$12.80	$25.60	$64.00
10	$25.60	$51.60	$128.00
11	$51.20	$102.40	$256.00
12	$102.40	$204.80	$512.00
13	$204.80	$409.60	$1,024.00
14	$409.60	$819.20	$2,048.00
15	$819.20	$1,638.40	$4,096.00
16	$1,638.40	$3,276.80	$8,192.00
17	$3,276.80	$6,553.60	$16,384.00
18	$6,553.60	$13,107.20	$32,768.00
19	$13,107.20	$26,214.40	$65,536.00
20	$26,214.40	$52,428.80	$131,072.00
21	$52,428.80	$104,857.60	$262,144.00
22	$014,857.60	$209,715.20	$524,288.00
23	$209,715.20	$419,430.40	$1,048,576.00
24	$419,430.40	$838,860.80	$2,097,152.00
25	$838,860.80	$1,677,721.60	$4,194,304.00
26	$1,677,721.60	$3,355,443.20	$8,388,608.00
27	$3,355,443.20	$6,710,886.40	$16,777,216.00
28	$6,710,886.40	$13,421,772.80	$33,554,432.00
29	$13,421,772.80	$26,843,545.60	$67,108,864.00
30	$26,843,545.60	$53,687,091.20	$134,217,728.00

a letter to David Whitin (who worked with John on this project) summarizing what actually happened at home. Several of their letters follow.

Dear Mr. Whitin,
I learned that my parents are smarter than I thought because my dad said no way. This is the conversation I had:
Me: Hey Dad! Will you give me one cent the first day and double it every day for a month?
Dad: Why? Why should I do that?
Me: Because I want you to.
Dad: That's a lot of money! You'd get a fair amount of change!
Me: That isn't a lot of money!
Dad: Huh! By the 10th day you'd have over $10.00! No way! I'm not that dumb.
Me: Oh well! At least I tried.

FIGURE 3–12

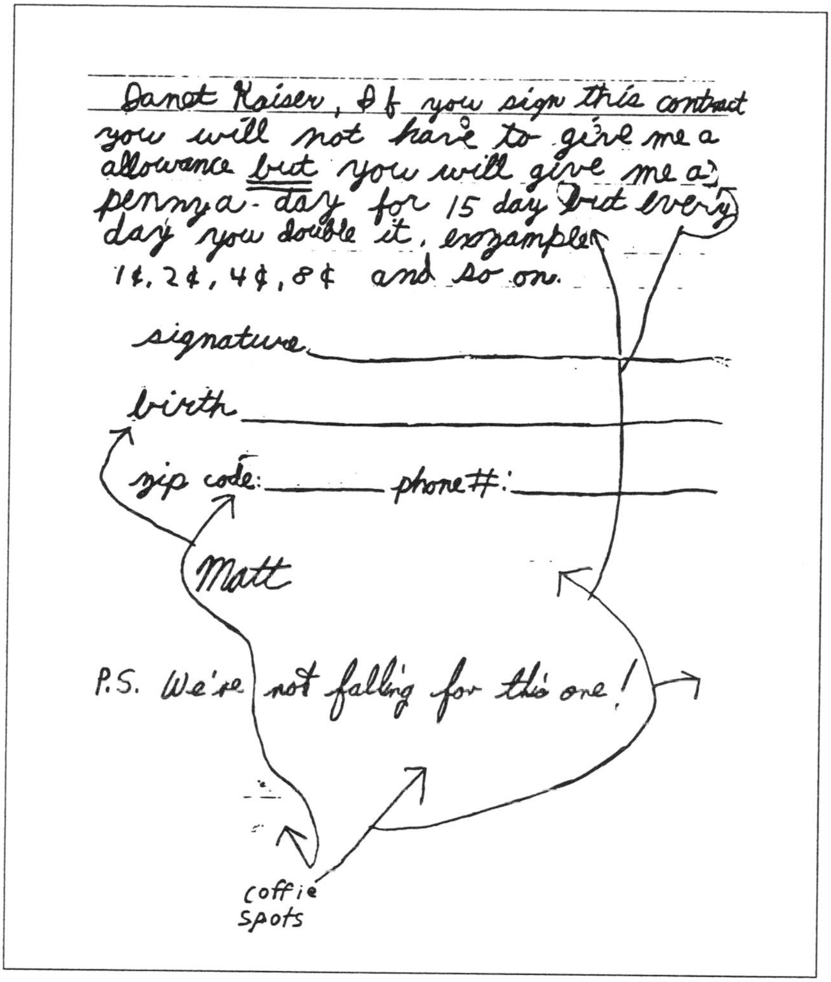
Danot Kaiser, If you sign this contract you will not have to give me a allowance but you will give me a penny a day for 15 day but every day you double it, exzample 1¢, 2¢, 4¢, 8¢ and so on.

signature ____________

birth ____________

zip code: ______ phone#: ______

Matt

P.S. We're not falling for this one!

coffie spots

Dear Mr. Whitin,

When I asked my dad about this he said no way! Kids should not get that much money!! The way my dad figured it out was he asked my mom and she said no way and showed my dad the graph. The rest of the day he called me slickster.

Dear Mr. Whitin,

1. *As I discussed the project with my mom, she said that she would think about it. After a few minutes she said no.*
2. *The deal I tried to make with my mom was "I will buy a movie tonight if you pay me a cent today and double it every day. Then she said "I want to figure it out first to see if I can afford it." Then I showed her the chart we made.*
3. *The experience that I learned was that you don't get everything you want, and some things sound better than they really are.*

4. *What surprised me was one cent could turn into $5,368,709.02 in thirty days.*

Dear Mr. Whitin,

When I asked my mom if she would give me a penny a day and then just keep doubling it she said "No" because she wanted to stick with the allowance stuff we do now. And she said it would be too much money anyways. At first I think my mom believed me but not for long. I learned that just because you start out with something small doesn't mean it can't end up big. Also what surprised me was how much something small can turn into in only thirty days. I liked that math a lot. Thanks for coming to see us. P.S. Please come back!!!

Dear Mr. Whitin,

When I discussed this with my mom she said I could get my allowance and take it to the bank and exchange it for pennies. I showed her the sheet and she said "No." Me and my mom sat in our two chairs and I asked my mom if I could change my allowance. Our conversation was pretty good, we sat and talked for about ten minutes. I learned from this experience that pennies can add up to a lot. I never knew that pennies could be so much money.

Dear Mr. Whitin,

It was on Sunday when I talked this over with my parents. At first I thought that I had tricked my mom into it. We talked about the checkerboard and the doubling. When she caught on to the idea, she said that I would make a good loan shark. You trick some but not a suspicious mom. It surprised me when my mom wrote "Not in this lifetime, kid!!"

Dear Mr. Whitin,

I tried your method for an allowance but my parents were too quick. As my parents and I discussed the project, we found that small things can double into large things very quickly. We also talked about how much things can deceive you at first, and then when you see what happens, it can change your decision. What surprised me was that by the end of 2 weeks, I would have over 373 dollars.

Dear Mr. Whitin,

I hope you come back to see us some day. I loved your math class. I talked with my mom if she would go for the "Money Deal," but she said, "No way!" She asked if she would be living in the woods without anything except a piece of clothing by the end of the month. I said, "You will probably be living in the woods in 21 days unless you are a millionaire." I wasn't surprised at all even though I wish she would have gone with the deal! I now know that if someone asks me to do a "deal" with them I will think twice and ask how much is it going to cost me. I sure wouldn't want to be living in the woods. Thank you for teaching me to always think twice if someone wants to talk about a "deal." Come back very soon!

P.S. I love Math a lot!!!

These letters clearly show children and parents enjoying a good mathematical conversation. Together they play with a geometric progression and have fun imagining the results of this consecutive doubling process. Perhaps most interesting are the consumer lessons that parents and children come to understand together.

The teacher's role in fostering mathematical discussions

Interesting discussions about books do not just happen. Teachers work hard to establish the conditions that foster these productive conversations. Looking back at the conversations recorded in this chapter, we discover several important strategies these teachers used:

1. Valuing anomalies. The teachers in this chapter encouraged children to talk about parts of the text that did not seem to make sense to them. For instance, when Donna Caprell read *The Doorbell Rang,* Zach could not understand why the number of cookies per child did not follow a "halving" pattern of six, three, one and a half. She reread the story so Zach could investigate this anomaly for himself. Good teachers know that anomalies are not something to avoid but rather are the driving force of inquiry; when teachers see children questioning, doubting, or puzzling over a part of text, they support that uncomfortable feeling because they know it is the seed for further discussion and examination.
2. Encouraging hypothesizing. One of the students in Christie Forrest's classroom asked if a factorial would work going backward. A child with whom Pet Harper worked was intrigued by penguins living in Australia and hypothesized, "I wonder if the fact that they are so small has anything to do with why they live in a warm climate?" Encouraging these kinds of hypotheses lays the groundwork for further questioning and research.
3. Supporting children in discussing the language of mathematics. Teachers who read *How Much Is a Million?* to their students encouraged them to explain the term *million* in their own way. Elaine Cope's third graders discussed the various meanings of *foot* and *feet,* and Deborah Cotherman's children tried to distinguish between *halves* and *thirds.*
4. Supporting different explanations. When teachers value the learning process, they focus not on the answers but the way children explain their answers. The letters John Gorman's children wrote demonstrate a rich variety of explanations for the concept of a progression. Good teachers frequently ask their students to explain their answer in another way. Even though many children may use the same strategy, their explanation of *how* they used it broadens the group's understanding of the process.
5. Pushing for clarification. During her students' discussion of *The Half-Birthday Party,* Deborah Cotherman asked, "How is a friendship bracelet half a

present?" and "What do you mean by three thirds?" In the first instance Deborah was asking her children to explain a relationship they had made; in the second she wanted them to clarify a fractional term they had used. Because of their past instructional history, children are sometimes used to giving short answers. Good teachers extend the conversation, ask their students to tell them more about an idea, thereby helping children explain as well as explore their current understanding of that idea.

6. Asking open-ended questions. Good teachers keep asking questions that invite all students to contribute: Who would like to say something about this story? What did you notice? What did this story remind you of? After hearing this story, what are you now wondering about? These divergent questions can often lead the conversation in unpredictable ways; good teachers are ready for those unanticipated excursions because they know the children will help shape them and set them in motion?
7. Encouraging children to answer their own questions. Good teachers support a class in solving problems together rather than presenting themselves as the sole source of knowledge and the final arbiter in all decisions. When a child heard *Anno's Mysterious Multiplying Jar* and asked Christie Forrest, "How did it get to be that many jars?" Christie let the children answer that question. Good teachers constantly turn individual questions back to the group by saying, Who can help us answer that question? or What do other people think of this idea? or How could we figure out the answer to this question? The group develops a sense of ownership and responsibility for the problems and explorations that are to follow.

References

Anno, Mitsumasa. 1983. *Anno's mysterious multiplying jar.* New York: Philomel.

Barnes, Douglas. 1987. *From communication to curriculum.* New York: Penguin.

Birch, David. 1988. *The king's chessboard.* New York: Dial.

Brown, Stephen, and Marion Walter. 1983. *The art of problem posing.* Hillsdale, NJ: Lawrence Erlbaum.

Cole, Joanna. 1985a. *Large as life: Daytime animals.* New York: Knopf.

———. 1985b. *Large as life: Nighttime animals.* New York: Knopf.

———. 1990. *Large as life animals: In beautiful life-size paintings.* New York: Knopf.

Ekker, Ernst. 1985. *What is beyond the hill?* New York: Lippincott.

Harste, Jerome, Kathy Short, and Carolyn Burke. 1988. *Creating classrooms for authors: The reading-writing connection.* Portsmouth, NH: Heinemann.

Harste, Jerome, Virginia Woodward, and Carolyn Burke. 1984. *Language stories and literacy lessons.* Portsmouth, NH: Heinemann.

Hutchins, Pat. 1986. *The doorbell rang.* New York: Greenwillow.

Karp, Walter. 1985. Why Johnny can't think. *Harper's* (June): 69–73.

Mazer, Anne. 1990. *The yellow button.* New York: Knopf.

Moerbeck, Kees, and Carla Dijs. 1987. *Hot pursuit.* Los Angeles: Intervisual Communications.

National Council of Teachers of Mathematics. 1989. *Curriculum and evaluation standards for school mathematics.* Reston, VA: National Council of Teachers of Mathematics.

Pomerantz, Charlotte. 1984. *The half-birthday party.* New York: Clarion.

Russo, Marisabina. 1986. *The line up book.* New York: Greenwillow.

Schwartz, David. 1985. *How much is a million?* New York: Lothrop, Lee & Shepard.

Thaler, Mike. 1982. *Owly.* New York: Harper and Row.

4 *Talking About Books*

If we want to understand the power children's books have for promoting mathematical thinking in our classrooms, we must listen to the children and teachers who read and talk about them. Their insights and reflections on the mathematics/literature connection help us all see more clearly the potential that stories hold for explaining and exploring mathematical ideas.

Children speak out

As Lisa Jordan, an undergraduate teacher-education student, prepares to read a story to some third graders during their math time, Brian seems a bit confused: "A math book? You can't *read* a math book, you can only *do* a math book!" For Brian, mathematics is done only within the pages of his math workbook, and when we look at those pages, the "doing" usually involves crunching numbers together in computational silence. Based on his past instruction, Brian (with good reason) wonders what reading a book has to do with mathematics. When teachers share stories that have a mathematical dimension, they demonstrate to their students that mathematics is more than numbers; they are saying that mathematics is a natural part of daily living.

EXPANDING THE VISION

Seven-year-old Matt writes (see Figure 4–1), "It was fun stories and I was adding and subtracting and didn't even know it." Matt reminds us that stories break down the wall that sometimes exists between "math time" and the rest of the school day. Good stories do not announce themselves as mathematics lessons; they are just engaging tales to tell. The mathematics arises naturally from the children's personal connections, observations, and questions.

Six-year-old Allison is just getting ready to enter first grade, but she already sees the potential that books hold for expanding her vision of what

FIGURE 4–1

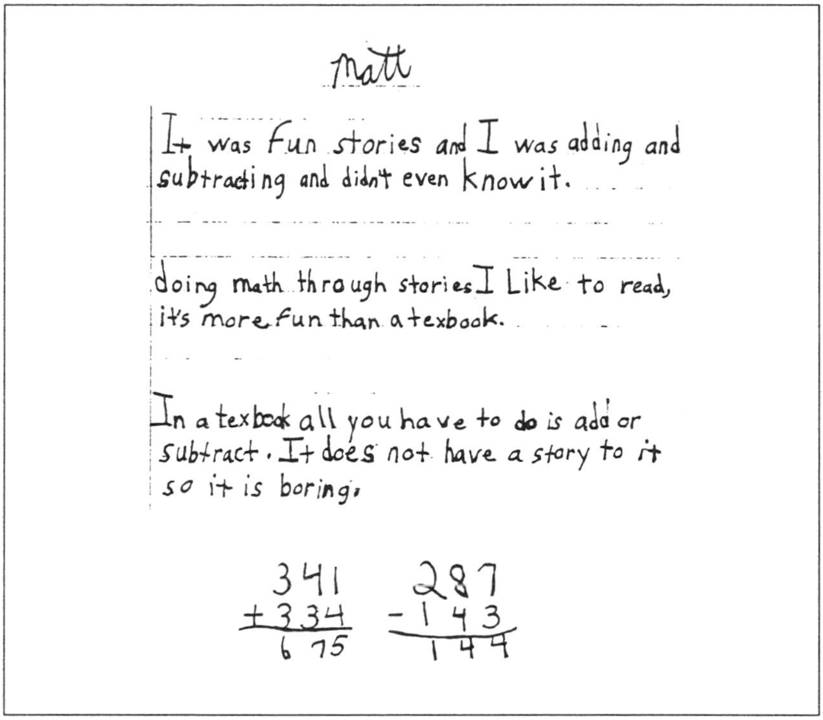
Matt

It was fun stories and I was adding and subtracting and didn't even know it.

doing math through stories I Like to read, it's more fun than a texbook.

In a texbook all you have to do is add or subtract. It does not have a story to it so it is boring.

341 + 334 = 675

287 − 143 = 144

mathematics can be. She writes (see Figure 4–2): "It's more fun reading in the book because you read the book and not just look down on papers." Good pieces of literature help learners go beyond the papers; they help them see that mathematics is not the act of looking down on numbers but of looking out at the world, inward at ourselves, and across at our peers as we discuss the stories of our own lives.

Eight-year-old Cassie shows us that stories can break down the myth that mathematics is primarily a pencil-and-paper activity: "You don't have to have a pencil. You don't have to write. It is easier. It is funner. It's better." Stories help learners see that mathematics is a way of thinking, not just a written exercise in a math workbook. Unfortunately, some children have already learned that unless they have pencils in hand they are incapable of thinking mathematically. This perception is clearly the antithesis of the NCTM standards, which advocate the importance of producing flexible problem solvers who adapt to changing situations and who draw upon a variety of strategies and tools—estimation, mental computation, calculators, computers, as well as paper and pencil—to solve their problems. Stories invite children to think mathematically without an intravenous hookup to a #2 pencil.

Seven-year-old Brannon sees that stories can expand our vision of what mathematics can encompass: "What can we learn from reading books about math? Doing math without numbers." Stories help learners see that mathematics is more than numbers on a page. Rather, it is a tool for measuring, counting, estimating, comparing, designing, locating, and predicting. It is a system for making patterns of

FIGURE 4–2

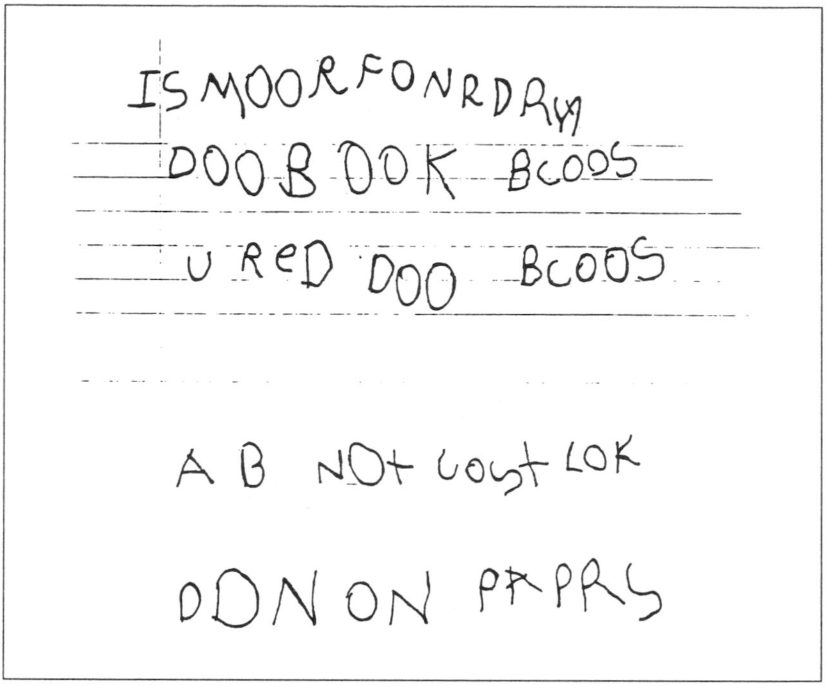

all sorts: numerical, algebraic, geometric. Books help expand children's vision of what it means to think mathematically.

Sixth grader Tawanda writes that stories allow learners time to think about problem situations: "You can learn to think about a question before you answer it. Like in a textbook it just be a lot of problems. In literature books you can learn to solve problems. I liked the books you read, they were interesting." Mathematics textbooks seem to demand answers right away; Tawanda appreciates stories because they give learners time to mull things over, reconsider possibilities, make personal connections, and wonder about other possible story scenarios. Here again, books provide an opportunity for thinking and reflecting, not computing and responding.

Fifth grader Tameka comments that the role of the teacher may change if we begin to share stories during math time: "It's fun to use math stories because then the teacher will not have to go to the board." Tameka has been led to think that mathematical learning occurs when the teacher stands beside the chalkboard. Stories can be a way for all learners, including the teacher, to sit down together and discuss mathematical ideas.

The perception that mathematics is not an enjoyable experience is addressed by third grader Delethia: "How can books and stories help people understand math? You can learn and have fun at the same time." As children go through school, their attitude toward mathematics begins to turn negative. They view it as dull and boring, with no room for exploring, no opportunity for connecting it to their lives. However, stories provide the connecting tissue between symbols on a page and living in the world. Delethia is right; learning is a lot more fun that way.

FIGURE 4–3

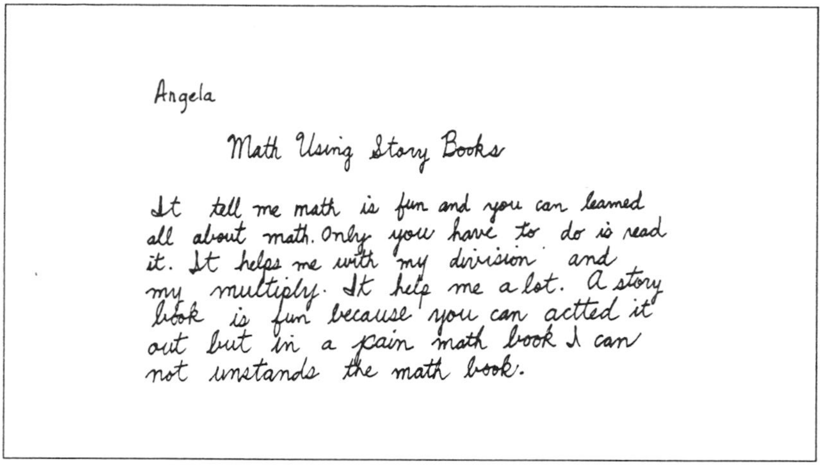
Angela

Math Using Story Books

It tell me math is fun and you can learned all about math. Only you have to do is read it. It helps me with my division and my multiply. It help me a lot. A story book is fun because you can acted it out but in a pain math book I can not unstands the math book.

Students in Elaine Cope's third-grade classroom read numerous mathematical texts and then created some of their own stories based on these texts. For instance, they read Paul Giganti's *Each Orange Had 8 Slices* (1992) and Joy Hulme's *Sea Squares* (1991) and then created their own counting and multiplication books. Brandon comments about the benefits of writing and drawing to learn mathematics: "Now that writing math stories is being taught to us I'm understanding better on math problems. They show me more things than my math book can. It has showed me lots more things in division that my math book didn't show me. It helped me learn two-digit division better. Drawing out my picture is better than flipping pages." Brandon is referring to *The Doorbell Rang* (Hutchins 1986) as a helpful story for understanding division. He knows that he learns mathematics best by writing and drawing his own stories, not by flipping the pages of a math workbook.

Angela, a student from this same third-grade class, adds another benefit (see Figure 4–3): "A storybook is fun because you can act it out but in a plain [notice her spelling, *pain*!] math book I cannot understand the math book." She and her classmates acted out *The Doorbell Rang,* as well as several of their own versions of this story. They also created some of their own timing records based on David Lloyd's *The Stopwatch* (1986). Angela views literature as a starting point for acting out mathematical understanding and investigation. She recognizes that as we increase opportunities for expression, we increase avenues for understanding.

One last aspect of what mathematics can be involves the role of estimating. Third grader Bradley comments, "Stories can help you because you can guess what might come next. My teacher won't let me guess math answers. I want my teacher to read stories for math time." Bradley notices that his teacher allows him to predict in reading but forbids him to do so in math. He shrewdly reasons that if his teacher would only read him more mathematical texts he could do some more predicting and estimating in his head and his teacher would have no way of stopping him! Part of the role of stories in mathematical learning is to support this crucial strategy of estimation.

The comments of all these students demonstrate that literature can be a powerful vehicle for demystifying many of the harmful assumptions that students learn about the nature of mathematics. Literature can help us replace myths about mathematics with a more realistic perspective of what it is really all about.

Myths About Mathematics	*Perspectives Gained Through Literature*
1. Math is something you do in a math book.	1. Math is a way of thinking about the world.
2. Math is not a part of anything else.	2. Math is an integral part of living.
3. Math is looking down at your paper.	3. Math is a vehicle for looking up and looking out at our world.
4. Math always involves using your pencil.	4. Math involves sharing stories and discussing ideas.
5. Math only involves numbers.	5. Math involves reasoning, communicating, measuring, and thinking geometrically.
6. Math is answering questions very quickly.	6. Math is mulling over ideas and making personal connections.
7. Math is the teacher standing at the board.	7. Math is the teacher working as a collaborative learner.
8. Math is not something you should enjoy.	8. Math is intrinsically rewarding.
9. Math is turning pages and completing a long list of problems.	9. Math is turning out our own stories and posing our own problems.
10. Math doesn't involve any guessing; it is about getting the right answers.	10. Math involves a lot of messing around; sometimes there are multiple solutions or no solution at all.

SEEING THE RELEVANCE

Many students have commented that children's literature helps them see the relevance of mathematics. Twelve-year-old Regina emphasizes this point:

> *Literature books can help people better understand mathematics by relating math with an object to give you a kind of mental illustration. It's easy to understand something when you have something else to relate it to. Literature books give you that mental illustration to relate math with understanding. When you read about something you don't quite understand, and it's described fully, it triggers something in your brain and you never forget about what you read.*

Learning is making connections, and stories can help us make those connections. When mathematics is reduced to numbers and symbols on a page, children view it as a world of fragmented and isolated bits of information. Stories preserve the wholeness of the mathematical experience, giving learners "mental illustrations" of how it is used in the real world. Eisner (1991) argues that images (Regina's mental illustrations) are the wellspring of conceptual development. If we want learners to think mathematically, they must be able to think conceptually. Stories can help build this conceptual base by providing images of these concepts in action.

When third grader Nickolas writes about the relevance of mathematical stories, he gives a specific example:

> *Literature books are neat because you're having fun and learning. When I hear literature books it makes me think of my own life experience. It is like what you have been through in your daily life. I'm also surprised at how much reality is in them. Let's say I like baseball a lot, which I do. I'm going to figure out how many home runs Willie Mays hit. That's the kind of math I like. The kids that don't like math may start to like it if the teacher read books that they like instead of the textbooks.*

When mathematics is relevant to the lives of children, fun and learning can occur simultaneously. The calculations that Nickolas performs about the accomplishments of Willie Mays are meaningful mathematics because they are tied to a subject that he enjoys and knows something about.

The importance of stories for helping learners understand mathematics is reiterated by Maggie, a sixth grader:

> *I think that reading about math is a lot more fun than out of a textbook. Reading about it makes it easier to understand because it communicates math with everyday things. Sometimes I learn more from reading about math because to me it makes math interesting. I understand things better when they are interesting and about things we see everyday.*

One of the goals of the NCTM standards is for students to be able to communicate mathematically. Stories can help them do that. When mathematics is tied to "everyday things" in a story, children can connect that mathematics to their own experiences as they learn from the personal connections of others. A single story can lead to other stories, as together we see the relevance of mathematics in our daily lives.

Children have also commented that stories are useful because they can be interpreted in different ways. Third grader Cindy remarks:

> *We practice reading while we're really thinking. We don't just get an answer but we think and get lots of answers. We can think about things in a different way. It makes me feel smart to learn this way. It is not boring.*

Children see that stories are open to multiple interpretations and extensions and they value this potential. For instance, look at how children have imagined alternative endings for two particular stories. Some readers wonder how the twelve children in *The Doorbell Rang* (Hutchins 1986) could have shared twelve cookies if more and more kids had kept arriving. Some have suggested not opening the door. Others have recommended giving everyone half a cookie and keeping the rest as leftovers. Children have suggested different ways that a line of *One Hundred*

Hungry Ants (Pinczes 1993) could have marched to a picnic and successfully carried off food. One thought they should march in four groups of twenty-five (5 rows × 5 columns); someone else suggested a group of sixty (5 × 12) and a group of forty (4 × 10). It is this playing around with problem variables that Brown and Walter advocate in *The Art of Problem Posing* (1983). Generating alternative possibilities challenges children and makes mathematics an exciting enterprise.

Stories show mathematics being put to good use. William, age eleven, explains: "Books show pictures of things being done. My math book only makes me do it from numbers." Numbers are merely the remnants of a story. As Harold Rosen (1987) reminds us, "Every chemical reaction is a story compressed into the strait-jacket of an equation" (p. 16). William sees that children's literature can reintroduce the story to the often abstract numbers and symbols he finds in his math book. Stories help demonstrate to William that mathematics is not a meaningless abstraction but a useful tool for getting things done.

Books also provide a natural and supportive context for mathematics. Twelve-year-old Marin finds that "math is interesting and makes more sense with books. It relates to the brain better. It uses things that [readers] find funny, things in their environment. Books are more like things they know about." Lisa, also twelve, says, "Books integrate lots of things, like science, math, and home ec." Mathematics, like language, music, art, and dance, is a system for making meaning and occurs quite naturally in story situations. Children notice that it is an integral part of science and home economics and that it is more easily understood in those contexts.

Joel, age eight, also writes about the reality of mathematics in stories: "Books make math fun. It looks like it's real. It makes math important, so you can get the hang of it. It is not fun writing the numbers." He explains, "In math books [i.e., textbooks] you only have problems to write: no pictures, no words, just problems like 13 − 8 and 9 + 6. Sometimes it don't make sense to write so much." When mathematics is relevant to children's lives, as it is in story situations, they see it as a useful tool for describing and thinking about their world; it makes good sense and enables learners to get the hang of how it works. However, when children do not have stories to fall back on, but only a series of dictatorially imposed rules, then mathematics becomes nonsensical.

Children have described the relevance of mathematics in children's literature in still other ways:

> *[A story] helps you better understand math by having lots and lots of math difficulties, for example, Alexander [Viorst 1978] had a difficult time with his money (math).*
> —Coleman, age ten

> *Reading can help you understand mathematics because when you read you learn more about problems that might happen any day.*
> —Stephanie, age ten

> *Books can give many different examples to help your mind comprehend the mathematical principles being stated. They can also make math more interesting by using different situations. They can use math to give a lot of interesting facts about everyday life. They can teach math through a character's life.*
> —Stephen, age twelve

A story book has character development and a textbook doesn't.

—Chris, age eight

Comments like these clearly show that children see the value of storybooks that portray flesh-and-blood mathematics; they enjoy problem situations, like Alexander's struggle to keep track of his dollar in Judith Viorst's *Alexander, Who Used to Be Rich Last Sunday* (1978). Stephen notes that books represent mathematical ideas in various situations. He may be referring to *Counting on Frank* (Clement 1991), a story he really enjoyed and in which he saw mathematical concepts like time, capacity, volume, and length in use. Representing mathematical concepts in different contexts deepens our understanding of those abstract ideas.

LEARNING TO LOVE IT

Literature can help reverse the negative attitude toward mathematics that many children develop. Children sense this potential themselves:

Reading funny stories makes it a lot better because you can sit back and relax instead of having to work!

—Chris, age ten

I think that children that like to read would rather learn math through books. I'd rather listen to a story than do about twenty math problems. In the book Sea Squares it shows you how to add and multiply. Colorful pictures also inspire you in the book. I enjoyed multiplying ten squids with ten tails each. One day five fisherman caught three dolphins and they each weighed three hundred pounds. How much did three weigh?

—Casey, age eight (see Figure 4–4)

Math is very boring but I like to read.

—Emily, age seven

The books that you read made me like math a little more than I did before. I used to detest math, now I like it a lot better. The literature books talk about other things in the world relating to math. I think you should keep on reading books throughout the year.

—Monica, age twelve

The books didn't have an effect on me about liking math. I still don't like math. It's boring. But the books and activities we sometimes do make it better. Don't take it personal about me not liking math. I just don't like the subject, not you. One thing is for sure, I like reading fun books better than textbooks.

—Stewart, age twelve

From the books Miss Shealy had read to us I think they were useful because they gave educational skills to my personal abilities. Most of all I can [relate] back to the books and get answers of problems. The skills are used in my life every day. The books give math a boost of interestment to my knowledge. Thank you for reading the books to our class.

—Amanda, age twelve

FIGURE 4–4

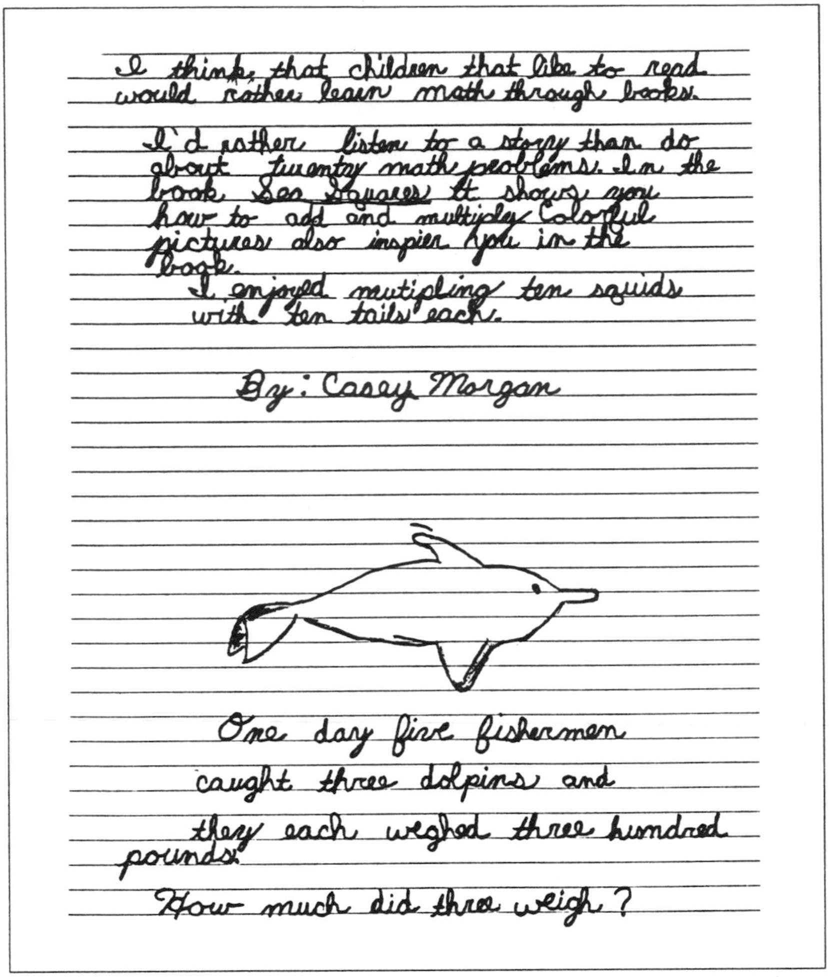

I think that children that like to read would rather learn math through books.

I'd rather listen to a story than do about twenty math problems. In the book Sea Squares It shows you how to add and multiply. Colorful pictures also inspier you in the book.

I enjoyed mutipling ten squids with ten tails each.

By: Casey Morgan

One day five fishermen caught three dolpins and they each weghed three hundred pounds.

How much did three weigh?

Learning with math with storybooks is fun because you get excited. I like the jump rope contest because it is fun to see how much you could really jump altogether, and it was fun, fun fun [à la the Beach Boys' classic hit!]. And the crocodile was 12 feet long and the babies were 9 inches long. Measuring the crocodile was a lot of fun. A crocodile is very long, and it took all of April, and all of Malcolm, and Quay down to his knees. And I would like to measure me and see how many feet I am.

—Eric, age eight (see Figure 4–5)

Plain math books are boring. Just plain math all the way through. In a literature book it uses mathematical skills, at the same time giving an enjoyable story. In literature books there are exciting pictures of stuff that goes along with the story, but at the same time talks about shapes and numbers. So a child would rather learn math in a literature book than a math book.

—Ewell, age twelve

Eric Leaning

Leaning with math with story book is fun because you get exited. I liked the jump rope contest Because it is fun to see how much you could realy jump altogether and it was fun fun fun.

and the crodile was 17 feet long and the dadys (babies) were 9 inches long measer-ring the crocodile was a lot of fun a crocodile is very long

and it took all of April and all of malcome and Quay down to his kness and I would like to measer me and see how many feet I am.

FIGURE 4–5

Literature books are better because they make learning fun. A student could read a math-related fairy tale and learn something. If you like the story you'll give it to someone else, and so on. This results in a lot of people reading that book. Even if you don't realize it's math-related, you'll think about it later. If a student sees that math just isn't two plus two but fits into even the most enjoyable activity that will make them more eager. It would prove that learning can be fun and exciting. It could change a person that doesn't like math into a person that may love it eventually. We would owe it all to the literature book pointing out a different side of math.

—Amanda, age thirteen

To better appreciate the insights of these children, let's contrast them with the comments of a bright, math-avoidant woman who portrays a very different image of mathematics: "Math makes me think of a stainless steel wall—hard, cold, smooth, offering no handhold, all it does is glint back at me. Edge up to it, put your nose against it, it doesn't give anything back, you can't put a dent in it, it doesn't take your shape, it doesn't have any smell, all it does is make your nose cold" (quoted in Borasi 1992, p. 185). The use of children's literature can help change this perception of mathematics; the children's comments document this transformative potential. Children's books portray mathematics not as a hard, impenetrable wall but as a soft, malleable story that learners can interpret and extend in different ways. For instance, Eric enjoyed reading *The Stopwatch* (Lloyd 1986) and then having class members use a stopwatch to set their own jump-rope records. He enjoyed reading *Large as Life* (Cole 1985a, 1985b) and then doing some of his own measuring, such as discovering that three of his classmates lying foot to head would approximate the length of a twelve-foot crocodile. Instead of offering *no* handhold for understanding, mathematics through children's literature offers *many* places to grab on to concepts and discuss and explore them. Nor is mathematics a hard, cold discipline when it is revealed through stories; Casey finds listening to stories an enjoyable experience and notes that colorful pictures can "inspire you"; Chris comments that he can "sit back and relax" while listening to a story; Amanda sees that books give math a "boost of interestment" by allowing her to explore the problems in various stories and relate them to her own life. The children's comments demonstrate that through literature we can edge up to mathematical ideas, put our noses into mathematical situations; the things that happen in literature shape and are shaped by our own experiences, as we discuss, interpret, and extend these stories in our own way.

EMPOWERING LEARNERS

When teachers share children's literature with their students in open-ended ways, they can empower their students as literacy learners. Children develop an increasing responsibility for and ownership of their own learning when they are given the opportunity not to regurgitate the facts of stories but rather to interpret and extend these stories in meaningful ways. In supportive classrooms children can question an author's purpose, disagree with a character's decision, hypothesize about an alternative ending, or tie a group of stories together in a new way. They can choose how they wish to respond. Dustin, age nine, appreciates this last benefit:

> *Reading books is more fun. When Mrs. Strickland reads a story I get to decide what we're going to do. I decide what I'm going to learn. I am in charge. When you read a story first and talk about it, you get to thinking "What if?" or "How?" just like I didn't believe the pig was 100 inches around. That's almost as big as a washing machine. This makes you want to know. A plain old math class don't give you a choice. You just do what the teacher says.*

Dustin likes being in charge and deciding how he will respond to a story. He had read *Farmer Mack Measures His Pig* (Johnston 1986) and was intrigued by pigs that had a girth of 100 inches. Dustin wanted to find something else that had a perimeter of 100 inches so he could get a better feel for the size of the animal. When he found that the distance around his family's washing machine was about 100 inches he was amazed. Dustin also enjoys the opportunity to discuss stories and hypothesize about some of the attributes of those stories, such as wondering "What if?" and "How?" This is the same kind of quality that is attractive to Joshua, ten, when he writes: "Reading books don't have division signs and lots of problems. They have nice pictures and lots of stories. I like to read because I can imagine."

Imagining is empowering; it frees us from the bounds of a single right answer and supports multiple interpretations and personally meaningful extensions. Amanda, age thirteen, discusses the perspective we gain about ourselves as problem solvers when we are given this kind of support:

> *Literature books help people understand mathematics in many ways. One way is that it can make math easier to understand. It can explain it instead of just showing the steps. When a student reads a book and figures it out by his/herself it gives them a feeling of self-success. The more you succeed, the better you feel about yourself. Therefore when you find something you do well you'll continue doing it, resulting in a love for math. Of course if you love math then you'll become a better student. This is one way literature books help people understand mathematics better.*

Amanda insinuates that learning mathematics by memorizing a series of steps is an insult to the intelligence of an empowered learner. One of the qualities of an empowered learner is that feeling of self-success that says, I can learn to solve problems in my own way. Stories invite discussions about how problems can be solved in different ways; lockstep procedures cut off discussions and reduce learners to automatons. Eight-year-old Charnell resents this subservient role and writes eloquently about the injustice she sees occurring:

> *I can learn a lot from reading books that I can't learn from a math book. Some of the things are different ways of doing things that you can relate to. That way the teacher wouldn't have to say "You missed a step" or "Your answer is wrong" or "I've tried everything! What else can I do to get this through your head?" We as children are tired of teachers blaming us and not allowing us to express our ways of doing things if it is right. It is always the math book, or the teacher's way, or none at all. I will be glad when we as students will be able to stand up and be heard. There are lots of neat ideas in our minds but you as teachers and the old math book are stopping us from sharing them.*

Charnell sees that literature books demonstrate different ways to solve problems. She can relate to those story situations, and enjoys solving problems in alternative ways. However, it is her incisive analysis of a suppressive learning environment, written when she had just finished the third grade, that reveals how even young children can sense the potential that schools hold for them if they are only given the chance. Encountering mathematical ideas through the world of literature is one avenue for enabling learners to explore and investigate their own ideas—and thus become the empowered learners that Charnell knows they can and should be.

Teachers reflect

Teachers who regularly share literature books with their students become very aware of the potential these books hold for supporting the understanding of mathematical concepts. Their voices give us an inside look at what they have learned about themselves as well as their students. David Whitin asked a number of teachers to respond to a four-question survey and found their responses most informative. Here is a selective sample:

1. How have literature books helped give you insights about your children?

Books tend to bring out the best in children, making this an easy and natural way to foster mathematical thinking. —Jackie Bankert

The books have made me realize that children wonder about many things and have a lot of unanswered questions. They rarely ask interesting questions while using a textbook but seem to bubble on after listening to a story.
—Patricia Black

By using literature books to teach math, I have come to understand that all children can learn mathematics regardless of what their IQs have been shown to be. I have seen that each and every child is capable of deep reflection and problem solving. I have realized that different children relate to books in different ways and comment on things that are intriguing to them. Finally, I have observed that giving children the opportunity to wonder about things and to further investigate their "wonders" makes them more excited about learning and thus gives them a much more active involvement in their own learning.
—Kathryn Shand

I realized that children can identify with literature books in real-life situations. Children learn to appreciate mathematics in new ways. The literature books take them above and beyond regular classroom texts and give them the fun and knowledge of math as a way of life. They begin to "think" mathematically.
—Melissa Smith

Children enjoy giving their opinions and ideas rather than listening to me lecture all the time. They also reveal more about themselves when they relate to events or characters in a book. —Barbara Creighton

Using stories and books helps me really know my children and the thinking processes they use. Children express themselves and their understanding through things they can relate to. I've learned to listen to my children.
—Pam Brett

Some of the lower-level predictable books (such as The Doorbell Rang*) caught the interest of two boys who just completed fourth grade. I think one of the most enjoyable moments I had working with Zach and Michael was to sit back and to listen to their mathematical conversations, their questioning, and their discovery of how something does really work out. It was so interesting to see them share their ideas with each other, to witness moments when one boy's thoughts inspired yet more creative thoughts and discoveries.*

—Donna Caprell

Literature books have given me great insights about children. Reading and listening allow the children to formulate problems in their minds, explore them, and create different ways of solving them. They have the opportunity to suppose and wonder.

—Mary Wright

I had a wide variety of books for the children to choose from. I found out from their choices that they were interested in the sea and the animal life that goes with it. I also realized the value in rereading a book over and over. I thought they would get bored but in reality they explored their own thoughts further.

—Kristin Temple

I think it is interesting that although we may all be looking at or talking about the same thing, we don't always (if ever) see things in the same way. I have seen children in my own classroom take ideas from books that I didn't see and use them to solve their own problems, compare similarities and differences among problems, and generate rules based on their understanding. I have also noted that the stories in children's literature tend to open the students' minds to wondering about things, fantasizing about things, and exploring things that might otherwise be left untapped.

—Rhonda Singleton

Literature books have helped me understand my children more. Their comments and reflections about stories often reveal inner feelings they are either hesitant or unable to express otherwise. Their likes and dislikes become more apparent, as do their personalities and strengths.

—Carolyn Webber

2. What other value do you see in using children's books to foster mathematical understanding?

Mathematical thinkers are interested in the thinking of others. Books offer an author's thinking for us to examine. Several of my students have told me that books help them to understand concepts better.

—Robin Cox

The best thing to ever happen to teaching volume was one of Anno's books [Anno 1989]. There was a chapter called "Counting Water" that not only explained a need for volume measure but introduced the metric measures. In all my years of teaching, it was the first time I had been able to provide a "why" this is done instead of just telling them to do it.

—Erica Swimmie

The story of the process is what's interesting, not the right or wrong results. Children's books open an unending conversation with mathematics.

—Marilyn Crosby

It provides a basis for the students to explore mathematical ideas. Children's literature can combat the frequent perception that math is essentially a written system composed of symbols rather than words. It is not just something to be performed on paper, but a vehicle for oral communication.

—Deanna Burroughs

I think it shows children how math is used in everyday living. It also gives them a background against which to discuss math. I think it starts children thinking about math all around them and they become more observant.

—Linda Mook

Historically, stories have been a wonderful teaching tool for all subjects. Even the Bible presents profound lessons through familiar stories. Why not use stories for learning about counting, shapes, money, or fractions? Numbers on a page will never have the meaning to a child that a real story will have.

—Pet Harper

Besides meeting the needs of a wide range of learners, using children's books to foster mathematical understanding promotes deeper, more analytical thinking. It fosters collaboration and increases curiosity about mathematics.

—Kathryn Shand

Through the use of children's literature, the aesthetic dimension of mathematics can be explored. Open-ended investigations show students that mathematics can be viewed in many ways—patterns, numerical relationships, symmetry, and so on.

—Linda Nance

Children are more willing to take risks in their thinking and not always look for the right answer. Children of all abilities can learn math through literature. Math becomes a social experience in which children learn and create together. Children gain self-esteem because they feel they are being treated as respected learners.

—Barbara Creighton

3. How have you grown as a teacher-researcher by using literature books with your children?

I found a new world of possibilities. I have always enjoyed reading aloud and sharing books with my students, but I was the one who did most of the talking. And when I asked questions about the books, they were usually fact based. Through sharing literature with children this summer, I have learned how to listen to them, how to follow their lead and how to explore problem situations with them.

—Deb Cotterman

A valuable lesson has been to value the ideas and creativeness of kids as well as how they think and view things. What they have to share is important for me and for their classmates. So often kids can put things into language that other kids seem to understand.

—Donna Caprell

I have grown as a teacher-researcher by understanding a little better that you don't need a structured setting or the standard textbook to prove that learning is taking place.

—Mary Wright

I have come to realize that my role as a teacher should be one of an active participant, not merely a facilitator of knowledge. Through children's literature I can provide my students with open-ended situations that encourage them to explore mathematical concepts by using their own strategies and sharing their findings with the group, thereby giving them a sense of ownership and deeper insight.

—Linda Nance

I have gained more trust in my students' ability to generate their own mathematical explorations and have realized that their explorations are just as important, if not more important, than the activities I create for them. Children's literature teaches my students so much more than the humdrum worksheets and math textbooks that have been so overused by many teachers in schools.

—Kathryn Shand

I've become a better listener to what children have to say. I try to look for ways to extend ideas that the children come up with. I see math as more exciting and interesting and hope I convey that to the children.

—Barbara Creighton

Although I could complete math problems, math has never been a strong point of mine. I finally understand the "whys" and will use this new insight to make my students better mathematicians in the real world.

—Debbie Poston

4. What other thoughts do you have about this literature/mathematics connection?

Capitalizing on the children's interest and questions can lead to wonderful investigations and new ways of recording their results.

—Patricia Black

I am more aware of what I am looking for in the books I purchase for my class and trust my own judgment rather than always following recommended book lists.

—Carolyn Webber

We need to make mathematics real, to make it a part of everyday life. In many classrooms math has become nothing more than numbers on a page; only facts and skills are stressed. Children become bored with the paper-and-pencil drill. Many quit trying because they don't get the "right" answer. We have all heard a child say, "I'm no good at math anyway." I think we can eliminate those negative thoughts and feelings, and literature is one way to do it. Using literature gives mathematics meaning and purpose. It shows children that thinking and problem solving can be done in different ways and that many times there is no one "right" answer.

—Deb Cotterman

Using children's literature allows us to be more real, to look at problems to be solved holistically rather than piece by piece. —Belinda Lay

I'm glad math is finally integrating with the other subjects. It has always been "thematic learning," then math. The books bring math into the theme as a natural part of the lesson. —Erica Swimmie

As Jackie Bankert says, "Books tend to bring out the best in children." The comments of these teachers confirm that observation. When these teachers share books with their students, they feel a renewed interest and enthusiasm for mathematics, which "bubble on" even after the story is over. Marilyn Crosby notes that "children's books open an unending conversation with mathematics," and other teachers reiterate this point. Books invite everyone into the mathematical conversation because good books are good for all learners; everyone can participate, contribute, and grow from these conversations. Donna Caprell notes the generative nature of these conversations, as children build on one another's discoveries and questions. Others comment about the open-ended potential that stories hold for allowing their children to wonder, imagine, and explore. Still other teachers see that stories give them a better window through which to view their children's mathematical understanding because these stories are tied to familiar situations.

Many teachers feel that stories promote a mathematical view of the world. Concepts are better understood in meaningful contexts. Erica Swimmie marvels at how *Anno's Math Games II* helped her children understand the concept of capacity. Kathryn Shand notes that books "foster collaboration and increase curiosity about mathematics," implying that conversations about books help build a supportive classroom community. Other teachers see books as helping to foster a spirit of risk taking, since stories can encourage a diversity of responses and children are not tied down to a single "right" answer. Linda Nance notes that stories often represent mathematical relationships. For instance, the pattern of counting by twos is nicely conveyed in Diane Hamm's *How Many Feet in the Bed?* (1991) and the Liberian folktale *Two Ways to Count to Ten* (Dee 1988).

As teachers use these books with their students they also gain a new perspective about themselves. Several mention that they have become better listeners, more observant of their students' intentions. Others have gained a renewed appreciation for the kind of mathematical language their children use to explain their insights and understanding. Still others see the empowering potential for all learners when they, as teachers, look to the children's comments and questions as the beginning points for mathematical investigations.

This chapter has resounded with the voices of children and teachers. We believe that learning is a collaborative enterprise and that everyone grows when more voices enter the conversation. The reflections by these children and teachers point to some of the restrictive practices of the past, as well as celebrate the potential of the future. Using children's books in an open, supportive way can radically change the nature of the teaching and learning of mathematics. As we scan the mathematical horizon before us, we agree with Stuart Little that the future holds great promise: "As he peered ahead into the great land that stretched before him, the way seemed long. But the sky was bright, and he somehow felt he was headed in the right direction" (White 1945, p. 131).

References

Anno, Mitsumasa. 1989. *Anno's math games II.* New York: Philomel.

Borasi, Raffaella. 1992. *Learning mathematics through inquiry.* Portsmouth, NH: Heinemann.

Brown, Stephen, and Marion Walter. 1983. *The art of problem posing.* Hillsdale, NJ: Lawrence Erlbaum.

Clement, Rod. 1991. *Counting on Frank.* Milwaukee: Gareth Stevens.

Cole, Joanna. 1985a. *Large as life: Daytime animals.* New York: Knopf.

———. 1985b. *Large as life: Nighttime animals.* New York: Knopf.

Dee, Ruby. 1988. *Two ways to count to ten.* New York: Henry Holt.

Eisner, Elliot. 1991. *The enlightened eye.* New York: Macmillan.

Giganti, Paul, Jr. 1992. *Each orange had 8 slices: A counting book.* New York: Greenwillow.

Hamm, Diane. 1991. *How many feet in the bed?* New York: Simon and Schuster.

Hulme, Joy. 1991. *Sea squares.* Westport, CT: Hyperion.

Hutchins, Pat. 1986. *The doorbell rang.* New York: Greenwillow.

Johnston, Tony. 1986. *Farmer Mack measures his pig.* New York: Harper and Row.

Lloyd, David. 1986. *The stopwatch.* New York: Lippincott.

National Council of Teachers of Mathematics. 1989. *Curriculum and evaluation standards for school mathematics.* Reston, VA: National Council of Teachers of Mathematics.

Pinczes, Elinor. 1993. *One hundred hungry ants.* Boston: Houghton Mifflin.

Rosen, Harold. 1987. *Stories and meaning.* Sheffield, England: National Association for the Teaching of English.

Viorst, Judith. 1978. *Alexander who used to be rich last Sunday.* New York: Macmillan.

White, E. B. 1945. *Stuart Little.* New York: Harper and Row.

5 *Listening to Tana Hoban and David M. Schwartz*

Tana Hoban, a photographer, has created enchanting books of visual exploration, many of them related to mathematical themes like shape and number. David M. Schwartz is the author of *How Much Is a Million?* (1985) and *If You Made a Million* (1989), picture-book investigations (illustrated by Stephen Kellogg) of large numbers up to a trillion and of monetary concepts from spending to mortgages. We interviewed each of these authors to find out about the origins and development of their books, which have been such an inspiration to children and their teachers.

Tana Hoban

Tana Hoban has been a photographer since her studies at Philadelphia's School of Design for Women in the 1930s; she's been creating photographic concept-books for children since 1970 (always with the same editor, Susan Hirschman, formerly with Macmillan and now at Greenwillow, of which she is the founding editor). Hoban has also taught a course on photography as communication, used poetry in work with mental patients, and made an occasional short film. After many years in Philadelphia and New York, she now lives in Paris with her husband, John Morris, former director of the Magnum photographic agency and currently the Paris correspondent for *National Geographic*. During the interview, we were impressed by her strong intuitive aesthetic sense; the mathematical content of her books emerges through her strong and witty interactions with the visual world around her. Portions of the interview are presented below under headings reflecting some of the important topics and themes of Hoban's work.

HOW I GET MY IDEAS

TANA HOBAN: Of course the mathematics and geometry in my books are intuitive. I don't think I could pass a test on it. I don't know how you explain intuition.

SANDRA WILDE: One of the reasons we chose you to interview is that you do subtle things. You do what you do, and the mathematical concepts grow out of it.

TH: Mainly what I'm trying to do is say, Don't miss anything. Observe and notice and examine. In the context of that concept, it comes out mathematically sometimes. And I'm always fascinated by groups of things, and how they're arranged, the patterns.

SW: Maybe we could talk about some specific books. *Shadows and Reflections* [1990b] is interesting because it's not just reflections in mirrors; the shapes get distorted. How did you get the idea to do this one, and how did you find some of the images?

TH: Sometimes the title just happens in conversation. It might be a phrase, and I say, Gee, that sounds like a good title. I think this might have been something like that. And then, looking for the reflections, I didn't want to just do the stereotyped reflection, so I looked for interesting things, and I looked for things children relate to. I'm always trying to use the things that they see every day. This [*a shot of clouds reflected in windows*] is in Paris, and I love clouds, and that's something I think is not too corny; it's a nice reflection of clouds, and then you have the clouds up here, and you have the reflection. And of course this is a common one: the man on the street and the big puddle. I've used puddles before with garbage and trash in a shapes book, because you find all kinds of marvelous shapes there. This [*flamingoes reflected in a pond*] was at the zoo. I went to shoot, and I got this shot very early in that shoot, and I went back again just to see what I'd get, and it never, never was like that again.

ON NOT BEING BORED

TH: I have another book that I'm working on, where a fish fascinated me because it was so unusual. It might be presumptuous, but I like to think that a child will look at that and say, Wow! I wonder what kind of fish it is? Then if I identify it in the back, then the child will be interested in going to the aquarium like I would. What I'm trying to do is arouse their curiosity. Too many people just get turned off. Maybe they don't try hard enough, or maybe they're just too bored. And that's what I'm trying to stay away from: boredom, trying to stay away from being numb to the world. I do want to feel everything, to sense everything, and I think I do these books for me, to see if I can do that. Not lose my sensitivity.

THE MAN WITH THE HORN

TH: This [*a man playing—and being reflected in—a large brass horn*] is one of my favorite pictures of all time. I love this. When I use people or children, I like them to be universal, not specific, just like this man. The horn is important, not if he's a handsome man with a beard or without a beard or young or old. So children can be all children.

SW: The man reflected in the horn is pretty sophisticated mathematically in terms of the curvature distorting the reflection.

TH: I think it's fun to have children play with curves and shiny things, and see what they pick up.

THE NATURE OF THE IMAGE

TH: Sometimes you have the perfect mirror image; the pelicans in this picture I think children would find amusing. And this is just a nice big puddle, and I guess I was fascinated by the pattern. I try to get a strong graphic image, something so when the children look at my pictures, it registers; it's not as though they have to try to find it; I want it to be very clear.

STAGED AND FOUND IMAGES

SW: What about staged images versus found images?

TH: When I stage them, I usually am copying something natural, it's not totally fiction. I mean, this [*an image of a cat's cradle, seen only as a shadow*] is a game children play, and I played it when I was a child, and a lot of the images come from my childhood. I remember certain things, the way my mother cut an apple across to get the star. Things like that. And this is one of them. And now to take a picture like this, of course you can take it on the table, you can take it on the rug. I like the background to be unobtrusive, but not just dead, not a dead white paper. So this was the steps of the Musée d'Orsay in Paris. We were there, and it happened to be nice. I like it to be a universal background. You can't tell where it is, it doesn't get in the way, and it's graphic.

ON PLANNING AND RESULTS

SW: Did you know that *Shadows and Reflections* would come out like this, with fractured and distorted reflections?

TH: No, because I never thought of it that way. I never thought, Well, okay, this is a good fractured one, this is a good clear one. I just thought of reflections.

SW: It's great that through your intuitive photography, it came out with a whole universe of what reflections might be like.

TH: It's marvelous. Of course everything is mathematical.

CITY, COUNTRY, AND CHILDHOOD

SW: You seem to have a real balance between the natural world and the urban landscape.

TH: Yes, because I live in the city in Paris, I lived in Manhattan. I grew up in the country; in the country we had pigeons and chickens and dogs and cats. We had all that. And we lived in the country because my mother and father thought it was healthy for the children. Way before people did it, my father screened in the porch, and we'd sleep outside.

DAVID WHITIN: Were there some experiences you had early on that influenced what you're doing today?

TH: Not in any conscious way, I guess. We always had books, we had a room upstairs that was called the library. And when I was growing up, that wasn't a common thing to have. I doubt if any of our friends had it. And the whole room was lined with books. And you'd go up to read. My father would save magazines; he would save newspapers.

BECOMING A PHOTOGRAPHER

SW: How did your visual sense develop as a child? When did you get interested in photography?

TH: I always drew, I'd make drawings to show my father when he came home at night, I would copy things. And then I would always go to art class, and I was always the youngest student. I'd go to Saturday morning art classes, then I went to a sketch class. And I was also the youngest when I was in life classes. And I guess I always thought I'd be an artist, an illustrator. I took in art school a class on the illustration of paintings, and I got the award for painting. I took photography in the last semester of art school, and it was the first time they ever had photography. My father had a Graflex, I have a picture of him with it under his arm, the big hood, the four-by-five lens. And by a strange coincidence, the teacher went to buy everybody a camera, a used camera, and the one he bought for me, without knowing anything about my father, was a Graflex, like my father's, with this beautiful lens, and it was a two-five [*2.5*] Cooke lens. I became known for my pictures of children, with selective focus; I would take these moody pictures of children, and focus on their eyes. And I became known for these moody children, introspective pictures, and I would do them for myself. I always felt if I did commercial work, I'd still want to balance it with personal work, that it was okay to do commercial if you did some art. So that's what I tried to do, and I became known as one of the best photographers of children, and then I'd do advertising. I did children, and I did people, and I free-lanced all my life. I worked for Eastman Kodak, I worked for Polaroid free-lance. I could just take whatever I wanted, work a whole summer. They would give me a retainer fee, and then they'd pick out things at the end of the summer. It was a very interesting time.

SW: So then what led you into doing books for children?

TH: When you do advertising, it's all art directors and things like that, and if they change art directors the new one drops the old sources. And I said, Well, I don't want to be doing this forever, and it has a certain amount of stress. Is it going to turn out? Is the light going to work? And I always use natural light, or when I use artificial light, I imitate natural light. And I got tired of doing that, and then a friend of mine had a baby. I used to do some medical photography, and I photographed the delivery. I had shown those pictures to John Morris, who's now my husband. He was working for one of the magazines, and he said, "Oh, you have a book here." I said, "If you lay it out, we'll do it together." He had a friend at Doubleday, and we thought maybe we'd have somebody write a text. Well, we never sold it, and the couple who had the baby got divorced, so they didn't want me to use the pictures! I had made a very careful dummy, and after that I had some ideas. I did a book about a rabbit. I just took a lot of pictures of a rabbit and picked out the best pictures to try to make a story. When I showed that to Susan Hirschman, she didn't like it but said come back next week, So in three weeks I showed her three dummies, and the rabbit was first, and the second was *Look Again* [1971]. When I brought it in, they thought at first maybe it was too gimmicky, so they said come in again next week, and the third week I brought in *Shapes and Things* [1970], which is photograms [*images printed directly on photographic paper*], and she called in other editors and they got excited about that, and they took the two books. And that's what started them. And I thought photograms was such a simple idea, somebody's going to come up with it, and I just did it as fast as I could.

LOOK AGAIN AND ITS SEQUELS

DW: We were curious how you came up with the idea behind *Look Again* [*cutouts in the pages focusing attention on part of an image*].

TH: Oftentimes you cut a little mat to look at things, how to crop a picture, and I think maybe a piece of paper with a hole in it was lying on something. And that must have given me the idea. When you get an idea, something clicks. If I'm riding in a bus, riding in a car, riding on a train, there's nothing to do but sit and have my mind wander. And that's when I get ideas. If you give children a strip of paper with a little frame, they can put it on their skin, they can put it on an eye, put it on the hair; they can just go around and look at things, outdoors or indoors, wherever they are. I always try with my pictures to say, come closer, so they'll really look at it. And of course this makes them think of all kinds of things, and I love it because their mind does go far afield to come up with something.

DW: I've seen kids try to predict what one of these pictures is, and when they turn the page and find it, even though it may not be what they have predicted, they've already begun to make comparisons: well, it wasn't this, but in a way it's similar. They begin to make comparisons between things in the world. One of the things that's interesting mathematically about these books with the frames is differences of scale, like one picture looks like it's going to be a flower or something, and then it's a Ferris wheel.

TH: There's one of a dandelion, and children would come up with, it's broken glass, a bird's nest, it would be so far off, but it doesn't matter; what matters is that they're thinking of things. And with the counting book, *Count and See* [1972a], that one, when I would go to schools, I'd show that, and they'd say, one fire hydrant. And they'd all sing-song it. But then if I said, one what else? that was sort of a key. They'd begin to see things that aren't there and things that are there. One crack in the pavement, one shadow, one building, one street curb; and that's really what I want them to do. I just want the wheels to turn. I don't want the pictures to be a passive experience.

SHAPES

DW: Let's talk about *Round and Round and Round* [1983c], *Circles, Triangles and Squares* [1974a], and *Shapes, Shapes, Shapes* [1986a].

TH: I'm fascinated by shapes.

DW: And your intent is certainly more than to have kids merely identify shapes, knowing that's a circle, that's a square . . .

TH: Right. So that garbage in the street isn't always just garbage, it's triangles, and circles, and squares, and it might be textures.

SW: This picture in *Round and Round and Round* is a nice lead-in to why things are the shape they are. A hoop is round so you can roll it. Why is a pea round, why is a colander?

DW: That's one of the questions I often ask kids, not so much what is the shape, but why do you suppose it's shaped that way? One of my favorite stories is about a five-year-old, while we were looking at *Round and Round and Round.* There were wheels on a car or a truck, and I kept asking, "Why do you suppose they're round? What if they were square?" And he thought for a minute and he said, "Then we'd rock instead of roll."

JUXTAPOSITION

DW: When juxtaposing certain photographs with each other, how do you go about it?

TH: I take pictures separately, without thinking of them together, and then when I do a book, when I go to lay it out, first of all I accumulate pictures, accumulate the images, and then I lay the pictures all out, and then I pick up two at a time, to make each two-page spread, and usually this first way I've arranged it stays pretty much the same, what seem like natural juxtapositions. There's a French librarian who has a whole theory about my pairings! I just feel that images go together, and it might be because it's a pairing of natural and man-made, or it might be that they look alike, you don't know. In most cases there's something that puts them together.

DW: There's one in *Dots, Spots, Speckles and Stripes* [1987b], a freckled boy and a lobster across from him.

TH: The little boy was out to lunch at the next table one day. And I said, "Oh, look at that kid with freckles." And I was doing *Dots and Spots.* So I asked the father and mother if I could do one of the boy, and I just moved the chair out and shot it.

SW: It keeps the idea of a nonspecific child, because it's the freckles that we focus on.

TH: The freckles, and he's not looking right at the camera. I love his expression.

DW: The point of clarity is the freckles rather than the eyes.

TH: I got the idea for this book with a bouquet of flowers. I was at my daughter's in Rochester, and she had these flowers on the table. And I just looked at them and thought about dots and spots and freckles. And that's how I got the idea.

DW: So you're always looking?

TH: I guess unconsciously. Not, what book will I do next? It's just that I go about what I'm doing, and something clicks.

DW: But you're looking for little things; you're looking for patterns; you're looking for relationships, interesting shapes, and we don't all do that. We need to learn to see the world in that particular way. That's part of what your books do for kids.

SW: It's interesting the way you're moving now into more subtle, less defined shapes. You're not just doing things like circles, but you're going into spirals and fanshapes and dots and speckles.

26 LETTERS AND 99 CENTS

SW: Some of your books involve a more formal teaching of concepts. We could talk particularly of the ninety-nine cents part of *26 Letters and 99 Cents* [1987a], how you got the idea.

TH: I think I got the idea because I read in the newspaper that children by a certain age should know how to count thirty-nine cents and know the letters of the alphabet. The original idea was twenty-six letters and thirty-nine cents. But then, with inflation it needed to be higher, because it's an amount for lunch money or something. So Susan said, let's make it ninety-nine cents, because a dollar doesn't sound right for a title. I was fascinated by this. I had started this book a while back, and she didn't seem to like the idea, but then I made a dummy. She doesn't understand my books very well if I just tell her a title. So here you have a particular way to do it, and then the money is actual size, so they can lay the money here. I think that's kind of fun to do. And then it was my editor's idea to turn the book upside down for the letters, and I found the lowercase [ones] but not the capitals, and I contacted the people who made them, and they didn't have capitals and they were in England. So they said they needed a certain twelve-hundred-dollar machine to do it and so I lent them the money to do it because I wanted the letters. And I never got the money back because they went out of business eventually. And I probably have the only set of letters they made. I didn't want to just have flat, dead letters; these look so juicy and so I find them very appealing. And now I think there are books that come packaged with letters like these.

NUMBERS AND SHAPES

SW: With the counting books, the fun is in picking what images to use.

DW: In *Count and See* [1972a], you found some unique objects in the environment that were grouped in a particular way, and that was really appealing to us and to kids.

TH: I looked at it recently, and I thought, Gee, this is really good, in all modesty! I really liked it. I did just take ordinary things, the paper bag with the peanuts. Even when I arranged things, I'd just dump them out.

SW: In *Shapes, Shapes, Shapes* [1986a], one thing I liked is that you did identify the shapes in outline form at the beginning.

TH: My editor thought it would add to it, and it does.

SW: When you look at the photos, what I think is fun, when I shared it with first graders, we talked about the shapes in the beginning so they had a vocabulary.

TH: Then it is really geometry. And you don't always realize that it is.

SW: It seems like you were really having fun with some. One in particular is the lunch box. It's got every shape you could think of. I especially like having the egg because *oval* comes from a word meaning egg.

TH: What amazes me is the oval and the circle [*of the yolk in a hard-boiled egg*] together.

SW: Was it your intention when you planned the book to have the specific shapes that are listed at the front?

TH: No, Susan made the list after I did the book. I like each picture to be more than one thing, not just to have one answer. So they can keep searching and keep thinking.

URBAN LIFE

SW: Weren't you one of the first photographers for children that was noted for doing urban scenes?

TH: I think Susan [Hirschman] thinks I was a pioneer. It's because I lived in the city, one week they're digging up Twenty-third Street, the next week they'd be digging up another block. And so I did *Push/Pull, Empty/Full* [1972b]. That was from all that. Another day there were trash cans, four trash cans, the sun was hitting them, and I counted them. That gave me the idea for *Count and See* [1972a]. So then I was thinking, I live in the city; I'm raising my child in the city, and I was concerned about the urban child, children who just live in the city, who never get to the country. I grew up in the country, so I knew how wonderful it was, and so I was trying to do things for the urban child, and to use what they saw with their eyes every day. At Bank Street School, they would ask the children, What did you see on the way to school? And the children said, Oh, nothing, nothing. Then, when they gave them cameras, they had a focus. You can give them tubes, like from toilet paper or paper towels, and just say, Look around. When I talk to them I say, Do it with your hands, and look close. Get the wide angle, and then use your hands to narrow your focus and get the closeup, so it's like a telephoto. And you can do that with children; it gives them another way to look. Instead of seeing the whole room, the whole thing, it kind of picks out things like a camera. Children just discovered the world, they discovered the buildings going up, and they discovered the river, and they discovered the market. It sort of turned them on. So that's what made me think, what am I not seeing right where I'm living? I don't have to go to the Sahara or somewhere to do glamorous pictures. I can do my pictures right here. I had a child, I didn't want to have to travel. Sometimes if you think, I want to take great pictures, you think you have to go somewhere far away. I always remember my son-in-law taking my granddaughter, she was little and he'd carry her around, he'd take her up to a tree to just touch a leaf. And I think things like that are important.

DW: I think very young kids can help us adults see the world in new ways.

TH: Absolutely.

ARE YOU MATHEMATICAL?

SW: Do you consider yourself a mathematically minded person?

TH: I don't know if I am. I never thought of myself as that, but maybe I am without realizing it, without doing it deliberately. Because I must think that way. Where I work is a mess, but I know where things are, and I get things done. Having it in order is not my priority, but I do like to have things in order, and in my disorder, in my chaos I have some order. And I guess that's mathematical.

SW: You're so attuned to both shape and number in the world that that may be a kind of mathematical mind-set.

TH: I think it is, so maybe I use my mind mathematically, and get the result without the equations. I think it's marvelous that you think I'm mathematical! The way they teach mathematics today, don't they teach it more interestingly than they used to when it was just *x* plus *y* or something? It's more practical; you're doing something, right?

SW: Not in all classrooms, but that's the direction the schools are going in.

TH: Yes, and I think that's very good.

DW: Geometry, which of course is what your books focus on so much, often gets shortchanged in schools.

TH: Maybe I should do some more shape books. I had this in mind because a long time ago somebody said, Your books are about geometry. And I thought I really should figure it out, do it specifically. But maybe I can just do it with more shapes, more sophisticated shapes, more classic geometry.

SW: And the thing that you're really doing that nobody else is is to go beyond the regular shapes and into the curves and so on.

TH: I think that the people who imitate me miss something. I don't want to say they're bad, but I think they're either too pedantic or they don't go beyond the basic shapes. Whereas I think I do.

SW: Especially in geometry, but all of math really, there's an aesthetic to it, even in a simple book, like *26 Letters and 99 Cents.*

TH: Definitely, in the four parts of the page. For me it is appealing, and I like the way the money looks.

SW: You can really see the difference between seventeen and eighteen.

TH: It's not arranged so everything is straight on, not all heads. I just did it kind of at random. I did it on purpose because I thought that's the way you see money.

SW: The nice thing about counting books is that you start to develop an intuitive sense of what does six look like? and so on.

TALKING TO TEACHERS

DW: Is there anything you would want to tell teachers that you haven't already mentioned?

TH: It's important to nurture curiosity and wonder.

SW: Do you have any thoughts about how *not* to use your books with kids?

TH: Well, I don't think there should be one answer. There's what it says on the cover, and if they see something else in it, I think not to squelch them. I think it's not written in stone, so if they digress, it starts with one concept, but there's no right and wrong answer to my books. If the teacher says, Look for this, look for that, I think that's wrong. It's not just a tool.

DW: The books, as you've said so well, are a basis for helping kids think and view the world.

TH: Yes; enthusiasm is also what they're for. You know, I think so many people get that squelched out of them at an early age. Then they're afraid to talk about it.

DW: It would be very easy with one of your books, say *Round and Round and Round* [1983d], just to go through it and quiz kids on finding the circles, and not allow more conversation than that.

TH: I think you need to enlarge on it. So what else is round? And to look at the book and then, what in this room is round? The top of the chair, the table, see what there is right where they are, because I often say, what is there right where I am standing that I don't notice, that I don't see? Because it's like when you misplace something, and you can't find it, and all it is, is turned over on your desk.

SW: One of the things you've done in these, where a lot of the images are found images, like a variety of clothes with polka-dots on them, what these should do for kids is help them to learn to frame the world themselves so they can see in this way.

TH: In one of my books, I went to take a picture of a peacock, and then it never occurred to me to shoot the back of the peacock, and the peacock turned around, and I thought, my gosh, it's fantastic! And lots of my books, it's like each time I do a book I go down the street, so I'm going down the street and I'm going to the market, but each time I'm looking for something else. Something new.

SW: Framing different things.

TH: Then, of course, I'm counting, for a counting book I'm counting everything in sight. It's hard to break that habit.

DW: There's such a diversity in the photographs you take, such as urban and rural and things that appeal to kids. One of the things about your books, no matter where kids are, no matter where they're living, they can connect with those photographs and think, there's beautiful things where I am too.

TH: Absolutely. And I think that's good to point that out.

David M. Schwartz

David M. Schwartz, born in 1951, was a biology major in college and never intended to be a writer. His two mathematical children's books have drawn a great deal of attention, however, because they make challenging concepts not only extremely accessible but also a lot of fun. Before he began writing for a living in 1980, he worked as an elementary schoolteacher and college associate dean, along with briefer stints as a carpenter, lumberjack, and veterinary assistant. In his conversation with David Whitin, he reveals an approach somewhat different from Tana Hoban's; where she is intuitive, his books and work with children are grounded in a precise sense of number. These differences reflect the diversity of the field: there are many different ways to explore mathematical topics with children through literature.

DAVID WHITIN: What got you intrigued with mathematics?

DAVID M. SCHWARTZ: When I was a kid, and I was interested in what we might now call math or science, it wasn't so much math per se, it was the concepts that math could be applied to. For example, I was fascinated with things that came in large numbers, and things that were large, like the magnitude of the stars, in relation to my own life. And the same with tiny things.

So I would ride my bicycle during the day. I liked to ride my bike. A lot of kids do. And maybe I went on a long ride, maybe ten, fifteen, or twenty miles, which for me then was a lot. And I would be really tired. And as I was riding along, I'd be thinking, Well, this seems like a long way, but imagine riding all the way across the country. How long would that take? And I'd try to figure that out. And then, how long would it take if I kept going, and I could go all around the world? And my mind would be boggled about how large the world was. But then I would think, Yeah, but the earth is small compared to Jupiter. How long would that take? Or if I could ride my bike to the sun, ninety-three million miles.

I would wonder about stuff like that. How long would it take me to count all the stars up there? I learned that stars were in the trillions, how long it would take to count to one trillion. Those sorts of things fascinated me. Not things I was obsessed with, but just things I liked to think about. I liked that mind-boggled feeling I got from thinking of things like that. Then I sort of put it aside for a few decades. It was in fact the stars, seeing them on one particular night, when I happened to be freshly in love, one beautiful early spring night, that was a flashback to the stuff I used to like to think about and wonder about as a kid.

The name of a book by Rachel Carson, *The Sense of Wonder* (1956), came to mind. This is a book she wrote for parents to try to get them to cultivate that sense of awe and wonder that's native to children. And I remember that I had read this when I was a teacher, and I remembered the part where she talks about how if the stars could only be seen in one place on earth, there would be this huge migration of people, this pilgrimage to see the stars. Or if they could only be seen on one night of the year, everybody would go out to see them. Many people will go through their whole lives and never really take stock of how beautiful that sight is on a clear night, because it's there all the time. So in a way we devalue it because it's so common. Anyway, the whole book was about that idea, cultivating a sense of wonder.

Those words, a sense of wonder, came back to me that night, and so did my childhood memories of being fascinated by things that were hugely numerous and gigantic, so large compared to the scale of human life we could relate to that it was mind-boggling. So I thought I'd write a book to help kids get that same feeling I had. I played around with different approaches to the book, but in the end I decided to orient the book around the numbers, because every time I tried something else I ended up using these big numbers to describe whatever it was

I was talking about, like how many lifetimes it would take to count the stars, so why not first write the book that explains what these big numbers are? And that's how *How Much Is a Million?* came about.

DW: Has the writing of the book regenerated this sense of wonder that you had as a child?

DMS: Well, I started maybe taking note more carefully when I would see things that you really want to stop and pause and think about. Look at any day's issue of the newspaper and you'll probably find some big numbers. Or somewhere you see some boring statistic like Americans eat 620 million avocados every year and then you can think about that. How big a volume is that? I wouldn't say, though, that it has particularly changed my life, except my professional life, of course.

DW: How did you come to write *If You Made a Million*?

DMS: After I wrote *How Much Is a Million?,* I discovered that what people were really interested in wasn't so much millions of stars or goldfish or millions of days of counting, but millions of dollars. When people hear the word *million* they like to think of dollars. When I'd go to a school, a teacher would introduce the book and say, This is called *How Much Is a Million?* but what we'd really like to know is how much is a million dollars. So it led me to realize that people were interested in associating millions with dollars, but also there were some good value lessons that I might be able to communicate, such as making money means making choices, and there are a lot of concepts about money that kids don't understand and sometimes I thought adults didn't really understand. I thought if I could tie all that together into a book, it would be a natural sequel.

I also wanted to do something called *How Much Is a Millionth?* focusing on small things. I've never done it. No particular idea of how to do it came to mind. I might actually be able to make that part of the measuring book [*a book on the metric system, in progress*]. You know, get down to millimeters and microns and so forth.

DW: Have you seen *Powers of Ten* [Morrison & Morrison 1982]?

DMS: Yes, that's a wonderful approach.

DW: Are there any other childhood experiences that nurtured your interest in mathematics?

DMS: I collected coins as a kid, and I liked to think about how they added up or multiplied.

DW: Do you remember any good mathematics teachers?

DMS: When I think about the good teachers I had, math isn't really what comes to mind. However, in junior high school, I remember the rule about you can't have a fraction with a zero in the denominator. You can't divide by zero. Being a little bit of a rebel, but not a math genius, I started thinking, Well, suppose we had a system where you could divide by zero, or suppose we had a geometry where three points didn't necessarily define a plane, and I wondered about these things. And I remember one day sitting down and trying to write out this new mathematics, but I didn't get anywhere. I thought it was a fun thing to think about, but I didn't know what to do with it.

DW: It's interesting you mention that, because for me one of the most powerful words in *How Much Is a Million?* is the word *if. If* a million kids stood on each other's shoulders, or *if* you counted from one to one million, and it's that kind of intellectual leaping that ought to be encouraged with kids in school.

DMS: That's interesting. Here is something that's a little bit related to the counting of the stars. I would say, What would I find if I could go to the end of the universe? What would be there? As if it were a yard or something. Would there be a brick wall there and a sign that says, Do not go beyond this point? What would there be on the other side of the wall? *If* enables you to violate all the assumptions of the universe, of our life, and of our thought processes. It takes you into other worlds mentally. That's an interesting point that nobody ever said before about the book. Every couplet in that book starts with *if,* doesn't it?

DW: I have found when teachers share *How Much Is a Million?* with children, a lot of times kids will say at the end of the story, Is that book true? And when teachers ask, What do you mean by that? children will talk about how kids couldn't really stand on each other's shoulders, that couldn't be possible.

DMS: I think what they're saying is, Should we believe you or not? Are you making this up? Are you lying to us? How do you know how big this goldfish bowl would be? Did you just pick this out of thin air? Interestingly on a few occasions I have received in the mail some books made by kids or classes that are takeoffs on *How Much Is a Million?* where they come up with their own inventions. Looking through them I see that they don't figure out things. Well, occasionally they do, but usually they'll be a lot of examples like, A million teddy bears would fill eight and a half rooms of the school or it would take such an amount of time to eat a million pizzas. I think they pulled those things out of thin air; they don't look true to me. I wish I had those here to show you. Every time I've made a little mental calculation it's been way off. I still think that's a valuable thing for them to do; they're imagining how much they think it would be.

DW: Your sense of humor somehow reminds me of the sense of humor in Stephen Kellogg's illustrations. Did you know each other before you wrote your books?

DMS: People always ask me this. I had nothing to do with hiring him on to the book; it was done by the publisher even before they agreed to take it on. When I got a call from my agent to tell me that Lothrop wanted to publish *How Much Is a Million?* and Stephen Kellogg was going to illustrate it, I said, Great! Can I meet him? He said no. I said, Just to talk about the illustrations? He said no. [*It's common for authors and illustrators not to communicate with each other.*] So I had written out some ideas for the illustrations already, which were included in the manuscript when I wrote the book. He followed only half of them, roughly. In fact, one he illustrated in a very odd way. It was the one with the million stars spread out. I had to reword my text to fit his illustration because by the time I saw it, it was too late to change the illustration. So I added, "It's pages spread side by side." I felt that people couldn't understand what was going on in that picture based on the way I had originally written it.

DW: Do you think children's own observations and questions make good starting points for mathematical investigations?

DMS: When I go to schools I use popcorn as a way to develop the idea of a million, starting with one and going through the powers of ten, at least up to 100,000, with popcorn. I have 100,000 kernels. I don't have a million, and we have to imagine the size of that bag of popcorn. Kids are always disappointed at that point because I have so astonished them by actually having 100,000 kernels. So we discuss a million, and then I ask them to imagine a billion kernels of popcorn. Imagine not just one bowl like this [*filled with a million kernels*], or ten bowls like this, not a hundred bowls, but a thousand of these millions, and that's called a billion. And then I say, Do you think a billion kernels of popcorn would fill up this school? Now that's a good question that I've never figured out. Probably it wouldn't in most schools. But they want to know. And we could figure that out, because we could measure the 100,000 that I have, and then figure out the volume of the school.

DW: What about your interest in writing? I know you've done other kinds of writing before the publication of these two books for children.

DMS: You know, I never wrote with any particular interest through college. And then I became an elementary school teacher, and I taught in a school where we had to write out our report cards, basically like a letter to the parents. Another teacher in the school read mine and said I really ought to do some more writing. Then he proposed an idea a few weeks later when my class was studying weather and we went and looked at weather vanes. The kids made weather vanes, and the weather vanes didn't point in the right direction. Instead of pointing into the wind they pointed away from the wind. And I said, Let's go look at some real ones up on the rooftops and let's see if we can figure out what makes them point into the wind. This was in Vermont, and we went around in the school's van and looked at a bunch of weather vanes and we were amazed at the variety. My friend came along, and he suggested that we do an article on weather vanes. I would write it and he would do the pictures. And so we did, although he never did the pictures, but *Smithsonian* magazine bought the article and they commissioned a photographer they had worked with before. That was the beginning of my writing career, and I did magazine writing, which I still do.

So then I moved over to writing about scientific nature, wildlife, the environment. That's really where my strongest interest is, for that kind of writing. About fourteen years ago a friend of mine had this idea about writing books about food, or restaurants I should say, that were near the interstate highway, near the freeways. We self-published it and then Simon and Schuster wanted it to be a series, so we spent a few years driving around the country working on this as part of a national series called *The Interstate Gourmet.* That led to me doing a lot of food writing for magazines.

I always think I want to write a serious, long book but I've never found a subject I felt I wanted to dig into for two years. Maybe because I'm naturally a dilettante and I like to play around with things. Also I like writing for a magazine, because I can explore a lot of different subjects. I'll spend two months working on egg collecting or working on otters, or working on a profile of some interesting person, and then I'll go on to something else. I do sometimes think I need to be a little bit more sustained in my interests.

DW: What kind of interesting letters or reactions have you received from kids about your books?

DMS: I've been to schools where they have done things like if I had a million dollars, and each kid gets a green million-dollar bill to write on it what he or she would spend it on. A lot of schools have tried to collect a million of something and they call me in to see it and to visit and talk to them. A million pop-tops, a million pages of reading by the whole school, a million things they might print out on the computer—or a million computer holes [*from the edges of sprocket-fed paper*], one school in Connecticut did that.

Here's another interesting reaction I've gotten from kids. I've gotten a couple of letters telling me there's a mistake in *If You Made a Million.* And there is. I recorded the wrong height for nickels. I said a million of them stacked up would go this high. And when they pointed that out to me, I was shocked. How could I have gotten that wrong? And then I remembered how I did it. When I was writing it, I didn't have the roll of nickels to measure. Measuring one or two isn't quite accurate enough with a crude measuring implement. So I wrote something in there with the intention of going to the bank, getting a roll of nickels, measuring it, and replacing it with the right number but I forgot to do that. I just used my guess. I just took a guess, a temporary measure, and forgot to replace it. So kids went and checked it, the same way that they checked that counting to one million lasted twenty-three days. There's one other letter as well. I got a letter from a guy shortly after the book came out who was a parent and told me that he really liked my book but why did I use those archaic measurements instead of metric measurements? And he was part of some metric society and he worked out the whole book using metric measurements.

DW: Are there any comments that you'd like to make about literature and mathematics? I feel that stories can be a powerful avenue for kids to think about and explore mathematical ideas. Do you have any thoughts yourself on the importance of story?

DMS: I think different kinds of kids have different kinds of reactions to the world. I used to think about things that I did in terms of numbers sometimes, like riding my bike. Similarly, when I read books as a child, sometimes what would stand out in my memory would be something that was a little bit quantitative. For instance, when I read *Cheaper by the Dozen* [Gilbreth & Carey 1948] one of the things that stood out was, well, the very title has a number in it. It's about a family that has a dozen kids, except one of them died, so they really had eleven, but they kept the title. The father used to like to say, Oh, I had all these kids because it's cheaper by the dozen. I always thought, Yeah, a dozen is a nice word, it means twelve but we don't have any nice word that means eleven, so that's why he had to say that. It's sort of biased in favor of certain numbers.

The other thing that really stood out in my memory was an incident in the book in which the father brings to the cottage on Nantucket, where they go for the summers, a piece of graph paper that has one thousand vertical lines and one thousand horizontal lines across it. He says to the children, Do you see this piece of paper? This piece of paper has one million little squares that are made by these lines, one thousand down and one thousand across. If a man had one million dollars he would have as many dollars as there are squares on this piece of paper. And one of the little kids says, Do you have a million dollars, daddy? And he says, No, I have a million children instead! Somewhere along the line a man has to make a choice! Anyway, for some odd reason, perhaps because that's the way my mind worked, that's what I remembered about the book, one thousand lines by one thousand lines made a million squares, and that's as many squares as a million dollars. And if you saw that piece of paper you could see a million of something. I thought to myself, Gee, that's really neat. I wish I could see a million of something in one place. So there's a childhood experience that involves literature.

There are other books. There was *Homer Price* and the doughnut machine [McCloskey 1943], a takeoff on "The Sorcerer's Apprentice." There was also *Henry Reed, Inc.* [Robertson 1974], one of my favorite books. It was about a kid who had his own business and figured out how to do all kinds of things that needed to be done around town and make some money at it, but I don't remember the details too well. But I do remember being fascinated, not by the aggrandizement of wealth, but by the way money was tied to activities of certain kinds. Certain things are worth different amounts of money.

DW: Based on your fascination with large numbers I can see how *Cheaper by the Dozen* would appeal to you. Part of my interest in all this is that I don't think kids have enough stories that are tied to the mathematical concepts that they are supposed to learn in school. Like the second graders I told you about who wanted to represent one million in some way after they read your book. And one child said, How about body parts? Then someone said noses, and someone else said eyes. They finally tried to use all their fingers. A group of two hundred teachers and kids lined the hallway to count all their fingers hoping to reach one million and learned that they needed five hundred more hallways like that one to reach their goal.

DMS: I love that story. I have told it to some kids in a few schools. One of the questions I often ask kids as I work in individual classrooms is, What do you think we have a million of in this school? Then I tell them about that story of putting down the fingers in the hall, and videotaping it, and how many times you'd have to run the videotape, and they really like it. Then they come up with all kinds of ideas for what there might be a million of. One of the most common ones is, if the room has carpeting, there are a million of those little nubs in the carpeting. Or if the room has acoustic tiles with holes in it there must be a million holes. Grains of sand is one that I always wondered about as a child. You know, how many grains are on this beach or are in the world?

DW: I'm sure when you go out and visit schools they know about the word *googol.*

DMS: They do, and *googolplex.*

DW: Do they ask you about that?

DMS: Sometimes they do. Sometimes I ask them. I say, What's the largest number in the world? The most common answers are *infinity, zillion,* and *googol* or *googolplex.* When I do my thing where I build up by powers of ten to one million, I make the point with the kids: Why use exponents? When we get to really big numbers I say, Now let's suppose I want to write out the number googol [*one followed by one hundred zeroes, or* 10^{100}], and I start doing it, and my arm is getting tired. Is there an easier way to write this number? Personally I find it utterly fascinating that the number googol is larger than the estimated number of molecules in the universe, which is somewhere around ten to the sixty-ninth power or ten to the seventieth power. Isn't that something?

DW: Yes. The number of grains of sand needed to fill a sphere the size of the earth has been estimated to be ten to the thirty-second power.

DMS: And those grains of sand have a lot more molecules. And there's a lot more than grains of sand in the universe.

DW: I bet you find that kids are really fascinated with large numbers.

DMS: They are. They really are. It's just sort of an inherently interesting subject. It's the same thing as kids being fascinated with dinosaurs: huge!

DW: Do you have any comments about the condition of mathematics education in this country?

DMS: That's not something I'm especially knowledgeable about. I don't get the sense there's a lot of integration of mathematics into the rest of the curriculum. That's why I do a workshop for teachers on integrating math. I think it's unfortunate that many teachers feel so uncomfortable with math.

DW: It's interesting you mention integration, because in your comments today you've talked a lot about science.

DMS: Also geography was a childhood interest of mine.

DW: Did you enjoy maps?

DMS: Yeah, I loved maps. Some of my favorite activities to do with children now involve maps. They involve relating big numbers to maps. If we had a million kids, a million fourth graders just like you, and they were holding hands along the side of the road, starting right here in Wallingford, Connecticut, how far would they go? Would they reach Florida? Let's figure it out. We get ten of them up there measuring to figure it out. If we had a car that could go over anything, the oceans, the deserts, the mountains, and it wanted to go a million miles, how many times around the world would that be? You can give them the circumference of the earth, or they could figure it out from the scale of miles, they can look it up, or whatever. And they see it's about forty times around the earth. You can take a string and wrap it forty times around a globe. Or just measure it off so we know what that would be. And then stretch that string out and see a million miles compared to the globe. So that's a million miles on the scale of the globe. And then, when you get that stretched out, you say, Now how many miles to the sun? Ninety-three million. So how many strings like this? Ninety-three strings like this to show the distance from the earth to the sun, if the earth were the size of this globe. And if you really wanted to, you could go outside and see how far that would be.

Then suppose we wanted to show in a book a scale drawing that showed the earth and the sun and the distance between them. Could we do that? How small would we have to make this earth? It would have to be microscopic. So none of those pictures you ever see of the solar system are to scale. Except in Peoria, Illinois, the Peoria Museum of Science did a project where they set up a scale model of the solar system in town. They had to use the whole county! They used a twelve-inch earth. They had either the earth or the sun in the museum; they had something else in the airport, something else ten miles down the road. You could drive around and look at all these things and see where they are in relation to each other. I think it may still be there. You might want to check it out.

I remember in fifth grade, when I was in school, one of the hardest things to understand was ratio. But there are so many activities like that, making maps or drawing things to scale, that could be used to explore ratio. I think what made it hard to understand ratio was not knowing what it was for, not having any concrete sense of ratio. It's such an abstract principle.

DW: You mean having an understanding of why people might use it?

DMS: Yes. I think if we had done something that involved ratio maybe I would have understood it.

DW: Are you familiar with base-ten blocks? They would be a good model for you to share with kids as you discuss one million. Kids can imagine that one thousand of the big base-ten cubes would equal one million centimeter cubes. They often call the one thousand block the ten hundred block because that describes how ten flats [*the "hundred" pieces*] constitute the block.

DMS: When I do my popcorn math we take a bag filled with a hundred kernels and we count by hundreds ten times to get to one thousand. We count eight hundred, nine hundred, and then a lot of the kids say ten hundred. And so I point that out. First I show them the bag of one thousand kernels, and if they're young they are quite impressed, but if they're older, that doesn't impress them. The older ones get impressed though when we get up to 100,000. So then I say, Let's go back a minute. Remember when we were counting by hundreds, and you said eight hundred, nine hundred, ten hundred? Is there anything wrong with that? They say no. They all recognize that ten hundred is the same thing as one thousand. I say, Let's remember that, and I write "1,000 = ten hundred." We come back to that, because later when we're counting by 100,000's: 700,000, 800,000, 900,000, one million, we've finally reach a million, right? Then we go back and I say, Remember when we were counting by 100,000, and we said 800,000, 900,000, and I heard a lot of people say ten hundred thousand.? Anything wrong with that? They say, No, it's the same thing. So we write "1,000,000 = ten hundred thousand." I circle the ten hundred and I say, What did we already say that ten hundred was the same as? They say, One thousand. So we can erase ten hundred and write one thousand, and you see a million equals a thousand thousands. I hold up the bag of a thousand kernels and I say, Okay, if I had a thousand bags like this I would have . . .? That all sounds good to you and me but what ends up happening a lot of times is that it really makes me wonder how kids think, or whether in their answering of questions they try to figure out what answer you want rather than what the answer is. When I say, What is ten hundred equal to? they will often say, A million.

DW: Yes, you're associated with being the "million man." It's like the minister who conducts a time for children at the front of the church. Kids learn that when the minister asks a question, if they answer *Jesus* they're usually right. Is there anything else I should have asked you during this interview?

DMS: That's how I end all interviews too! I can't think of anything. And you brought out things I hadn't thought about for months or years anyway. There is one thing, though. Kids sometimes ask me how come I didn't do the pictures for my book. I tell them when I was young somebody told me I couldn't draw, that I shouldn't draw. So I stopped drawing. And I figured, I'll never need to draw. Now I write these books and if I could draw the pictures I could be doing both. So I say to them as a lesson, Don't listen to anybody who tells you you can't do anything. If you want to do it, and practice it, you'll get good at it.

References

Carson, Rachel. 1956. *The sense of wonder.* New York: Harper and Row.

Gilbreth, Frank, and Ernestine Carey. 1948. *Cheaper by the dozen.* New York: Bantam.

Hoban, Tana. 1970. *Shapes and things.* New York: Macmillan.

———. 1971. *Look again!* New York: Macmillan.

———. 1972a. *Count and see.* New York: Macmillan.

———. 1972b. *Push/pull, empty/full.* New York: Macmillan.

———. 1973. *Over, under and through.* New York: Macmillan.

———. 1974a. *Circles, triangles and squares.* New York: Macmillan.

———. 1974b. *Where is it?* New York: Macmillan.

———. 1975. *Dig/drill, dump/fill.* New York: Greenwillow.

———. 1976. *Big ones, little ones.* New York: Greenwillow.

———. 1978. *Is it red? Is it yellow? Is it blue?* New York: Greenwillow.

———. 1979. *One little kitten.* New York: Greenwillow.

———. 1981a. *More than one.* New York: Greenwillow.

———. 1981b. *Take another look.* New York: Greenwillow.

———. 1982. *A, B, see!* New York: Greenwillow.

———. 1983a. *I read signs.* New York: Greenwillow.

———. 1983b. *I read symbols.* New York: Greenwillow.

———. 1983c. *Round and round and round.* New York: Greenwillow.

——— . 1984a. *I walk and read.* New York: Greenwillow.

——— . 1984b. *Is it rough? Is it smooth? Is it shiny?* New York: Greenwillow.

——— . 1985a. *1, 2, 3.* New York: Greenwillow.

——— . 1985b. *A children's zoo.* New York: Mulberry.

——— . 1985c. *Is it larger? Is it smaller?* New York: Greenwillow.

——— . 1985d. *What is it?* New York: Greenwillow.

——— . 1986a. *Shapes, shapes, shapes.* New York: Greenwillow.

——— . 1986b. *Panda, panda.* New York: Greenwillow.

——— . 1986c. *Red, blue, yellow shoe.* New York: Greenwillow.

——— . 1987a. *26 letters and 99 cents.* New York: Greenwillow.

——— . 1987b. *Dots, spots, speckles and stripes.* New York: Greenwillow.

——— . 1988. *Look! look! look!* New York: Greenwillow.

——— . 1989. *Of colors and things.* New York: Greenwillow.

——— . 1990a. *Exactly the opposite.* New York: Greenwillow.

——— . 1990b. *Shadows and reflections.* New York: Greenwillow.

——— . 1991a. *All about where.* New York: Greenwillow.

——— . 1991b. Tana Hoban. *Something about the Author: Autobiography Series* 12:157–75.

——— . 1992a. *Look up, look down.* New York: Greenwillow.

——— . 1992b. *Spirals, curves, fanshapes and lines.* New York: Greenwillow.

——— . 1993a. *Black on white.* New York: Greenwillow.

——— . 1993b. *The moon was the best.* New York: Greenwillow.

——— . 1993c. *White on black.* New York: Greenwillow.

——— . 1994a. *Little elephant.* New York: Greenwillow.

——— . 1994b. *What is that?* New York: Greenwillow.

——— . 1994c. *Who are they?* New York: Greenwillow.

McCloskey, Robert. 1943. *Homer Price.* New York: Viking.

Morrison, Philip, and Phylis Morrison. 1982. *Powers of ten.* New York: Scientific American Library.

Robertson, Keith. 1974. *Henry Reed, Inc.* New York: Dell.

Schwartz, David M. 1985. *How much is a million?* New York: Scholastic.

——— . 1989. *If you made a million.* New York: Lothrop, Lee & Shepard.

——— . 1991. *Supergrandpa.* New York: Lothrop, Lee & Shepard.

Part Two

Books, Books, and More Books

The Number System, Statistics, and Probability

6

Mary O'Neill, in her book-length poetic meditation on numbers, *Take a Number* (1968), comments: "All numbers are related/As links in a long chain/To be detached and put to use/By the human brain" (p. 32). Margery Facklam and Margaret Thomas, in *The Kids' World Almanac of Amazing Facts About Numbers, Math and Money* (1992), fill over two hundred pages with real-life number applications, from Celsius and Fahrenheit scales to a poem about the 206 bones in the human body. These two books exemplify the two very different treatments of numbers that we explore in this chapter: first, the number system (the theoretical underpinnings of how our mathematical system works), and second, statistics and probability (which involve application of numbers to real-world problems).

Although these topics overlap with other topics that we devoted chapters to in *Read Any Good Math Lately?* (as well as sections in Chapter 9 of this book), particularly place value and big numbers, the number system and statistics are topics that are especially interesting as explorations in their own right. As mathematics education has become more and more grounded in its applicability to real-life situations, resources on statistics and probability have proliferated, particularly trivia books aimed at adults but accessible to children. (We use *statistics* here both to refer to the formal study of statistics and probability and in the vernacular sense of a collection of numerical data like that found in the census.) Most books on number theory, by contrast, are from the 1970s and are likely to be out of print. These books were to some extent a response to the "New Math" of that era, with its focus on sets, different bases, and so on. We have chosen to write about these books because of the value of exploring mathematics as a pure intellectual exercise as well as a tool for use in the world.

Perhaps earlier attempts to examine number theory with children were not fully successful because an understanding of mathematical premises was seen as a *prerequisite* to using numbers; today's children, increasingly comfortable with applied mathematics as they explore it through literature and hands-on activities, may be ready to turn to a more abstract look at numbers *after* a practical grounding in their use.

Teachers will be able to find many of the older books on the number system in libraries (or at least through Interlibrary Loan); perhaps with the growing interest in children's literature as a part of the mathematics curriculum, publishers will be encouraged to bring them back into print.

The number system

Numbers are such an essential part of North Americans' intellectual life from such a young age that we tend to forget that mathematics is a system developed by human beings over time and that it works the way it does because of a collection of formally designed, internally consistent properties. Although a deep technical and philosophical understanding of number theory is the stuff of college-level and professional mathematics, some features of it are highly accessible to elementary school students and their teachers. Perhaps the history of our number system is a good place to start.

THE HISTORY OF NUMBERS

How Did Numbers Begin? (Sitomer & Sitomer 1976) takes readers through a psychological exploration of how numbers are likely to have evolved. The authors ask us to imagine an early herder of animals: having no number system to count how many animals come back each night from the pasture, he may well have developed a simple matching scheme of one pebble laid down for each animal. We have historical and anthropological evidence about the next logical step in the process, naming small numbers, with the word for five being the same as the word for hand in some languages. The book concludes by discussing the concept of counting as an outgrowth of both matching and naming numbers: a set of objects is matched in order with the set of counting numbers. *How Did Numbers Begin?* does a nice job of developing a sense of life before numbers and the human experiences that made the evolution of numbers necessary, and provides a good sense of the most basic properties of counting (sets, names, increasing by one, sequence).

Roman Numerals (D. Adler 1977) looks at number history with a narrower and more recent focus. As Adler points out, Roman numerals are still familiar today, because they are sometimes used on clocks and in a few other special contexts. The book invites students to make cards with the numbers 1, 5, and 10 on one side and the Roman numerals I, V, and X on the other, in order to create numbers using the additive Roman system and to explore other features, such as the shortcuts for writing 4 as IV and 9 as IX (underscoring the importance of ordering, even though the system isn't a place value system like ours).

How to Count Like a Martian (St. John 1975), which we discussed in *Read Any Good Math Lately?*, takes a broader historical view by discussing a number of ancient numeration systems and how they worked.

Students might enjoy inventing their own number systems. Could they invent symbols analogous to a handlike figure for five, such as a triangle for three and a spider for eight? Or perhaps more modern symbols—a stylized traffic signal for three or a Ninja Turtle to represent a set of four? This would be a chance both to explore what represents "fourness" or "eightness" to people living in today's world and to understand that symbols for numbers are arbitrary yet may have evolved out of meaning-based associations. Older students could research different number systems throughout history; small groups could each develop activities to help the class learn about the system they've studied, and the class as a whole could compare features across different number systems, such as the role of place value and the base used in each system.

ODDS AND EVENS, POSITIVES AND NEGATIVES, AND OTHER NUMBER FAMILIES

The abstract beauty of numbers, for those who are able to appreciate it, derives in large part from the order and symmetry of the number system. A number of children's books help students develop the appropriate concepts and begin to appreciate the patterns involved.

Odds and Evens (O'Brien 1971) is a basic introduction to the idea that all integers belong to either the set of even numbers or the set of odd numbers. The book helps readers understand the difference intuitively through a number of distinctions: odd numbers will never produce a tie in a two-way vote; pairs of matched fingers always produce even numbers; adding two odds or two evens always produces an even number while adding one of each always produces an odd number.

Zero Is Not Nothing (Sitomer & Sitomer 1978) deals with the number that is both the fulcrum of the integers and the great invention of our place value system. The authors clearly lay out information about zero that goes well beyond the sense that most children will have of it as representing nothing, none of something, the empty set (such as the set of cookies after they've all been eaten). Zero is shown also to be the starting point of any measurement, illustrated by the zero that appears on a scale with nothing on it and that is understood at the left-hand edge of a ruler; zero is also the separation point of a measure that also includes negative numbers, like a thermometer. Children playing marbles who end up with the same number they started with and a storekeeper finishing a day with neither profit nor loss illustrate zero as a break-even point. Finally, the role of zero in a place value system is developed at some length; without zero, there would be no way of seeing that the 3 in 305 stands for 3 hundreds.

A good companion to this book is *Less than Nothing Is Really Something* (Froman 1973), which uses examples like friends owing each other money, underwater depth, and the seconds of a countdown to explore negative numbers. Negative numbers are shown in their relation to subtraction (e.g., $0 - 2 = -2$), and a number line is then used to show how arithmetic operations work when negative numbers are involved.

Number Families (Srivastava 1979) helps readers explore a number of different number families (defined as groups of numbers that go together in some way). Children are invited to place small objects like buttons in arrays that model the characteristics of the number families; for instance, numbers in the even family can be placed in two equal rows, while numbers in the odd family will always have one left over when an equal-row array is attempted. The even family is then identified as equivalent to the two-times family, with the same principle then extended to the three-times and four-times families, and so on. The same visual model is then extended to defining primes, square numbers, and triangular numbers, so that a variety of sets of numbers are linked in terms of highly visible arrays.

These books on various kinds of number patterns and families suggest a number of classroom activities. Teachers can, for instance, encourage children to create drawings or books of odd and even numbers of things they see in the world around them, and thus explore the functions of odd and even numbers (e.g., why does a starfish have an odd number of arms and an octopus an even number of tentacles? why does the Senate have an even number of members and the Supreme Court an odd number?). When students are engaged in activities that naturally involve negative numbers—recording winter temperatures (on the Celsius scale, anything below freezing is a negative temperature), learning about scientific or historical events that took place B.C., or talking about debt in a consumer context, to name just a few possibilities—they can think about how negative numbers work mathematically. Children can extend the visual arrays in *Number Families* to develop a highly elaborated sense of different numbers. Which number families does each number from one to fifty belong to? Is there a pattern to how often prime numbers appear? These explorations, of course, are an excellent lead-in to understanding factors, but perhaps even more important, they give children a deep intuitive understanding of numbers. When you have created arrays that show that 24 can be represented as 1 × 24, 2 × 12, 3 × 8, 4 × 6, and the reciprocals of each of these, while 23 (a prime) can only be represented as 1 × 23 and 23 × 1, you have a feeling for "23-ness" and "24-ness" that you would not have from working with only the abstract numbers.

DEEPER IN: LOGIC, BINARY NUMBERS, FINITE NUMBER SYSTEMS, AND ALGEBRA

More advanced mathematical topics are rarely dealt with in elementary schools and indeed are probably not even very familiar to teachers, but they have been explored in children's books, in particular the Crowell Young Math series from the 1970s.

Yes-No, Stop-Go (Gersting & Kuczkowski 1977) is a very clear and readable introduction to truth tables, a basic component of mathematical logic. In the book, a castle surrounded by a moat is approached on one side by two parallel drawbridges, so that if either bridge A or bridge B is down, one can cross over to the castle. On the other side of the castle, there are two consecutive drawbridges, so that bridge C *and* bridge D have to be down. This data is then put into the following tables:

A or B Pattern		
A down	B down	Cross?
yes	yes	yes
yes	no	yes
no	yes	yes
no	no	no

C and D Pattern		
C down	D down	Cross?
yes	yes	yes
yes	no	no
no	yes	no
no	no	no

The and/or pattern is then extended to a model of railroad switches and finally to its most general application of true and false statements:

A	B	A or B
true	true	true
true	false	true
false	true	true
false	false	false

A	B	A and B
true	true	true
true	false	false
false	true	false
false	false	false

Binary Numbers (Watson 1977) deals with a topic that is of ongoing interest and importance in our present computer age. The idea of base two is introduced here by inviting readers to take a ball of string, measure off a length of one foot, and then double it as many times as possible, thus not only producing but getting a feel for the numbers (1, 2, 4, 8, 16, 32, 64, . . .) of the binary number sequence (also known as the powers of two). Strips of paper in lengths of one, two, four, and eight centimeters are then used to illustrate the property of the binary bases to build all the numbers of the base-ten system. Illustrations of the use of binary-scale weights show the usefulness of having sixteen ounces in a pound (at least in the days when balance scales were necessary!): a set of weights of one, two, four, and eight ounces and pounds can conveniently weigh any amount up to fifteen pounds and fifteen ounces, to the nearest ounce. The book ends with showing binary notation (e.g., 14 in base ten is equivalent to 1110 in base two) in a way that connects directly with the previous models of strips of paper and weights. *Binary Numbers* also includes a short version of the chessboard puzzle that is developed at more length in *A Grain of Rice* (Pittman 1986) and *The King's Chessboard* (Birch 1988).

The term *finite number systems* is probably not a familiar one to most teachers, but *Solomon Grundy, Born on Oneday* (M. Weiss 1977) explores this somewhat obscure topic in an interesting and easily understandable way. The traditional rhyme "Solomon Grundy, born on Monday, christened on Tuesday, married on Wednesday . . ." makes sense because we have a finite system of days of the week (rather than an infinite sequence of *different* days), a seven-member set of days that repeats cyclically. Solomon Grundy, therefore, could have been christened one week and a day, or two weeks and a day, and so on, after his birth. In the words of the book, "all the rhyme tells us is that it was on *some* Tuesday that Solomon Grundy was christened. And there are lots of Tuesdays." The days of the week are then compared to numbers on a clock to show how arithmetic works in a finite number system: just as five hours after eleven o'clock is not sixteen o'clock but four o'clock—because the hours cycle around—five days after Wednesday is always Monday. If we convert the days to numbers, with Monday as 1, we can say that day 3 (Wednesday) plus 5 equals day 1 (Monday). The months and seasons are other finite systems.

Even some of the underlying principles of algebra have been turned into a children's book. *666 Jellybeans! All That?* (M. Weiss 1976) begins with a simple math trick: "Think of a number from 1 to 5. Add 1 to it. Double your answer. Then add 4. Divide what you get by 2. Now subtract 3." Adults will recognize that this can be represented sequentially as $x + 1$; $2x + 2$; $2x + 6$; $x + 3$; x, so that one ends up with the original number. This concept is made accessible to young readers by depicting x as a bag with an unknown number of jellybeans in it, and showing that no matter how many jellybeans are in the bag, at the end of the series of operations, you'll have exactly what you started with. The book then easily moves to greater abstraction by replacing the picture of a bag with the letter *B* and talking about how mathematicians use letters as symbols in the language of algebra.

Mathematics (I. Adler 1990), a more recent book by a prolific author on mathematical themes, explores a number of topics in number theory. Aimed at upper elementary and middle school readers, this book contains brief overviews of topics such as divisors, prime numbers, rectangular numbers, and the history of written numbers. It is made especially contemporary by its inclusion of simple computer and calculator activities; for instance, readers are guided to produce computer programs that will print a consecutive series of odd or even numbers. An especially interesting example is a procedure for finding square roots by using a calculator to make successive approximations. This, of course, is of little practical value today, since even the simplest calculators have square-root keys, but is valuable for the same reason that other explorations into number theory are valuable—as a way of deepening one's experience with numbers. A few decades ago, extracting square roots "by hand" was a necessary part of the mathematics curriculum, usually in high school; perhaps this forgotten topic is ripe for at least a small revival as an enrichment topic for elementary school children, in order to explore some of the uses of calculators.

Any of these books on more arcane number theory topics can lead to fuller explorations. Understanding binary numbers would give children a sense of the underlying logical structure of computers, and they could perhaps develop a computer program to write a series of numbers in binary notation. A series of binary weights (one, two, four, eight ounces, etc.) and a balance scale could be used for a variety of measuring activities. Students could use finite arithmetic to calculate the days since their last birthday or until the end of the school year. A number of hands-on algebra problems could be developed that would let students use algebraic principles to perform "math magic." In any case, books like these are an accessible, age-appropriate introduction to topics elementary school students are likely to encounter as part of the formal curriculum in higher grades.

ON THE LIGHTER SIDE

The books discussed so far in this chapter have all been fairly serious approaches to the number system, but there are also a few more playful ones. *Bears, 1, 2, 3* (Ziefert 1989) is a picture-book exploration of odd and even numbers; it has pictures of bears and text like "5 bears on a basketball team. That's odd. 10 bears on two basketball teams. That's not odd. That's even." *Take a Number* (O'Neill 1968) uses rhymed poetry to explore numbers. Each numeral from 1 to 5 gets a few pages of thoughts ("Quadruplets are four,/There's a four-poster bed,/A quarto and four-ply/Rope, yarn, and thread"), and the author also includes rhymed pages on base ten, sets, cardinal and ordinal numbers, and the uses of number ("Imagine a world/Without mathematics:/Unmeasured houses,/Cellars and attics"). *Doodle Soup* (Ciardi 1985), though not focused as directly on number theory, includes a number of poems with a mathematical focus. Some of them are rather philosophical: in "There's Nothing to It," the narrator, who has "no pie," imagines dividing it in half and in half again, and wonders who got less: the person who got half of no pie or the one who got half of a half of it. "How Time Goes" ponders the fact that "I have spent/My whole life—up to a minute ago—/Being younger than I am now."

The Science Book of Numbers (Challoner 1992) takes a highly hands-on approach to number theory. This brightly illustrated book shows how to make a number of math-related artifacts, such as an abacus, an addition slide rule, and a counting wheel that works on the same principle as an odometer. Finally, *Any Number Can Play* (Sullivan 1990), though not really about number theory, perhaps fits in here as well as anywhere. It is about the numbers that athletes wear on their uniforms: where they come from, how they are chosen, and so on. This is a good example of numbers serving as labels rather than quantities, but in a way that often has great symbolic weight (players frequently try to acquire numbers that previously belonged to their heroes). One interesting example is that of hockey star Wayne Gretzky, who, when he began playing at sixteen, wanted the jersey number 9, worn by previous greats Gordie Howe, Bobby Hull, and Maurice Richard. Since it wasn't available at the time, he chose 99 instead, and "it wasn't very long before Gretzky had made No. 99 one of the best-known numbers in the sports world" (p. 113).

Statistics and probability

A good understanding of principles of statistics and probability may be one of the most useful mathematical ideas to carry into adult life, since much of the news we read and hear about politics, health, and human behavior in general grows out of statistical data, and statistical data is often difficult for the layperson to interpret and may even be misreported or misunderstood by those presenting it to the public. Statistics, in the sense of collections of numbers about everything ranging from the number of laboratory mice and rats used by American researchers every year—forty-five million and fifteen million respectively (Heymann 1991b)—to the number of families in the country officially defined as poor—in 1991, 7.7 million, or 15 percent of the population (Krantz 1993)—pervade our lives.

The children's books discussed below either help children learn to use the tools of statistics and probability or provide interesting collections of numbers for them to work with. A number of other books, marketed to adults mostly as collections of trivia, contain a variety of statistics that children can read about and work with.

CHILDREN'S BOOKS

The initial step in statistical work is data collection, and displaying gathered information in visual form makes it more accessible and understandable. *Charts and Graphs* (Arnold 1984) is a useful introduction to about a dozen different ways of displaying information, with interesting illustrations of how to develop graphs and tables out of more concrete representations. For instance, you can ask the children in your class to form a circle, those born in the same state standing next to each other, and then use chalk to create a giant pie graph. Or they can make a 3-D bar graph from piles of blocks. There are also instructions for making a mileage chart, a baseball schedule, a family tree, and other forms of visual display. This book is a useful resource for students as they undertake research in different curriculum areas and need to decide how best to display the information. Would a bar graph or a pictograph work best to show the lengths of various dinosaurs? What do the examples of time lines suggest about how they might set up a time line of the Civil War? The book will also help students read charts and graphs.

Once students have collected and organized data and are ready to work with it in a mathematical way, one of the most basic statistical concepts they can use is that of averages, which encompasses three distinct concepts: the mean (arithmetic average), the median (middle point in a series), and the mode (most frequent value in a set of data). Two children's books do a comprehensive and effective job of making these concepts accessible to children.

Averages (Srivastava 1975) gives a brief overview of all three, using simple examples and talking about when each is most appropriate (the mode is descriptive of what "most of" a group is like, the median is useful when items in a group are not too different from each other, and the mean is most precise). *What Do You Mean by Average?* (James & Barkin 1978), aimed at older readers, develops the concept of average in more depth in the context of a brief novel about a girl who is running for student council on a platform of appealing to the "average" student. The book helps readers understand the three kinds of average and how to conduct a survey using a random sample (not just surveying your friends or the kids who are in detention, since either would be a skewed sample) and convert the results into percentages and graphs.

Either of these books could be used as the basis for a series of activities in collecting and analyzing data. Although the mean is the most familiar and probably the most commonly used average, students' earliest survey and research efforts may be better suited to mode or median. For instance, a survey of most-popular television programs or breakfast foods can have only a mode (because the data cannot be arranged in an ordered series or quantified), and the median is probably the simplest and most appropriate average for children to determine with regard to a tabulation of the heights of students in a class (even though adults could find the mean relatively easily). A textbook approach to averages is likely to focus most on the mean, since it involves the most computation; the value of these two children's books and the activities that might be carried out in conjunction with them is that students can be encouraged to really think through when the mean, mode, and median are usable and appropriate.

Winning with Numbers (Riedel 1978) consists of a series of brief vignettes on all aspects of statistics. It models different kinds of charts and averages and includes a useful section on lying with statistics. This book's special strength is that it helps students become critical thinkers and understand the reasons for different statistical techniques. For instance, the section on the mean includes the story of a student whose football yardage is lower than a competitor's in absolute terms but works out to a higher mean when divided by the number of attempts. In another passage a business owner exaggerates his success by truncating the bottom of a bar graph. Teachers can encourage students to bring in statistics from newspaper and magazine articles and then examine them critically based on the ideas in *Winning with Numbers.*

Zillions, the children's consumer magazine published by Consumers Union, is another excellent resource for this kind of exploration. The surveys in the magazine always include appropriate and clearly described statistics, and one of its specialties is helping young readers see through misleading and dishonest advertising claims.

Do You Wanna Bet? (Cushman 1991) engages children in a variety of probability experiences. The book begins with the classic coin-tossing experiment; two children try to predict whether the outcome will be heads or tails. This experience is nicely contrasted with weather predictions; children are encouraged to keep track of the weather forecast and the actual weather for several days, to see how accurate these forecasts really are. Readers are also asked to identify events as certain (the earth will revolve around the sun), probable (it will rain on Saturday), or impossible (there will be a live dinosaur at the zoo) as a way to understand various probability contexts. In a chapter entitled "The ABC's of Probability," readers examine letter frequency as a clue for breaking a secret code. Other experiences relate to the chances that two people in a group will have the same birthday, using sampling to determine how many different kinds of candy are in a jar or how many people in the world are left-handed, and the chances of winning a raffle or picking the right number on the "lucky wheel" at a carnival.

Lotteries: Who Wins, Who Loses (A. Weiss 1991), written for young adult readers, explores the history, mathematics, and ethics of the rapidly proliferating, most popular form of gambling in the United States. Numbers appear throughout the book as it describes the proportion of money taken in that goes to prizes and to the states' budgets, the total amount spent on legal and illegal gambling every year in the United States (in 1987, $1,000 per capita) and, most interesting, the odds of winning. For instance, the chance of being the single winner of a 115-million-dollar Pennsylvania jackpot were less than the chances of surviving eighty-eight rounds of Russian roulette or of living to the age of 115. Students who live in a state with a lottery or other forms of legalized gambling might be inspired by this book to research the amounts of money and the odds involved, thus perhaps providing useful consumer information to their parents! This is also a social-justice issue, since the poor spend more of their income on lotteries (2.1 percent versus 0.3 percent for the rich).

Two books aimed at young readers provide a wide variety of statistical information to learn from and calculate with. *The Kids' World Almanac of Amazing Facts About Numbers, Math and Money* (Facklam & Thomas 1992) has ten chapters, each one focusing on a different set or category of numbers. For instance, "Time and Dates" tabulates the number of seconds in a day, week, year, and leap year; "Weights and Measures" lists the number of calories burned up in an hour of various physical activities or contained in favorite snacks, and "People Numbers" includes some census figures (the 4 million Americans in 1790 had grown to 250 million in 1990). This book is useful as a reference (finding out the number of teaspoons in a tablespoon or cups in a quart) but also for browsing to discover interesting numerical facts like how many ways the fifty-two cards in a deck can be arranged (80,660 vigintillion, or 8.07^{67}) or the size of the largest house of cards ever built (twelve feet tall and ten inches wide, containing 15,714 cards).

Although *Kids Ending Hunger: What Can We Do?* (Howard 1992) has a social rather than a mathematical focus, it includes a good deal of statistical information in both defining the extent of the problem of hunger and suggesting solutions. For instance, six hundred million children in the world are hungry every day, and between thirteen and eighteen million people die of hunger every year, yet a mere dime can buy a packet of oral rehydration salts that can keep a child from dying of dehydration. The action-oriented focus of this book, which lists "Fifty Things Kids Can Do to End Hunger," will perhaps inspire children to research the statistics of hunger and poverty in their own communities, with a view to making a difference.

ADULT BOOKS AS SOURCES OF STATISTICAL INFORMATION

A number of books aimed at adult audiences can be useful as data sources for elementary school children. Teachers do need to remember, however, that appropriateness may be a concern—these books often contain "adults only" material—and that the books should therefore be previewed before they are used with students.

The most visually delightful of these books, and one that can serve as both a reference book and an idea book for students who wish to present information visually, is *Designer's Guide to Creating Charts and Diagrams* (Holmes 1984). The author is in charge of designing data displays for *Time* magazine. The book, aimed at professional designers, begins with an overview of the fever chart (line graph), bar chart, pie chart, and table, defining each and discussing appropriate and inappropriate uses. This section contains useful background information the teacher can use when working with students in planning graphs and charts. Holmes then takes a fascinating look at nine typical assignments to translate data into visual terms, showing their step-by-step progression from initial raw data to final product. The final portion of the book comprises a collection of good examples of charts and diagrams, many of them the author's own, and an expository section on sources of error and distortion. The book is vividly illustrated, delightful to browse, and highly informative.

A similarly practical book is *The Numbers You Need* (Hopkins, Mayne & Hudson 1992b), which includes sections on topics such as the Consumer Price Index, how the interest on bank deposits compounds, wind-chill factors, camera settings, and energy consumption of different appliances. Appendixes present a variety of tools and tables and a basic overview of probability and statistics. This book is very good as a reference rather than for browsing, and would be especially valuable in an upper elementary or middle school classroom where students are doing a lot of applied mathematics.

There are a number of books of facts and figures about how human beings live their lives. Three recent examples focus on facts and especially figures about the United States. *The Unofficial U.S. Census* (Heymann 1991b) draws on a wide variety of sources of information dealing with the "sometimes seamy, often embarrassing, and always revealing underside of American life" (p. viii). For teachers who wonder about the appropriateness of this book for classroom use, it's not as bad as it sounds! Although the book begins with the proportion of Americans born as the result of mistimed or unwanted pregnancies (about one third) and includes regional incidences of constipation (highest in the South, at 18.2 percent), much of the information is more innocuous, such as a compilation of pet peeves (people talking in movies is most common) and preferred sleeping locations of America's dogs (on top of a bed ranks highest). This book is a lot of fun to read, and could suggest a number of ideas for students to carry out their own surveys.

America by the Numbers (Krantz 1993) is a more serious yet still fascinating compilation, providing an alphabetical listing of factual and statistical miniessays on topics ranging from the number of actors in the country (seventy-seven thousand, competing for forty-nine thousand roles and earning an average income of $29,000) to wrongful convictions (a study found 420 of them since 1900, including twenty-three executions of innocent people). A few sections, like those on male sexuality and therapist-client sex, are inappropriate for elementary school children, but most of the book provides readers with fascinating statistics, and interpretations of statistics, on often unusual topics.

The most complex of the three books is *Who We Are: A Portrait of America Based on the Latest U.S. Census* (Roberts 1993), a well-written nonfiction account of the latest in American demographics, written by an urban-affairs columnist for the *New York Times*. This book, with chapters on topics such as how we live, where we dream, and how we commute, is crammed with statistics, in the text and in tables in each chapter, as well as in a series of appendixes, which show, for example, the population of each state, the ancestry of Americans, and income breakdowns. This excellent translation of the results of the latest census would be interesting for teachers to read as a whole, then share relevant aspects of with their students.

Finally, some adult books focus on probability: the odds, chances, and risks that we face in life. *What Are the Chances?* (Siskin, Staller & Rorvik 1989) is set up in a question-and-answer format under sections dealing with long shots (1 in 600,000 of being struck by lightning in your lifetime), good bets (every time you fall down, you are six times more likely to die than when you are in an airplane), and the usual medical, weather, and gambling odds (for instance, men have double the risk of dying of heart disease that women do).

What the Odds Are (Krantz 1992) is set up alphabetically, with each item defined, usually with an explanatory paragraph, and the odds then listed. For instance, the entry on multiple births explains why they appear to be more common these days, then states the likelihood of having one, ranging from 1 in 90 for twins and 1 in 85 million for quintuplets. Because of the way the two books are set up, this book is better for browsing and *What Are the Chances?* is better for absorbing varied information on a single topic, although the information in *What the Odds Are* is somewhat more detailed.

We hope these books on probability and statistics, both those written for children and those written for adults, will inspire you to explore these fascinating topics in the classroom. There is probably no single field of knowledge more important in enabling citizens and consumers in today's complex society to understand the numbers that the media barrage them with every day.

References: The number system

Adler, David A. 1977. *Roman numerals.* New York: Crowell.

Adler, Irving. 1972. *Integers—positive and negative.* New York: John Day.

———. 1990. *Mathematics.* New York: Doubleday.

Birch, David. 1988. *The king's chessboard.* New York: Dial.

Challoner, Jack. 1992. *The science book of numbers.* San Diego: Harcourt Brace Jovanovich.

Charosh, Mannis. 1974. *Number ideas through pictures.* New York: Crowell.

Ciardi, John. 1985. *Doodle soup.* Boston: Houghton Mifflin.

Froman, Robert. 1973. *Less than nothing is really something.* New York: Harper and Row.

———. 1974. *A game of functions.* New York: Crowell.

Gersting, Judith, and Joseph Kuczkowski. 1977. *Yes-no, stop-go: Some patterns in mathematical logic.* New York: Crowell.

Juster, Norton. 1961. *The phantom tollbooth.* New York: Knopf.

Luce, Marnie. 1969a. *One is unique.* Minneapolis: Lerner.

———. 1969b. *Primes are builders.* Minneapolis: Lerner.

———. 1969c. *Sets: What are they?* Minneapolis: Lerner.

———. 1969d. *Ten: Why is it important?* Minneapolis: Lerner.

O'Brien, Thomas. 1971. *Odds and evens.* New York: Crowell.

O'Neill, Mary. 1968. *Take a number.* New York: Doubleday.

Papy, Frédérique, and Georges Papy. 1971. *Graph games.* New York: Crowell.

Pittman, Helena. 1986. *A grain of rice.* New York: Hastings House.

St. John, Glory. 1975. *How to count like a Martian.* New York: H. Z. Walck.

Sitomer, Mindel, and Sitomer, Harry. 1976. *How did numbers begin?.* New York: Crowell.

———. 1978. *Zero is not nothing.* New York: Crowell.

Srivastava, Jane. 1979. *Number families.* New York: Crowell.

Sullivan, George. 1990. *Any number can play.* New York: Crowell.

Watson, Clyde. 1977. *Binary numbers.* New York: Crowell.

Weiss, Malcolm E. 1976. *666 jellybeans! All that?: An introduction to algebra.* New York: Crowell.

———. 1977. *Solomon Grundy, born on oneday.* New York: Crowell.

Ziefert, Harriet. 1989. *Bears, 1, 2, 3.* New York: Random House.

Zillions. Published by Consumers Union, Mt. Vernon, NY. Subscription address: P.O. Box 54861, Boulder, CO 80322.

References: Statistics and probability

CHILDREN'S BOOKS

Arnold, Caroline. 1984. *Charts and graphs: Fun, facts, and activities.* New York: Franklin Watts.

Cushman, Jean. 1991. *Do you wanna bet? Your chance to find out about probability.* New York: Clarion.

Facklam, Margery, and Margaret Thomas. 1992. *The kids' world almanac of amazing facts about numbers, math and money.* New York: Pharos.

Howard, Tracy A. 1992. *Kids ending hunger: What can we do?* Kansas City, MO: Andrews and McMeel.

James, Elizabeth, and Carol Barkin. 1978. *What do you mean by average?* New York: Lothrop, Lee & Shepard.

Linn, Charles F. 1972. *Probability.* New York: Crowell.

Riedel, Manfred G. 1978. *Winning with numbers: A kid's guide to statistics.* Englewood Cliffs, NJ: Prentice-Hall.

Sharmat, Marjorie. 1979. *The 329th friend.* New York: Four Winds.

Silverstein, Shel 1974. "Lester." In *Where the sidewalk ends.* New York: Harper and Row.

Srivastava, Jane. 1973. *Statistics.* New York: Crowell.

———. 1975. *Averages.* New York: Crowell.

Weiss, Ann E. 1991. *Lotteries: Who wins, who loses.* Hillsdale, NJ: Enslow.

ADULT BOOKS

Heymann, Tom. 1989. *On an average day in the United States.* New York: Fawcett Columbine.

———. 1991a. *In an average lifetime.* New York: Fawcett Columbine.

———. 1991b. *The unofficial U.S. census: What the U.S. census doesn't tell you.* New York: Fawcett Columbine.

———. 1992. *On an average day in Japan.* New York: Fawcett Columbine.

Holmes, Nigel. 1984. *Designer's guide to creating charts and diagrams.* New York: Watson-Guptill.

Hopkins, Nigel J., John W. Mayne, and John R. Hudson. 1992a. *Go figure!* Detroit: Visible Ink Press.

———. 1992b. *The numbers you need.* Detroit: Gale Research.

Krantz, Les. 1991. *The best and worst of everything.* New York: Prentice Hall.

———. 1992. *What the odds are: A-to-z odds on everything you hoped or feared could happen.* New York: HarperCollins.

———. 1993. *America by the numbers: Facts and figures from the weighty to the way-out.* Boston: Houghton Mifflin.

Patterson, James, and Peter Kim. 1991. *The day America told the truth: What people really believe about everything that really matters.* New York: Prentice Hall.

Roberts, Sam. 1993. *Who we are: A portrait of America based on the latest U.S. census.* New York: Times Books.

Shook, Michael, and Robert Shook. 1991. *The book of odds.* New York: Penguin Books.

Siskin, Bernard, Jerome Staller, and David Rorvik. 1989. *What are the chances?: Risks, odds & likelihood in everyday life.* New York: Crown.

Encouraging a Multicultural Perspective

7

Why are so many of the children in counting books white? What are people around the world doing at different times of the day? How do people count in Africa? These questions reveal a number of cultural issues related to mathematical children's books. Multiculturalism and diversity are among the most important educational issues to emerge in recent years, even in curricular areas like mathematics that appear on the surface to be less "cultural" than subjects like social studies.

In this chapter, we explore what a commitment to a multicultural, diverse curriculum means when using children's books to help students learn about mathematics: what kinds of representation are valuable, what stereotypes to watch out for, and what resources are available to help teachers build their own knowledge about multicultural mathematics and an equity-focused curriculum.

Three guiding principles in evaluating mathematical children's books from a multicultural perspective are inclusion, authenticity, and equity. If a book portrays a number of people, are they ethnically diverse? Within your own classroom collection, your school library's collection, and the books you use to explore mathematics throughout the school year, are the many good books that have only white protagonists at least balanced by other books that show people of color? Inclusion is important both in classrooms with African American, Latino, Native American, and Asian American children, who need to see themselves and their experiences reflected in literature, and in homogeneously white classrooms, because these students nonetheless live in an increasingly diverse society.

Mere inclusion is not sufficient; portrayals of different cultural groups need to be authentic or, at the very least, neutral and nonstereotyped. When children's books contain racial stereotypes, teachers, if they use these books at all, have an urgent responsibility to promote equity by discussing and exploring the issues head-on.

Positive representations

As we examined hundreds of children's books both for *Read Any Good Math Lately?* and for this volume, we noticed that books that portray people of color in positive ways fall into three major groups: those with neutral settings, in which various ethnic groups are represented but not in ways that focus on distinctive aspects of their culture; those in which mathematical ideas appear in the context of one or more specific cultural settings; and those which specifically emphasize the unique mathematical aspects of a culture or cultures. All three categories are important, because they include people in different ways: as people sharing universal mathematical experiences, as people sharing mathematically related experiences (such as building houses, cooking, and dealing with money) that take different forms in different cultures, and as members of cultures that have developed their own mathematical ideas.

Before discussing books that illustrate these themes, we offer two general observations: there are still far too few multicultural children's books in mathematics, and African Americans are the only group appearing with any frequency. There are no more than a handful of books with mathematical themes that represent Asians or Latinos (within or outside the United States) or Native Americans. Publishers have made a great deal of progress in increasing the diversity of their children's books generally, but this trend has not carried over sufficiently to books on mathematical themes.

NEUTRAL SETTINGS

My First Number Book (Heinst 1992), one of the best new mathematical books for younger children, is also an excellent example of how to make a book on a neutral topic culturally inclusive. It is illustrated entirely with photographs—of numbers, objects, and children—and the children are the diverse group one would find in many of today's North American classrooms. They are about half male and half female, with almost as many children of color as white children. As these children line up by height, stand in groups to be counted, and play together, they are just children and (because the numbers are so equal) nobody is a token. *My First Number Book* is a model of the kind of multicultural representation to look for in mathematical books where culture as such is not a focus but where, as always, inclusion matters.

Balance can also be achieved by incorporating culturally neutral books in which the main characters are people of color. We found a number of examples, all African American. Three counting books with minimal text, *Ten, Nine, Eight* (Bang 1983), *Aaron and Gayla's Counting Book* (Greenfield 1993), and *Feast for 10* (Falwell 1993), feature Black protagonists dealing with a common human experience (getting ready for bed, going out for a walk in the rain, and shopping for groceries and cooking a meal, respectively). *One of Three* (Johnson 1991) is narrated by the youngest of three African American sisters; her experiences are universal, but the urban setting (living over a flower shop and riding on the subway) grounds the story in a community setting that, even if it is not unique to one ethnic group, makes this book somewhat more culturally specific than the three counting books. *The Toothpaste Millionaire* (Merrill 1972) is a short novel about a black twelve-year-old boy who starts a toothpaste business. The supporting characters in the book are ethnically diverse. Race is mentioned, but only briefly and as one of many characteristics and perhaps less important than some; the narrator comments that not only does Rufus (the protagonist) not mind that she's white and he's Black, her gender doesn't bother him either. Rudine Sims (1982), however, in a book-length study of the African American experience in children's fiction, does wonder why Rufus was given a name that is possibly stereotypical; she also comments on how many books with African Americans as major characters have a white narrator, as this one does.

Teachers need to realize that books that are apparently culturally neutral must be assessed with care, particularly if they are stories or novels rather than brief picture-driven texts like counting books. The work of ethnic authors and illustrators possesses an authenticity that comes from a perspective inside the culture; although it is possible for authors to do a reasonable job of portraying cultures other than their own (at least in books where culture is not an essential part of the story), they risk being unaware of subtle cultural differences and turning characters into tokens (Cai & Bishop 1994).

CULTURALLY SPECIFIC SETTINGS

In a culturally neutral book, the skin color and facial features of the characters are perhaps the only indication of their ethnicity; in other books, however, the cultural setting, as depicted in text, pictures, or both, is integral. Three recent books, two dealing with money and one with big numbers, take place in rural African American communities and are grounded in the lives of those communities. *Picking Peas for a Penny* (Medearis 1990), based on the life of the author's mother on a farm during the Depression, is about children picking peas for a penny a pound and then enjoying what those pennies buy. The hard work is not glossed over, but the text and pictures create a sense of the value and rewards of a family's working together during hard times. *We Keep a Store* (Shelby 1990) also celebrates a family's shared economic venture, this time in a present-day context of running a country store. The store is not just a financial venture but a social one as well: "Our customers don't come just to buy things. They come to visit, too. In winter, the men circle their chairs around the stove and tell long stories."

A Million Fish . . . More or Less (McKissack 1992) is a wonderful tall tale, set in rural Louisiana, about a young boy who catches (or so he says!) a million and three fish but arrives home with only three and has to come up with a really good story to explain to Papa-Daddy and Elder Abbajon what happened to the rest. The story is all the richer for being grounded in the storytelling tradition of a specific African American culture, as well as catching the flavor of a specific variety of American English: "[The raccoon] was purely outdone. He went to grumbling and mumbling and swearing under his breath. But in the end he made good his word. 'I takes me lickin', and now I'll be takin' me fish.'"

Another book that grounds a mathematical concept in African American cultural experience is *The Hundred Penny Box* (Mathis 1975). The elderly protagonist treasures a box that holds a penny for every year of her life, and she recapitulates not only her own history but recent American history as she counts back through the years: "18 and 74. . . . Year I was born. Slavery over! Black men in Congress running things. They was in charge. It was the Reconstruction" (p. 26). As in *A Million Fish . . . More or Less*, the portrayal of the language of a culture adds authenticity to the text.

Two recent counting books that take place in the Caribbean illustrate some of what to watch for in the depiction of varied cultures. *One White Sail* (Garne 1992) is distinguished by its vividly colored pictures that embody the bright sunlight of the region. Four of the ten pictures contain people, all of them dark skinned, whose heads are abstract shapes without facial features, consistent with the bold design of the illustrations as a whole. The pictures do not seem offensive in their lack of realism—merely stylized—but they contrast with those in *One Smiling Grandma* (Linden 1992), in which specific, precisely drawn people appear on every page. Both books have pictures of steel-drum musicians, and both sets of drummers are easily counted, but those in *One White Sail* are abstractions while those in *One Smiling Grandma* are people, each one with his own individual face.

Several books examine universal mathematical experiences by looking at them through cross-cultural, often global perspectives. The books in the *Count Your Way Through . . .* series by Jim Haskins (see the reference list at the end of this chapter for titles and dates) are informational books about a number of different cultures, organized under the rubric of numerical information about each country. Three books by Ann Morris (1989a, 1989b, 1992) feature photographs of bread, hats, and houses around the world and thus provide classifying experiences that use data with a multicultural flavor. *This Is My House* (Dorros 1992) portrays houses around the world at a more sophisticated level, commenting on how each one was built in a way that is consistent with its environment.

Two books use a global perspective to help readers understand time zones. In *Nine O'clock Lullaby* (Singer 1991), we travel instantaneously to places in thirteen different time zones: Brooklyn, Puerto Rico, England, Zaire, Switzerland, Russia, India, China, Japan, Australia, Samoa, Alaska, Los Angeles, Mexico, and Wisconsin. We therefore see not only what people do at different times of the day but also what life looks like all around the world. Since these are brief stops, with a single picture and minimal text for each culture, we get only a surface view of each society, but the depictions are charming and create a sense of distinctness across time. *All in a Day* (Anno et al. 1986) depicts children in the United States, Brazil, England, Kenya, Russia, China, Japan, and Australia every three hours in a twenty-four-hour period, showing what is going on simultaneously in each of their time zones throughout the day and night. Most of the artists are from the country they have illustrated (thus guaranteeing authenticity), and the artists have written an introduction that emphasizes the universality of human experience and the need for all humans to learn to live together.

The mathematics connection in *Everybody Cooks Rice* (Dooley 1991) is cooking, and this delightful book comes complete with recipes. A young girl exploring her neighborhood discovers that families from Barbados, Puerto Rico, Vietnam, India, China, and Haiti, along with her own Italian-ancestry mother, are all cooking rice for dinner that night in their own ways.

Although books that explore mathematical ideas within the context of one or more specific cultures do not radically alter perspectives or focus on social issues, they play an important role in ensuring that the exploration of mathematical ideas takes place in a way that recognizes a variety of social and cultural contexts.

CULTURALLY UNIQUE MATHEMATICAL SETTINGS

Recent scholarship has begun to examine the indigenous mathematics of cultures around the world (see Nelson, Joseph & Williams 1993 and Zaslavsky 1979), and in a few cases this information has been used to develop children's books. Three such books look at counting in an African setting. *Moja Means One* (Feelings 1971) focuses on the Swahili language, a lingua franca for most of East Africa; this is both a counting book and an introduction to African culture. *Count on Your Fingers African Style* (Zaslavsky 1980) illuminates African mathematical systems by examining different finger-counting systems in specific cultures. Although having ten fingers is a human universal, different groups use fingers in different ways to represent numbers, so this book not only affirms the diversity of African culture but helps readers think about how number systems work and how they might have been invented. *Two Ways to Count to Ten*, by the well-known African American actress Ruby Dee (1988), looks at counting from another angle; in this Liberian folktale, animals compete to be king by attempting to throw a spear so high that they can count to ten before it comes down again. Try as they may, none of the animals can throw it high enough, but finally the antelope throws it up and counts, "Two! Four! Six! Eight! Ten! . . . King Leopard did not say how the count was to be made." The reader is left with the satisfying moral that sometimes the cleverest rather than the strongest wins the prize.

Geometry and time are the ideas explored in two other books of multicultural mathematics. *The Village of Round and Square Houses* (Grifalconi 1986) tells the true story of a village in the Cameroons, where the men live in square houses and the women in round ones; the narrator's grandmother, a storyteller, recounts the legendary origins of this practice. (See our discussion on pp. 156–59 of *Read Any Good Math Lately?* and also Whitin 1993a, for how this book can be used to develop the concept of optimal housing shape with students.) *Thirteen Moons on Turtle's Back* (Bruchac 1992) is a compilation of Native American moon stories; many North American tribal nations named the thirteen moons of the year to reflect what goes on in the natural world. Each moon is related to a legend, such as the winter Moon of Popping Trees of the Cheyenne, when the Frost Giant strikes the tree trunks, and the summer Strawberry Moon of the Seneca, commemorating the legendary gift of strawberries from a race of Little People. One sign of the book's authenticity is that traditional Native American names have not been anglicized;

the Cree trickster Wis-a-ked-jak, for example, has not, as in some versions, been turned into Whiskey Jack. The thirteen moons (of twenty-eight days each) that occur in a year are, of course, one more than our calendar's number of months; students can be encouraged to think about the reason for this discrepancy, and the conventions of time in modern industrial culture compared with those in the days when humans lived closer to nature.

A few children's books explore the universal, mathematically grounded ways in which games are practiced across cultures. Zaslavsky, in *Tic Tac Toe and Other Three-in-a-Row Games* (1982), speculates on how such games might have arisen early in human history. After exploring rules and strategies for tic-tac-toe, she describes related games from around the world. For example, the game known as Three Men's Morris in England occurs under different names with exactly the same rules in the Philippines, China, the Arab world, and northern Africa. The illustrations include not only diagrams of all the games but also pictures, both historical and contemporary, of people around the world playing the games. A map at the end of the book shows the thirty countries and regions, on every continent, in which these games are played. Three profusely illustrated books—Botermans, Burrett, van Delft & van Splunteren 1989; Slocum & Botermans 1986, 1992—are comprehensive collections of games and puzzles from around the world. These books often provide historical information (e.g., the legend of the Chinese emperor who saw a tortoise whose shell contained a magic-square pattern of dots) and photographs from around the world (e.g., children playing marbles in Nepal or jumping rope in Tanzania). The intent of these books, written for adults but reasonably accessible to children, is somewhat different from Zaslavsky's books about games, and teachers need to be aware of this difference. Zaslavsky, in describing three-in-a-row games around the world, is clearly intending to impart information about both mathematics and culture to young readers; Botermans et al., writing for adults and looking at games and puzzles comprehensively, include some offensive images, such as American string puzzles using cardboard figures of Aunt Jemima and a stereotypical Chinese image (Slocum & Botermans 1992, pp. 80–81). These books provide an excellent opportunity not only to examine games from around the world but also to discover how the sad history of racism and stereotyping made its way into even these playful aspects of human culture.

Another excellent resource book about games, published by UNICEF and available through the gift store of the United Nations, is *Games of the World* (Grunfeld 1975). It not only introduces readers to a wide range of games from around the world but also provides color photographs of people playing the games in their indigenous settings. For instance, we see two Kenyan warriors in tribal dress playing the game of wari in an open field, their spears stuck in the ground beside them; another photograph shows a group of young men in a Madagascar marketplace playing their national game of fanorona; we also see two Japanese workmen playing the well-known game of go in traditional fashion, seated on the ground and using a board with short, detachable legs. There are photographs of original playing boards as well as ancient paintings and pieces of sculpture that depict various people playing these games. The rules are carefully explained, and there are even directions for making your own game boards. However, it is the photographs of people of different cultures deeply engrossed in playing the games that gives this book such an appealing multicultural flavor.

CULTURALLY UNIQUE HISTORICAL SETTINGS

We found several books whose treatment of mathematics in a historical context helps children think about the contributions of diverse cultures and ethnic groups. First of all, although the formal mathematical system used today in North America and around the world grew from European (especially Greek) roots, mathematics was also invented independently in many other cultures. A book like *How to Count Like a Martian* (St. John 1975) both honors this history and helps students understand that our particular numeration system is not the only logical or possible one.

Another book that discusses a numeration system different from our own is *Senefer: A Young Genius in Old Egypt* (Lumpkin 1992). Readers learn about the Egyptian culture 3,500 years ago under the rule of Hatshepsut, one of its most famous female rulers. Much of the story focuses on the everyday use of mathematics, such as the bartering system at the marketplace and the Egyptian numerals used to record such transactions. Young Senefer learns numerals from his mother and from the scribes of the temple storehouse, who keep accurate records of the loaves of bread used to pay the wages of people who work in the temple. Later on, when Senefer is allowed to attend a special school, he learns a clever method for multiplying a two-digit number by another two-digit number by partitioning one number into smaller parts. This is the only book available that shows a numeration system grounded in its historical context.

Ten Mile Day and the Building of the Transcontinental Railroad (Fraser 1993) tells the story of a particular historical event that is relevant here because of the great amount of mathematical data it involves. Part of the story of the building of the transcontinental railroad is the story of the Chinese laborers who were brought over to work on it. The author's research ensured that illustrations of these men are as accurate and authentic as possible, and in a sidebar she speaks of the hardships and racism they experienced. The numbers of workers involved are telling: the railroad was built primarily by two thousand Irish workers and *eleven thousand* Chinese. The author's revisionist view of history is also revealed at the end of the book when she describes the impact of the railroad on the Native Americans who lived on the prairies: hunters slaughtered all but a few hundred of the thirteen million bison that had once roamed there, destroying the livelihood of tribal nations, whose land was shortly thereafter given away. For a more detailed account of the Chinese laborers, readers might want to consult Lawrence Yep's novel *Dragon's Gate* (1993), which describes the long hours, low pay, inadequate food, and dangerous and deplorable working conditions they experienced. (This story does not have a mathematics focus but would offer additional background for interested readers.)

The history of racism also enters into the story of Benjamin Banneker (Conley 1989), an African American mathematician and astronomer (1731–1806) who built an original wooden clock as a young adult, used his interest in astronomy to write almanacs, and helped survey the land for the District of Columbia. Although he was not a slave, the book makes it clear that he lived in a time when slavery was an integral part of the fabric of American life: indeed, he became a symbol of African American achievement used to give support to the abolitionist cause. (*Followers of the North Star* [Altman & Lechner 1993], a collection of poems about well-known and heroic African Americans, includes a poem about Banneker.) Another book for young readers describing Benjamin Banneker's many accomplishments is *What Are You Figuring Now?* by Jeri Ferris (1988), which includes a math problem devised by Banneker for readers to solve.

Stereotyped or problematic representations

It is always painful to talk or write about children's books whose representations of cultural groups are stereotyped, problematic, or otherwise offensive, since authors, illustrators, and publishers work with the best of intentions to provide exciting and satisfying works of information and art that will contribute to the lives of young readers. However, we feel it is important to alert teachers to some of the often subtle problems that arise. Teachers must be particularly vigilant about counting books, where there is the danger (and a history) of turning people into objects, because in these books the illustrations *are* the message. As teachers we have a moral obligation to discuss these images; otherwise we are guilty of perpetuating that particular stereotype. We discuss here only a small number of books, our aim being to alert the reader to the relevant issues and, we hope, open a dialogue about how to deal with them.

COUNTING ART: OMISSION AND DEHUMANIZATION

The counting book is a unique genre that inspires authors and illustrators to come up with new takes on an old topic. Two recent examples draw on the world of art to invite young viewers to pick out and count specific details found in paintings and other works of art. Unfortunately, neither *I Spy Two Eyes* (Micklethwait 1993) nor *The Folk Art Counting Book* (Watson et al. 1992) does so in a way that reflects diverse cultures in a positive way, in the former case because of omission and in the latter because of probably inadvertent dehumanization. We are not singling out *I Spy Two Eyes* as being unusually problematic in any way, but in its pictures illustrating the numbers from one to ten, all of the human beings realistic enough for readers to determine their race are white. As in so many other counting books (at least those by white authors and illustrators), images of white people were perhaps the easiest to find and include. No one book is the problem here, but rather a body of work that through the cumulative effect of books that portray only one culture gives children an unbalanced picture of not only the human race as a whole but North American society in particular.

As one would expect, *The Folk Art Counting Book* is more diverse, since folk art is the product of untrained artists who are likely to come from all sectors of society. However, the book contains a number of scenes depicting problematic historical events as images only, with no discussion of the issues. The image for the number 12, with the caption "Count 12 people," is of a painting entitled "The Old Plantation," by an unknown artist (with no mention of the artist's race), probably from South Carolina around 1800. Twelve African Americans, who we know to be slaves from the title and date of the painting, are shown playing music, dancing, and relaxing. Number 13 shows the well-known painting "The Peaceable Kingdom" (1832–1834) by Edward Hicks, with the caption "Count 13 animals. How many children?" The foreground of the picture shows the animals and three children sitting together peacefully, the lion lying down with the lamb, while on the shore in the background eight European men, apparently Quakers, are presenting a scroll to an equal-size group of Native American men, most of them wearing feathered headdresses. The image for the number 16 ("Count 16 Indians") is entitled "Indian War Dance" and attributed to the Baroness Hyde de Neuville. A faint handwritten French caption translates as "War paint. Savages before President J. Monroe, 1821." Seven men are seated in the background with a drum while nine men in front stand or dance in a loose circle, wearing varied headdresses and face paint, many of them carrying swords.

To an adult viewer with a sense of American history, these three images are resonant and disturbing, suggesting as they do the days of slavery and the colonization and demonization of Native Americans. Do these pictures belong so casually in a counting book along with images of whirligigs, quilts, and weather vanes? Although presenting people as objects for counting is not problematic per se (nineteen white members of a quilting party are also so presented), these contexts make the counting exercises unsettling (and we wonder about the use of *Indians* rather than *people* in the caption for the number 16).

The introduction to *The Folk Art Counting Book* mentions that the collection at the Abby Aldrich Rockefeller Folk Art Center, from which the images in the book were compiled, includes more than 2,600 objects; might it not have been possible to replace these three images with alternative ones by artists of color that represent the everyday life of their cultures, as so many of the works by white artists do? (Even if the unknown artist of "The Old Plantation" was an African American, and even though it depicts everyday life, a picture in a setting other than slavery would have been a better choice, since the book provides no context for discussing the attendant issues and feelings.) Older students can look at the images in *The Folk Art Counting Book* and with the teacher's support discuss the historical issues that surround an exploitive and inequitable relationship. However, young children, who are the primary audience for these counting books, will find the issues surrounding these images too complex to understand; rather than leave them with this image of slaves happily entertaining themselves on a Southern plantation, teachers ought to avoid the book altogether.

INAUTHENTICITY

Knots on a Counting Rope (Martin & Archambault 1987) is a highly popular and widely distributed book about a blind Native American child and his grandfather. The book has a beautiful southwestern setting. The book begins with the boy's asking his grandfather to tell him again the story of how he was born. The mathematical connection is the counting rope of the title; at the end of the book, the grandfather says, "Now that the story has been told again, I will tie another knot in the counting rope. When the rope is filled with knots, you will know the story by heart."

This book, written by non–Native Americans, is very popular among teachers for the loving relationship depicted between the boy and the grandfather. However, it received a lengthy, scathing review by Doris Seale in *Books Without Bias: Through Indian Eyes* (Slapin & Seale 1989), a compendium of discussions and reviews of the portrayal of Native Americans in children's books. The review attacks the book on a number of grounds: sentimentalizing Native Americans by making the boy blind and using overwrought, "poetic" language; using clothing and hairstyles that do not represent any one Native culture; and depicting an inauthentic relationship between the boy and the grandfather. Finally, Seale asks, "What is this 'counting rope' business anyway? Did the authors get the idea from the ancient Peruvian quipu? Or is this another of those 'old Indian customs' of which none of us have ever heard?"

This response to *Knots on a Counting Rope* may come as a shock to readers who love the book, but it illustrates the importance of understanding the issues involved in representing diverse cultural groups in children's literature. When white authors and illustrators write about people of color, they may, despite the best of intentions, distort, stereotype, or homogenize. It is crucial that teachers considering such books be aware of what to look for and, when possible, find a review of the book by a member of the culture depicted. (For an authentic discussion of the quipu, see Zepp 1992.)

DIVERSITY OF INTERPRETATION

Read Any Good Math Lately? mentions *Hey! Get Off Our Train* (Burningham 1989) as an example of an addition book that also features an environmental theme. In the book a boy dreams he is on a train that picks up representatives of endangered species, such as polar bears and seals, as passengers. Sandra Wilde mentioned this book in a presentation to reading teachers in Alaska and received the following response from Jeanette Schramm, a language arts specialist for the Anchorage School District:

> *[When I discovered Hey! Get Off Our Train] I was impressed with the wonderful illustrations, the repetitive phrasing, and the use of animals to tell this tale, all of which I thought gave it great potential for use with emergent readers and writers. During this time I was new to the job of Early Childhood Education Coordinator for the Bering Strait School District in northwest Alaska; 99 percent of the children in this district are Inupiaq Eskimos living in tiny villages spread over 80,000 square miles.*
>
> *What I had failed to realize when choosing this book was that the message it contained went against the traditions of this culture. To support their subsistence life style, the Eskimo people in this region hunt polar bears and seals [two of the*

> *animals used in the book]. This is an example of two cultures clashing. The experience was an eye-opener to me, making me more sensitive to the messages in children's literature that have the potential of offending cultures different from my own. Though I still enjoy the book, I soon packed it off to teacher friends in the Lower 48.*

Although this book is about animals and the environment rather than different cultural groups, its message is bound to be viewed very differently by members of a culture in which hunting is a traditional way of life, where bears are shot for fur, whales and seals for food. Imagine the reactions of people who see this way of life implicitly attacked in a children's book created by the culture whose predatory approach to the environment is the real cause of species' being endangered.

The responsibility of not assuming that our values are shared by everyone, a responsibility particularly incumbent on teachers working with children from a culture other than their own, obviously goes far beyond mathematically oriented children's books. But as a subject like mathematics, formerly seen as purely abstract and academic, becomes more and more connected to real life in school—as teachers use children's books to explore mathematical topics like time, money, sharing, and statistics, topics intimately bound up with the lives we live as members of particular cultures—we must always be alert to interpretations other than our own and to the possibility that a seemingly innocuous book may carry highly loaded meanings in some communities.

This does not mean that teachers should avoid using such books. *Hey! Get Off Our Train* could be used to trigger excellent discussions on how the environments these animals live in got so polluted or examinations of both an Inuit hunter's and a polluter's point of view or debates about whether some endangered species are more worth saving than others. These dialogues are more educational than a sentimentalized plea on behalf of polar bears and seals.

Who decides?

The book that we have thought about the most in the context of multicultural issues, indeed that was the catalyst for this chapter, is *Ten Little Rabbits* (Grossman & Long 1991), a counting book that portrays rabbits dressed as Native Americans from ten different nations. An afterword identifies each tribe and tells a little about it. The number 2, for instance, is represented by the picture seen in Figure 7–1 and the text "Two graceful dancers asking for some rain." The paragraph at the back of the book identifies the dancers as being of the Tewa tribe:

> *Traditionally, all Rio Grande pueblos stage a corn dance, generally in the Spring. The dancers wear crimson parrot feathers and cowrie shells from the Pacific and carry gourd rattles. The male dancers leap and stamp to wake up the spirits. Finally, their evergreen finery (symbolic of the fir tree that, according to legend, people used to climb up from the underworld) is thrown in the river in the hope of pleasing the Shiwana, the rain-cloud people.*

FIGURE 7–1

When the book first appeared, David Whitin wrote the following review of it for *Arithmetic Teacher*:

> *This unique counting book integrates certain aspects of [N]ative American culture. It features counting rhymes with illustrations of rabbits in native American costumes engaged in various traditional customs, such as hunting, rain dances, and storytelling. One of the strengths of the book is the glossary in the back that includes additional information on the customs that are illustrated. . . . Four members of the Menominee tribe are shown hunting bear; five members of the Blackfoot tribe huddle around a fire to tell stories; eight members of the Nez Percé tribe of the Northwest fish for salmon, one of their main staple foods; and ten members of the Navajo tribe wear the beautiful blankets that they have woven. Each set of rabbits is clearly shown on a double-page spread, and their distinctness is often accentuated by being silhouetted against a morning, evening, or night sky. This informative counting book would make a nice addition to a library of [N]ative American culture.*

Claudia Zaslavsky, well-known for her work in multicultural mathematics, wrote a letter to *Arithmetic Teacher* objecting to the review. Her letter prompted both David and Sandra to think a great deal about the issues involved and discuss them with teachers and other colleagues. We present several pieces of this dialogue as a way of provoking similar thinking and discussion in our readers.

RABBITS AS OBJECTIFICATION

Here is a section from Zaslavsky's letter:

> *I should like to take exception to [David Whitin's] favorable review of Ten Little Rabbits. . . . I first encountered a reference to this book in an ad that read: "Remember your counting rhymes from childhood? Well, this charming book takes the classic 'one little, two little, three little Indians' and does it one more. Each 'Indian' is a furry little rabbit."*
>
> *For many years I have been giving workshops and seminars on the infusion of multicultural perspectives into the mathematics curriculum. In early childhood workshops I discuss the negative image of Native American peoples conveyed by the counting rhyme, "One little, two little, three little Indians," in which Indians are treated as though they were objects. Substituting one's own ethnic or religious group for the word "Indians" brings home the point sharply.*

UNIQUENESS AND AUTHENTICITY

Responding to Claudia's letter, David described some of the conversations he had had that led him to write the review:

> *At first I shared Ten Little Rabbits with a local teacher-support group with which I meet every month. Mixed reactions were found; some were not sure why the illustration used rabbits, whereas others felt the uniqueness of each tribe was nicely represented through their traditional garb. . . .*
>
> *After receiving your letter I called the publisher. . . . They informed me that the book had been nominated for various prestigious awards. . . . They also said the story goes well beyond the old counting rhyme by using various verbs to describe unique cultural activities and to portray specific Native American garments. They said the book had been well received by many Native Americans, as well. . . .*

David had read other positive reviews of *Ten Little Rabbits* before he wrote his own; *Booklist* said, "The characters are rabbits dressed as Indians. Though this may sound a bit precious, it's not: the gravity of the characters' demeanor precludes any silliness here" (Phelan 1991), while *School Library Journal* described the book as "a quiet, respectful survey of some Native American customs organized through the structure of a counting rhyme, populated by rabbits dressed in traditional garb. . . . The rabbits have an earnest charm" (Litton 1991).

A NATIVE AMERICAN VIEW

David continued to solicit opinions on *Ten Little Rabbits;* a friend of his spoke to two Native American teachers, and David described their reactions in another letter to Zaslavsky:

> *These teachers did not like the way Native Americans were portrayed in this book. They said they could see how the author and illustrator made an attempt to portray the uniqueness of each tribe. However, they were disturbed by the use of rabbits, particularly rabbits that all looked about the same. They said that they themselves can tell the difference between a Navajo and a Sioux. These differences were not addressed in this book. . . . They saw the book treating Native Americans on a surface level, looking different on the outside [i.e., in their clothing] but representing a single homogeneous people on the inside.*

TEACHERS' VIEWS

Sandra Wilde has shared some of the concerns raised above with a number of groups of teachers (mostly white and rarely including Native Americans) and asked for reactions. For the most part, these teachers have liked the book because of the charm of the illustrations and the portrayal of a variety of tribes, clothing, and activities, and do not feel that the use of rabbits is a problem, since animals in human form appear so often in children's books.

THE AUTHOR'S VIEW

David shared his review and Zaslavsky's response with Virginia Grossman, the author of the text of *Ten Little Rabbits.* Her reply is excerpted below. (The illustrator, Sylvia Long, did not reply to David's letters.)

> *I understand, but do not share Ms. Zaslavsky's dislike of the use of animals in children's literature. . . . The use of warm, furry characters can also cause a more sympathetic feeling towards them. This was one of the reasons for our choice of rabbits. The criticism of counting as dehumanizing leaves me dumbfounded. Humans are counted as objects every day. Everyone is destined to be a statistic at least once. . . .*
>
> *My impressions [as a child] of Native Americans, or Indians as they were called then, were largely the result of the influence of my grandfathers. My paternal grandfather, who with my father published the weekly country newspaper, was a Zane Grey fan who took my sisters and me to every Technicolor Western that played at the local theater. There, we were terrified by the bloodcurdling screams of murderous Indians thundering across the Plains on their ponies, human scalps hanging from their spears. My maternal grandfather, who practiced medicine with my uncle in a neighboring community, showed me a much different picture. His practice included the only Indian settlement in Iowa, the Mesquakie Indian Settlement. . . . What I saw on the streets of Tama,*

Iowa, was an Indian people in despair, their way of life stolen, and nothing left in its place. This grandfather spent an occasional Sunday searching for body parts along the railroad tracks . . . after an Indian's Saturday night drinking led to a nap on the tracks on the way home.

As an adult I sought to reconcile these two disparate images, one terrifying, and one very sad. I tried to imagine Native American culture without the distortion caused by the influence of Europeans and without the conflict. In my research I found that in many works which claimed to be a history of the Native American, . . . Native American culture before 1492 was treated as insignificant. What we wanted for Ten Little Rabbits was an image of a non-threatening culture, going about life's daily business: traveling, finding food, creating, playing, interacting, living with dignity. In that, I think it succeeds.

[In previous children's books] there seemed to be a generic Indian: he lived in a tipi, wore buckskin, braids, feathers, and war paint, rode a horse, and hunted buffalo. That image had no meaning for a Tulalip child whose ancestors lived in a lodge, wore cedar clothes, traveled by dugout canoe, and ate salmon. Even today, many Native American children know little about the traditions of distant tribes. One of our goals was to show that there is diversity within Native American culture.

HOW SHOULD WE ASSESS BOOKS?

Seeing these different points of view, teachers may wonder how they can possibly make decisions about the appropriateness of multicultural books. One important consideration is that those who are not members of a particular cultural group may not even be aware of what the issues are; therefore, checklists like the one in Slapin, Seale, and Gonzales (1989) can help one make more informed judgments. Let's apply some of these criteria to *Ten Little Rabbits*. (We have included only criteria under which this book is found wanting; others, like the use of "generic Indian" illustrations and the use of racist adjectives, do not apply.)

1. Look at picture books: Are animals dressed as "Indians"? (In this case, yes.)
2. Look at the lifestyles: Are Native peoples discussed in the past tense only? (Most of the descriptions of tribes in the afterword are in the past tense.)
3. Look at the author's or illustrator's background. (Virginia Grossman described her background in her letter; the flap copy of the book makes the following comments about Sylvia Long: "Ms. Long lived on a reservation in Wyoming, while her husband, a physician, worked for the Indian Health Service. This experience, combined with a reading of *Watership Down*, inspired a series of Native American rabbit illustrations that later became the basis of this book.")

SOME FINAL THOUGHTS FROM SANDRA WILDE

Ten Little Rabbits is a highly popular and widely circulated book. When Virginia Grossman wrote to David Whitin in November 1993, she mentioned that there were 120,000 hardcover copies in print and that Trumpet Club was distributing a paperback version. I find myself wondering why books about Native Americans and other people of color written by people from within the culture do not seem to have the same runaway success. For instance, the counting book *Moja Means One* (Feelings 1971), written by an African American author, which informs us about African culture while portraying people as people, has certainly won awards and done well, but it has not had nearly the success of *Ten Little Rabbits*, which I have seen not only in the usual outlets but in gift stores that carry only a few books. I believe it is a result of the romanticization of Native Americans by many well-meaning whites that has replaced the earlier, more vicious stereotypes. Sims (1982; see also Cai & Bishop 1994) has suggested that sometimes African American characters appear in children's fiction by white authors primarily as a way of teaching about social issues such as integration rather than as full human beings; similarly, Native Americans are seen by some whites as closer to nature, as speaking more "poetically" than other Americans (as in *Knots on a Counting Rope*), or as exotic or charming in their colorful costumes. Native American parents and teachers, starved for curriculum materials that represent their cultures, may in some cases find a book like *Ten Little Rabbits* at least somewhat acceptable, but it is perhaps especially dangerous when non-Native children who desperately need to see more authentic portrayals of a group of Americans with whom most of them are likely to have little contact see primarily this kind of representation. A final comment on the use of animals: although animals of many kinds take on human characteristics in children's books, I do not believe it is appropriate when used for members of a distinct culture. One possible analogy is to imagine a picture book about world religions with bunnies dressed as priests and rabbis. (At least two of the images in *Ten Little Rabbits* show cultural practices of comparable seriousness.) In spite of the good intentions of the author and illustrator and the relative authenticity of the clothing and customs seen in the pictures, and *because of* the cuteness of the pictures that so many readers love, I would not use *Ten Little Rabbits* with children.

SOME FINAL THOUGHTS FROM DAVID WHITIN

I learned that even the best intentions by authors and illustrators are not a guarantee that a work will portray cultures in a sensitive and respectful manner; I learned again that reading is a constructivist enterprise and that our own culture is a filtering system that supports how we interpret text; most important, I learned that a diversity of voices enriches the collective conversation. The intent is not to arrive at the "right" or the "wrong" interpretation; it is not enough to determine the "politically correct" response and then smugly look down upon those who still don't see it "the right way." The real goal is not consensus but rather enlightened conversation. I heard the perspectives of various people: fellow teachers, librarians, publishers, an ethnomathematician, Native American teachers in Minnesota, and the author herself. Each interpreted the issue from his or her own vantage point, their collective voices raising important issues that help us examine the many books that have a multicultural as well as a mathematical dimension with the aim of judging their effectiveness in portraying cultures sensitively and respectfully. This kind of examination has been the aim of this chapter as a whole, and we hope our readers continue to look at multicultural mathematics materials with an informed and critical eye.

References

CHILDREN'S BOOKS: POSITIVE EXAMPLES

Altman, Susan, and Susan Lechner. 1993. *Followers of the North Star: Rhymes about African American heroes, heroines, and historical times.* Chicago: Children's Press.

Anno, Mitsumasa, et al. 1986. *All in a day.* New York: Philomel.

Bang, Molly. 1983. *Ten, nine, eight.* New York: Penguin.

Botermans, Jack, Tony Burrett, Pieter van Delft, and Carla van Splunteren. 1989. *The world of games.* New York: Facts on File.

Bruchac, Joseph. 1992. *Thirteen moons on turtle's back: A Native American year of moons.* New York: Philomel.

Clifton, Lucille. 1970. *Some of the days of Everett Anderson.* New York: Henry Holt.

———. 1978. *Everett Anderson's nine month long.* New York: Henry Holt.

Conley, Kevin. 1989. *Benjamin Banneker.* New York: Chelsea House.

Dee, Ruby. 1988. *Two ways to count to ten: A Liberian folktale.* New York: Henry Holt.

Dooley, Norah. 1991. *Everybody cooks rice.* Minneapolis: Carolrhoda.

Dorros, Arthur. 1992. *This is my house.* New York: Scholastic.

Falwell, Cathryn. 1993. *Feast for 10.* New York: Clarion.

Feelings, Muriel. 1971. *Moja means one.* New York: Dial.

Ferris, Jeri. 1988. *What are you figuring now? A story about Benjamin Banneker.* New York: Scholastic.

Flournoy, Valerie. 1978. *The best time of day.* New York: Random House.

Fraser, Mary Ann. 1993. *Ten Mile Day and the building of the transcontinental railroad.* New York: Henry Holt.

Garne, S. T. 1992. *One white sail.* New York: Simon & Schuster.

Greenfield, Eloise. 1993. *Aaron and Gayla's counting book.* New York: Black Butterfly.

Grifalconi, Ann. 1986. *The village of round and square houses.* Boston: Little, Brown.

Grunfeld, Frederic. 1975. *Games of the world.* Zurich: Swiss Committee for UNICEF.

Haskins, Jim. 1987. *Count your way through the Arab World.* Minneapolis: Carolrhoda.

———. 1987. *Count your way through China.* Minneapolis: Carolrhoda.

———. 1987. *Count your way through Japan.* Minneapolis: Carolrhoda.

———. 1987. *Count your way through Russia.* Minneapolis: Carolrhoda.
———. 1989. *Count your way through Africa.* Minneapolis: Carolrhoda.
———. 1989. *Count your way through Canada.* Minneapolis: Carolrhoda.
———. 1989. *Count your way through Mexico.* Minneapolis: Carolrhoda.
———. 1990. *Count your way through Germany.* Minneapolis: Carolrhoda.
———. 1990. *Count your way through India.* Minneapolis: Carolrhoda.
———. 1990. *Count your way through Israel.* Minneapolis: Carolrhoda.
———. 1990. *Count your way through Italy.* Minneapolis: Carolrhoda.
Heinst, Marie. 1992. *My first number book.* New York: Dorling Kindersley.
Johnson, Angela. 1991. *One of three.* New York: Orchard.
Linden, Ann M. 1992. *One smiling grandma: A Caribbean counting book.* New York: Dial.
Lumpkin, Beatrice. 1992. *Senefer: A young genius in old Egypt.* Trenton, NJ: Africa World Press.
Mathis, Sharon Bell. 1975. *The hundred penny box.* New York: Puffin.
McKissack, Patricia. 1992. *A million fish . . . more or less.* New York: Knopf.
Medearis, Angela S. 1990. *Picking peas for a penny.* Austin, TX: State House Press.
Merrill, Jean. 1972. *The toothpaste millionaire.* Boston: Houghton Mifflin.
Morris, Ann. 1989a. *Bread, bread, bread.* New York: Lothrop, Lee & Shepard.
———. 1989b. *Hats, hats, hats.* New York: Lothrop, Lee & Shepard.
———. 1992. *Houses and homes.* New York: Lothrop, Lee & Shepard.
St. John, Glory. 1975. *How to count like a Martian.* New York: Henry Z. Walck.
Seltzer, Isadore. 1992. *The house I live in: At home in America.* New York: Macmillan.
Shelby, Anne. 1990. *We keep a store.* New York: Orchard.
Singer, Marilyn. 1991. *Nine o'clock lullaby.* New York: HarperCollins.
Slocum, Jerry, and Jack Botermans. 1986. *Puzzles old and new: How to make and solve them.* Seattle: University of Washington Press.
———. 1992. *New book of puzzles: 101 classic and modern puzzles to make and solve.* New York: W. H. Freeman.
Yep, Lawrence. 1993. *Dragon's gate.* New York: HarperCollins.
Zaslavsky, Claudia. 1980. *Count on your fingers African style.* New York: Crowell.
———. 1982. *Tic tac toe and other three-in-a-row games.* New York: Crowell.

CHILDREN'S BOOKS: STEREOTYPED OR NEGATIVE EXAMPLES

Burningham, John. 1989. *Hey! Get off our train.* New York: Crown.
Grossman, Virginia, and Sylvia Long. 1991. *Ten little rabbits.* San Francisco: Chronicle.
Martin, Bill, Jr., and John Archambault. 1987. *Knots on a counting rope.* New York: Henry Holt.

Micklethwait, Lucy. 1993. *I spy two eyes: Numbers in art.* New York: Greenwillow.

Watson, Amy, and the staff of the Abby Aldrich Rockefeller Folk Art Center. 1992. *The folk art counting book.* Williamsburg, VA: Colonial Williamsburg Foundation. New York: Abrams.

TEACHER RESOURCES

Cai, Mingshui, and Rudine S. Bishop. 1994. Multicultural literature for children: Towards a clarification of the concept. In *The need for story: Cultural diversity in classroom and community,* edited by Anne H. Dyson and Celia Genishi, pp. 57–71. Urbana, IL: National Council of Teachers of English.

Closs, Michael P., ed. 1986. *Native American mathematics.* Austin: University of Texas Press.

Litton, Karen. 1991. Review of *Ten Little Rabbits* (Grossman and Long). *School Library Journal* 37:77.

Nelson, David, George G. Joseph, and Julian Williams. 1993. *Multicultural mathematics.* New York: Oxford.

Perl, Teri. 1978. *Math equals.* Menlo Park, CA: Addison-Wesley.

———. 1993. *Women and numbers.* San Carlos, CA: Wide World/Tetra.

Phelan, Carolyn. 1991. Review of *Ten Little Rabbits* (Grossman and Long). *Booklist* 87: 1570.

Seale, Doris. 1989. Book reviews. In Slapin and Seale, pp. 149–387. Berkeley, CA: Oyate.

Sims, Rudine. 1982. *Shadow and substance: Afro-American experience in contemporary children's fiction.* Urbana, IL: National Council of Teachers of English.

Slapin, Beverly, and Doris Seale, eds. 1989. *Books without bias: Through Indian eyes.* Berkeley, CA: Oyate.

Slapin, Beverly, Doris Seale, and Rosemary Gonzeles. 1989. How to tell the difference: A checklist. In Slapin and Seale, pp. 117–47. Berkeley, CA: Oyate.

Van Sertime, Ivan, ed. 1983. *Blacks in science: Ancient and modern.* New Brunswick, NJ: Transaction.

Whitin, David J. 1992. Review of *Ten Little Rabbits* (Grossman and Long). *Arithmetic Teacher* 39 (September): 56–57.

———. 1993a. Looking at the world from a mathematical perspective. *Arithmetic Teacher* 40 (January): 438–41.

———. 1993b. Letter to the editor. *Arithmetic Teacher* 41 (October): 114.

Zaslavsky, Claudia. 1979. *Africa counts: Number and pattern in African culture.* Brooklyn, NY: Lawrence Hill.

———. 1989. People who live in round houses. *Arithmetic Teacher* 36 (September): 18–21.

Zepp, Raymond. 1992. Numbers and codes in ancient Peru: The Quipu. *Arithmetic Teacher* 39 (May): 42–44.

8 *Books for Grownups*

Just as many teachers who have expanded their classroom literature programs participate in book groups that read and discuss serious adult fiction, we hope that teachers who have begun to introduce children's literature into their mathematics curriculum will be inspired to read some of the wonderful new books written for adults who are not mathematicians but who find mathematics at least interesting enough to read about in their spare time. Many of you may be thinking at this point, Whoa! Not me! But if your previous experience with reading about mathematics at an adult level has been limited to textbooks, you may be surprised at the range of books available today. Just as children's books can make mathematics more accessible to children, particularly those who don't think of themselves as mathematical, good nonfiction books give many adults an entrée into a topic they have long feared as beyond them or avoided as hopelessly boring.

We have purposely avoided the books that talk about how much fun it is to multiply large numbers in your head or provide a zillion ideas for math tricks at cocktail parties. (Spare us!) We have also not included any textbooks, no matter how appealing. Instead, we focus on the many books that introduce readers to the lore of numbers throughout history, the wonder of mathematical ideas, and interesting applications of mathematics. Although we cited adult books often throughout *Read Any Good Math Lately?* and in this book as well, most of those are resources that come in handy when exploring particular mathematical topics with children. The books presented here are aimed more directly at adults who would like to explore mathematics as an intellectual interest of their own. We do, however, include ideas for classroom applications that might grow out of the books.

We begin with books for readers least likely to want to read about mathematics: books on fear of math or math anxiety. Then there are sections on books about numeracy (as a parallel term to literacy) and innumeracy; what we describe as "pop math," highly accessible books written for a popular audience; games and puzzles; mathematical applications; more serious books on mathematics that reward a close reading;

and finally, for the truly bold and experienced, books of "hard-core math." In most cases, we note three or four outstanding books for each topic.

We are happy to report that the mathematics sections of many larger bookstores now carry, along with the textbooks and the abstruse monographs aimed at specialists, a healthy selection of books aimed at general readers with backgrounds in math that range from minimal to competent. We hope you will pick up at least one or two of these books in the same spirit with which you share mathematical children's books with your students.

Math anxiety and how to overcome it

Sheila Tobias, the author of *Overcoming Math Anxiety* (1993), is the most widely recognized expert on why so many people are uncomfortable with mathematics to the extent that it limits their career opportunities and damages their self-esteem. Interestingly, Tobias is neither a mathematician nor a math educator; her concern about the topic crystallized when she read a 1972 survey that showed that 92 percent of female students entering the University of California at Berkeley had not taken four years of high school mathematics and were therefore ineligible to enter ten out of twelve colleges at Berkeley. Her feminist perspective on the occupational segregation of women (she teaches politics and women's studies at the University of Arizona) led her to begin a personal campaign against math avoidance. This 1993 revised edition of her groundbreaking 1978 book includes new material on brain research as well as expanded exercises and activities.

Overcoming Math Anxiety consists of both an explanation of what math anxiety is and where it comes from and a series of lessons on how to overcome it. Tobias makes a strong case for the importance of mathematics in today's world, and encourages readers not to let their life chances be limited by a lack of competence in a subject that is not nearly as mysterious and difficult as its mystique has led many people to believe. She disparages the idea that lack of a "mathematical mind" makes the subject inaccessible to many people, attributing the problem instead to inadequate instruction, gender stereotyping, and a mythology of innate differences. In particular, she demolishes the commonly held popular idea that males are genetically better equipped to do mathematics, showing how the studies that have been cited in support of this conclusion have typically been either flawed or misinterpreted, particularly in regard to the assumption that differences between the sexes are likely to be innate rather than culturally determined. In the second half of the book, Tobias focuses on solutions, giving brief introductions to the topics of word problems, everyday math, and even calculus, and describing courses and programs in overcoming math anxiety. For the many elementary school teachers, particularly women, who may teach mathematics very successfully but still feel like incompetents or impostors, *Overcoming Math Anxiety* is the obvious starting point not only for improving one's proficiency in mathematics but also for understanding the social and psychological underpinnings of why people are so insecure about the subject in the first place.

Claudia Zaslavsky, in her charmingly titled *Fear of Math: How to Get Over It and Get on with Your Life* (1994), explores the same topic from a different angle, focusing especially on how not only women but also people of color have been excluded from mathematics and stereotyped as not being good at it. Interspersing her comments with excerpts from math autobiographies written by adults, she challenges elements of our educational and social systems—IQ tests, narrowly defined and misinterpreted research, cultural attitudes—that have limited so many potential learners of mathematics. She blames an overly rigid system of teaching mathematics for fostering myths about one right answer and the solitary math genius and overemphasizing memorization of rules and procedures. Zaslavsky's solutions emphasize incorporating more mathematics into family life by building on the ways you already use mathematics and taking a commonsense approach to new topics rather than being intimidated by them, with an eye to raising a new generation that is more comfortable with mathematics right from the start. Zaslavsky also includes an extensive list of resources, focusing on programs, organizations, and materials that can help both adults and young people develop mathematical competence.

One of the most intriguing features of *Fear of Math* is the sidebars, one every few pages, on topics ranging from summaries of research to the language of mathematics to tips on temperature conversion, but especially focusing on examples of numbers from real life (many with a socially conscious flavor) and how to interpret them. Examples include what the infant mortality rate for the United States really means, figures on how the gap between rich and poor is growing, and an interpretation of how the rates of smoking for men and women have changed over time. One of our favorite examples describes President Ronald Reagan's reaction to a $900,000 land claim settlement with the Pequot Indians in 1983. He felt it was too high, suggesting instead paying the worth of the land at the time it was originally sold ($8,091.17) plus interest. He lacked the mathematical knowledge to realize that a 5 percent interest rate compounded quarterly from 1856 to 1983 would create a final sum of $4.5 million! A letter writer to the *New York Times* suggested that "the Pequots might be well advised to take the President up on his generous offer" (p. 154).

A third book on math anxiety, *Where Do I Put the Decimal Point?* (Ruedy & Nirenberg 1990), is also a useful resource, particularly for those who are ready to work on specific math topics. The first third of the book explores what math anxiety is, how to know if it's affected your life, and its cultural roots, while the remainder of the book consists of two dozen lessons on standard math topics like fractions and algebra as well as on real-life applications like understanding pay increases, adjusting quantities in recipes, and balancing your checkbook.

All three of these books contain information teachers can apply in elementary school classrooms. All have a number of general ideas for making mathematics topics easier to learn and understand, and each also has its own special emphasis. *Overcoming Math Anxiety* encourages teachers to think about whether they are letting stereotypes get in the way of helping both sexes enjoy and do well in mathematics; *Fear of Math* helps teachers think about mathematics from a multicultural and social-justice perspective; *Where Do I Put the Decimal Point?* provides a good math anxiety questionnaire that challenges myths about mathematics in ways that can be adapted for use with children and also includes the most specific and detailed lessons on particular math topics.

Numeracy and innumeracy

When a society is made up of many people who are either uncomfortable with mathematics or know how to do the computations but don't always apply them accurately in real life, it faces what some might call a crisis of *innumeracy,* a term popularized by John A. Paulos (1988) as analogous to *illiteracy.* We leave it to the pollsters and pundits to decide how rampant innumeracy really is in North America, but we can recommend three books about the topic that are well written and explore a number of interesting mathematical byways and blind spots. Some mathematical facts and patterns are counterintuitive enough that even those of us who are relatively comfortable with mathematics may be surprised at the pitfalls associated with numbers we come across in our daily lives.

The classic book to start with is, of course, Paulos's best-seller, *Innumeracy* (1988). He begins by discussing how large numbers are difficult for many of us to grasp intuitively, yet are not really that hard to understand when looked at logically or in relation to other numbers. For instance, the 45,000 Americans killed in car accidents every year is equivalent to the number of American casualties in Vietnam, while the seventeen Americans killed by terrorists in 1985, which made so many people fearful of traveling outside of the country, were among 28 million Americans who traveled abroad that year, making the chances of being a victim about one in 1.6 million. (Paulos is driven especially crazy by people who respond to that statistic with, "Yes, but what if you're that one?" and feels that such overpersonalization is common among people who really don't take the time to understand numbers.)

Much of Paulos's book deals with probability and statistics, and although the discussions sometimes get overtechnical, he has wonderful examples of how lack of mathematical understanding contributes to superstitions, scams, and pseudoscience: he explains why the experience of meeting someone who knows a friend of a friend is so common (and doesn't require a belief in fate); why receiving a positive test result for AIDS or cancer, even if the test is 99 percent accurate, isn't necessarily cause for despair; and the mathematical reasons why the existence of UFOs is so unlikely.

Innumeracy is perhaps most valuable not for its specific examples (although they are numerous, diverse, and intriguing) but for the attitude of skepticism it creates, particularly when faced with misleading explanations for phenomena that are only apparently impossible (like a gambler's lucky run of the dice) or attempts to influence random mathematical phenomena (like a computer program that supposedly helps you pick winning lottery numbers).

A. K. Dewdney, known for his eight-year authorship of the "Mathematical Recreations" column in *Scientific American,* has written an excellent book about innumeracy, *200% of Nothing* (1993). His special focus is the misleading use of numbers by advertisers, politicians, and others who (intentionally or unintentionally) provide distorted information to the public. For instance, a car salesman might suggest financing a car rather than paying cash, pointing out that the amount earned by leaving the money in the bank at 7.5 percent interest would be more than the cost of financing (through the dealership) at 11 percent. But what the salesman doesn't point out is that if you were to pay cash for the car and put the amount of the monthly payments in the bank, you'd end up with more than four times as much extra money as doing it the other way.

Another example will be interesting to educators: in 1988, the federal Department of Education (under an administration that was not very committed to adequate funding for public education) issued a chart that appeared to show skyrocketing education costs and plummeting SAT scores during the years 1963–1986. However, Dewdney shows that the true trend of both figures was distorted, the SAT scores by using a scale ranging from 800 to 1000 rather than 400 to 1600 (the range of possible scores) and the spending amounts by not showing them in constant dollars. Superimposing these two misleading graphs on top of each other made the picture even more dramatically incorrect.

This is a terrific book that helps all of us be better consumers of mathematical information (and more of Dewdney's examples come from real life than Paulos's do). One of Dewdney's interesting comments is about lotteries: the combination 1, 2, 3, 4, 5, 6 is *exactly* as likely to win as a seemingly more random combination like 7, 12, 19, 28, 37, 41, yet what believer in mystical lottery luck would ever pick the former?

Our third innumeracy title is also a coined word: *Mathsemantics* (MacNeal 1994). The author, a business consultant, takes a very practical approach to mathematics, with the idea that making sense is what counts most and that traditional approaches to mathematics often get in the way of making sense. Much of the book is built around a math quiz that he has given to prospective employees, in which the mathematics is relatively simple but a lack of applied-math common sense leads to many wrong answers. (You may want to start by taking the quiz yourself—it's in his appendix.)

MacNeal addresses "mathsemantical" misunderstanding in a number of interesting chapters. One issue is the lack of care given to the underlying meanings of numbers. Two problems on his test involve adding decimals; most test takers produce the right answer for the one in which all the numbers have two decimal places and are lined up evenly, but about a third of the answers to the problem that involves adding figures with different numbers of decimal places and with the decimal points not aligned aren't even close, showing that when people have been taught to follow a formula rather than think about what they are doing, even a small variation in format can throw them way off.

One of the most amusing test items is the one designed to measure what MacNeal calls "number-related naming ability." The following deceptively easy problem resulted in 56 different answers from 196 test takers:

2 apples
<u>5 oranges</u>

The most common answer, "seven pieces of fruit," was the correct one, but many respondents either answered "2 apples + 5 oranges" (thus failing to add at all) or skipped the problem. Many of the test takers strongly protested the question, parroting the cliché that you can't add you-know-what; MacNeal had a lot of fun presenting them with two pencils and a pen and seeing how easily they were able to recognize that they now had three writing implements.

Teachers will be especially interested in topics they can explore with their students. In Chapter 10 ("Writer's Cramp"), for example, MacNeal describes a lesson his father taught him about mathematics. When he and his brother were about six and eight, their father invited them to start writing numbers in sequence beginning with one, and promised to pay them a set amount of money every time they reached a one followed only by zeroes. They cashed in quickly on 10 and before too long on 100, and then settled in for some long hauls before finally quitting at some point between 100,000 and 200,000. The real value of this seemingly pointless activity was in giving MacNeal a lifelong feel for the uniqueness of numbers and their arrangement in an infinite series, the flavor of which is captured in his writing:

> *Some [numbers] were lovely: 22222, 23456, 24680. Others were jagged: 31537, 35491. Some seemed like Mom's voice exercises: 46864, 57975. Others lack immediately discernible pattern: 58921, 61309. Some seemed to blare like trumpets: 67799, 88599. Others wasted away: 97421, 98310. (p. 102)*

All these books on innumeracy have extensive classroom applications; teachers will appreciate them both for the many specific treatments of mathematical topics and for the impetus they provide to always make sure that our students are using mathematics in commonsense ways and not just as rote number crunchers. *Innumeracy* is the classic introduction to the topic, *200% of Nothing* has the strongest consumer and citizen orientation, and *Mathsemantics* immerses readers most strongly in a meaningfully grounded sense of numbers.

Pop math

The books we have identified as "pop math" are designed to be playful, to deal with mathematical topics in brief vignettes or as fiction. The granddaddy of all pop math books is *Flatland* (Abbott [1884] 1982), written over a hundred years ago. The author's alter ego, Mr. A. Square, describes his two-dimensional world, where men of the lower classes are isosceles triangles and those of the middle and upper classes are equilateral triangles, squares, and so on; the nobility begin at hexagonality, going up to the circular priestly class. (Women, sadly, are straight lines in this clearly sexist world!) The first half of the book describes the customs and history of Flatland, the second half explores the narrator's difficult attempts to explain his country to the king of unidimensional Lineland and his startling visit from a Sphere from Spaceland and his own visit there. Even the Sphere is discombobulated, however, when Mr. Square suggests the possibility of a fourth dimension:

> *My Lord has shown me the intestines of all my countrymen in the Land of Two Dimensions by taking me with him into the Land of Three. What therefore more easy than now to take his servant on a second journey into the blessed region of the Fourth Dimension, where I shall look down . . . and see the inside of every three-dimensioned house, the secrets of the solid earth, the treasures of the mines in Spaceland, and the intestines of every solid living creature. (p. 100)*

Flatland is a blend of geometrical exploration, science fiction, and social satire, written in ornate nineteenth-century language, and remains a widely known classic.

More recent writers are still having fun with mathematical concepts. *Zero to Lazy Eight* (Humez, Humez & Maguire 1993) has chapters on each of the numbers from zero to thirteen, with a final chapter on some bigger numbers, including Mersenne's number, a seventy-digit whopper that it took a Cray supercomputer to factor. Each chapter uses its number as a jumping-off point for several mathematical explorations; for instance, the chapter on three touches down briefly on "odd man out," triage, the three degrees of burns, the Three Billy Goats Gruff, and TV dinners (yes, TV dinners!) before exploring the topics of number sequences, Golden Rectangles, and pi, all of it painless to the nonmathematician because the real math is mixed in with so much entertaining historical and cultural trivia. We get a sense of the unique nature and features of each number and are often prompted to see extremely familiar ideas in old ways. For instance, have you ever thought about why a group of people pushing to free a car stuck in the snow do it on the count of three? (The interval between "one" and "two" sets the rhythm, so that you know how soon you'll be hearing the "three" on which you push in unison.)

A more highly structured but still accessible overview of mathematical topics is *Beyond Numeracy* (Paulos 1991), the follow-up to *Innumeracy*. This collection of seventy brief essays includes both purely mathematical subjects (one chapter, entitled "E," is about the number with that name, which is roughly equal to 2.718, and its special mathematical properties) and more humanistic ones, like mathematical folklore and mathematics in ethics. This is a good book for those who feel ready to dip briefly into topics like calculus, imaginary and negative numbers, and prime numbers; the four pages or so on each topic are enough to give you a feel for what it is about but don't require you to make the commitment of learning about it formally and in depth. *Beyond Numeracy* is just detailed enough to make a layperson conversant with a large number of current mathematical ideas. Paulos also provides a good bibliography for further nontechnical reading in mathematics.

All three of these books can inspire classroom applications. *Flatland,* although its Victorian language and social satire might not be fully appreciated by elementary schoolchildren, could inspire activities in which students design their own two-dimensional countries and think through the issues of what houses would look like, how people would recognize each other, and so on; a teacher familiar with the book can intelligently guide such an exploration. The major value of both *Zero to Lazy Eight* and *Beyond Numeracy* is their expansion of teachers' knowledge base; they can help teachers plan activities relating to each of the numbers and to topics such as area and volume, pi, and probability.

Games and puzzles

In *Read Any Good Math Lately?* and in Chapter 9 of this volume, we identify children's books that feature games and puzzles as well as many adult resources on the topic that are in some way accessible to children. Those we describe here are not so much resource materials as books to sit down and read.

Ancient Puzzles (Olivastro 1993), as its title suggests, takes a historical look at puzzles through a brief tour of a number of mathematical topics. Chapter 1 begins with a picture of an 11,000-year-old bone, discovered in Africa, that has groups of notches down the sides. Although the notches do not fit into any single numerical pattern, Olivastro comments that they include incidences of doubling (a sequence of groups of 3, 6; 4, 8; and 10, 5, 5), numbers reflecting an interest in ten, and a series of prime numbers. Each of these patterns is then related to explorations of similar numbers throughout history, such as the mystical significance of ten in Egyptian and Buddhist religion; an ancient doubling method of multiplication; and the Sieve of Eratosthenes, an ancient Greek method of determining primes. Other chapters deal with the history of how pi is calculated (it involves geometric formulas, not measuring circles), the history and strategy of tic-tac-toe games, Chinese parallels to Pascal's Triangle and the Pythagorean Theorem, and many others. *Ancient Puzzles* provides clear evidence of how mathematics has always been a worldwide human endeavor.

Another Fine Math You've Got Me Into . . . (Stewart 1992) is a compilation of columns by one of the current authors of *Scientific American*'s "Mathematical Recreations" and follows in the tradition of the previous author of the column, Martin Gardner, but adds a lot of humor. The sixteen chapters in this volume each begin with a story that leads into a mathematical exploration of some kind. For instance, "The Lion, the Llama, and the Lettuce" is a rephrasing of the old wolf, goat, and cabbage puzzle. A farmer can only carry one of the three across a river at one time, but not all of the items can be safely left alone together: "A llama will guzzle an entire lettuce, however gigantic, at a single sitting. . . . When a lion is left alone with a llama it tends to see the creature more as llamaburger" (p. 2). Although the solution to the puzzle is fairly simple, Stewart uses it to explore graphical methods of illustrating the solution to this problem and others, such as the classic "Tower of Hanoi" (in which discs must be moved from one of three piles to another following specified rules). Other chapters deal with Venn diagrams and the more elaborate Edwards-Venn cogwheels, strategy games similar to "Prisoner's Dilemma," and the mathematics of moving a sofa around a corner. Although the mathematics in these columns is not for rank beginners (they were designed to be interesting to readers of science magazines), the book is clearly written, not difficult to follow, and full of charmingly corny humor (like the chapter title "A Vine Math You've Got Me Into").

Mind Sights (Shepard 1990) is a collection of recreational drawings created by a psychologist known for his work in perception and cognition. Shepard has been creating ink drawings of optical illusions for more than fifteen years and has here pulled them together into a collection in which he also writes autobiographically about how he came to draw these pictures (as an adolescent, he had a penchant

for perceptual pranks like moving all the furniture out of his sister's room).
The illusions are grouped into nine categories that relate to features such as depth, ambiguities, figure-ground relationships, and metamorphoses. Shepard often adds some unique twists to familiar illusions; for instance, in a picture of two identical monsters chasing down a corridor, not only does one appear larger because of the perspective of the corridor, but the same expression looks like rage on the face of the pursuer and fear on the pursued. Another group of puzzles plays with alternative ways of representing numbers, as in "Four in Five":

I
II
III
FIVE

A lengthy section following the illusions themselves describes how and why each works and gives an overview of the principles of human perception, including a discussion of the Ames room, the classic illusion in which a trapezoidal room, when looked at through a peephole, produces weird illusions of size and proportion because the brain misinterprets it as rectangular.

One of the most interesting new game and puzzle creations is not a book but a box (though widely available in bookstores); *The Paradox Box* (1993) is a collection of about forty optical illusions and visual puzzles, most of them unfamiliar ones from the nineteenth and early twentieth centuries. Also included is a little booklet of "Words at Play," which gives examples of paradoxes, bulls (sensible nonsense, like "Let's forget it never happened"), oxymorons, palindromes, and other forms of wordplay. Most of the illusions are on individual cards about the size of postcards. They include hidden pictures, cards meant to be held up to the light to reveal a hidden image, pictures that change into something else when turned upside down, and so on. The publishers are also planning a sequel of more recent optical illusions.

These three books and a box, each so different from the others, will not only delight teachers in their own perusal of them but provide interesting enrichment ideas for the classroom. *Ancient Puzzles* is full of many classic puzzles that lend themselves to exploration by elementary school students (for instance, there is one involving a set of containers holding three, five, and eight quarts, where one is asked to divide eight quarts of liquid into two equal measures just by pouring back and forth). The puzzles in *Another Fine Math You've Got Me Into . . .* are often more complicated but at least tend to begin with simple versions. And the illusions in both *Mind Sights* and *The Paradox Box* are accessible to anyone, with the postcard format of the latter making it especially amenable to classroom display.

Mathematical applications

Of the four outstanding and entertaining books about mathematical applications we have chosen, two are about the visual display of information and two are about lies! Of the latter, *How to Lie with Statistics* (Huff 1954) has been around longer and is, as one would guess, not a primer for con artists but a guide for readers to the kind of statistical information that appears so often in the news. Picking up on many of the same topics dealt with in *200% of Nothing,* this classic uses lively prose and cartoon illustrations to indicate the many ways that information can be slanted through judicious (and often unethical) distortions in how it is gathered and presented.

Statistics can be distorted even before they are tabulated by the way a sample is selected. Huff starts the book with a published statistic that the average Yale graduate from the class of 1924 earns $25,111 a year (which was a fair chunk of money when the book was written!). However, a little research showed that the figure was based on responses to a questionnaire sent to those with known addresses, thus leaving out many who "have not fulfilled any shining promise. They are clerks, mechanics, tramps, unemployed alcoholics, barely surviving writers and artists," or those who are not "making enough money to brag about" (p. 15). Similarly, a survey that asked Southern blacks during World War II, "Would Negroes be treated better or worse here if the Japanese conquered the U.S.A.?" got very different answers depending on whether the interviewers were black or white. *How to Lie with Statistics* also provides useful overviews of mean, median, and mode and other basic statistical concepts, and is perhaps best known for several illustrations that show how different presentations of the same data can produce very different impressions. For instance, a graph that shows moderate growth from $20 to $22 billion dollars over a twelve-month period can be made to look much more dramatic by chopping off the bottom range of the graph (the area below $18 billion where no figures appear) and even more by stretching the vertical axis in relation to the horizontal one. Similarly, a map distributed by a bank showing the portion of national income spent by the federal government as equivalent to the total incomes of people in shaded-in states is called "The Darkening Shadow" and shows almost everything west of the Mississippi fallen prey to the federalist monster. But if you start on the east coast, the area shaded in is about the size of Montana. (Huff points out that an honest map would have shaded in a group of moderately populated states whose income is roughly proportional to their area for the country as a whole.)

The author of *How to Lie with Maps* (Monmonier 1991) acknowledges his debt to *How to Lie with Statistics* for his title and accomplishes many of the same ends while also giving the reader a quick course in map geography, particularly in early chapters that survey the conventions of mapmaking, one of which is (of necessity) to gloss over extraneous detail although it may lead to distortions.

Some map errors are deliberate and relatively innocuous. For instance, commercial mapmakers often insert mythical, out-of-the-way streets in order to catch copyright violators; and a fan of the University of Michigan's football team, the Blues, supposedly implanted the mythical towns "Goblu" and "Beatosu" (the Blues' traditional rival is Ohio State) on a map of Michigan. Maps are often set up in a schematic way for ease of use (a subway map, for example), but maps are also used for propaganda purposes (the maps found even on postage stamps in Argentina that lay claim to the Malvinas Islands—called the Falklands by their British claimants—as well as part of Antarctica). This book also explores the use of maps in war and as a tool for understanding data and is a must for anyone who is interested in maps and their use.

Edward Tufte is the most exciting writer currently exploring the field of graphic design as a tool for presenting information. In two large-format books, *The Visual Display of Quantitative Information* (1983) and *Envisioning Information* (1990), he takes the reader on a whirlwind tour of good and bad examples of graphic design, historical and modern, and discusses the principles involved in great detail.

In his first book, Tufte makes a strong case for the power of a visual display to communicate in ways that raw numerical data, even in tabular form, cannot, by translating four sets of data into scatter diagrams that clearly show how greatly the data sets differ from each other. He spends a great deal of time discussing what he describes as possibly "the best statistical graphic ever drawn," a figurative map of Napoleon's disastrous Russian campaign of 1812 that plots six variables over a period of several months. He also has fun with bad examples, like the chart from an educational journal that uses five colors and three-dimensional perspective to report only 5 pieces of data and "may well be the worst graphic ever to find its way into print." He is a special foe of what he calls "chartjunk," defined as decorative graphics that often obscure rather than clarify information.

Envisioning Information focuses even more strongly than the earlier book on how to create powerful images that communicate information clearly and vividly, using principles such as micro/macroreadings (as in Washington, D.C.'s Vietnam Memorial, which makes a forceful impact both from a distance and up close, though for very different reasons), layout and separation (e.g., the judicious use of shading to separate and highlight information), small multiples (e.g., four maps that are identical except for the data, changing over time, plotted on them), and color (e.g., using different colors for primary and secondary roads on a map).

These books of mathematical applications are especially interesting to non-mathematicians, and their extensive use of visuals is a particular delight. All of them will also spark many ideas for helping elementary school children gather, organize, and display data of various kinds, and the two *How to Lie With* books can also be used to help children become more critical readers and consumers of mathematical and visual information. Many of the illustrations in the two books by Tufte are also accessible to young readers.

Serious mathematics

Some adult books about mathematics make more demands on the reader but are still not textbooks or technical books. The seven books we briefly summarize here are accessible even if you don't remember much math beyond basic algebra or geometry, although you may find yourself skipping over a few sections.

For those interested in the history of numbers or of mathematics, either *The Mathematical Experience* (Davis & Hersh 1981) or *From One to Zero* (Ifrah 1985) would be a good choice, although the two books are very different. *The Mathematical Experience* takes a more episodic approach, with brief, independently readable segments focusing on mathematical topics, philosophy, and personalities, as well as a number of historical vignettes about the development of various mathematical ideas, theories, and procedures. Unlike some of the other books we have described, this one focuses primarily on the formal Western mathematical tradition, and is filled with the names, work, and often pictures of mathematicians like Euclid, Archimedes, Euler, Fourier, and Riemann. *From One to Zero,* translated from the French, is a lengthy and structured history of numeration systems, beginning with speculation about the natural human faculties of number perception that must have underlain early counting, then exploring concrete counting tools like the hand, notching, pebbles, knotted strings, and the abacus. The bulk of the book discusses the many numeral systems developed around the world; the Roman, Sumerian, Egyptian, Greek, Arabic, Chinese, and Babylonian systems are discussed at length, others are mentioned more briefly.

Descartes' Dream (Davis & Hersh 1986), by the authors of *The Mathematical Experience,* focuses on human applications of mathematics, both practical and philosophical. For instance, a section entitled "Are We Drowning in Digits?" talks about the "mathematicization" of modern life, while other essays deal with computer dating services, standardized testing, and other uses of mathematics as a social filter. On a more abstract level the authors deal with issues such as whether computers think and whether mathematics has distorted our perhaps "truer" unfiltered perceptions of reality.

Ivars Peterson has written two books aimed at making recent developments in mathematics accessible to general readers: *The Mathematical Tourist* (1988) and *Islands of Truth* (1990), both of them collections of his columns from the magazine *Science News.* The brief chapters, arranged in sections according to common themes, are lively explorations of current hot topics like fractals, game theory, chaos, and computer models and graphics. Picking two examples at random, "Shadows and Slices," in *The Mathematical Tourist,* defines a four-dimensional solid (such as a hypercube) in mathematical terms, then talks about how computer graphics have vastly expanded mathematicians' ability to create and manipulate images of these structures, images that not only are aesthetically pleasing but can "suggest relationships and conjectures that don't arise easily just from equations or lists of data points" (p. 90). In *Islands of Truth,* "Musical Numbers" explores new mathematical concepts that have led to radically new acoustical designs for concert halls, designs using panels with wells of equal width and varying depths. This technology has arisen from number theory, seemingly the most abstract branch of mathematics, which nonetheless has practical applications not only in acoustics but in fields like cryptography.

Also very up-to-date is a brief book by Marilyn vos Savant of *Parade* magazine's "Ask Marilyn" column. *Is It Solved?* (1993) is a brief history of Fermat's Last Theorem, recently in the news because of the supposed proof, devised by a Princeton mathematician, to this seventeenth-century unsolved problem. (As of this writing, it's still uncertain whether the proof works or not.) The theorem is as follows: *The equation* $x^n + y^n = z^n$*, in which n is an integer greater than 2, has no solution in positive integers.* Vos Savant makes the theorem, the history of attempts to solve it, and the ramifications of the recent possible proof surprisingly accessible. She also enlightens readers with brief chapters on what it means to prove a mathematical theorem and on a number of mathematical paradoxes and mysteries, solved and unsolved. One brief but tantalizing one is Goldbach's Conjecture that every even number greater than two is the sum of two primes (e.g., 8 = 3 + 5, 36 = 17 + 19). The conjecture has never been proven, but no exception has ever been found either.

Martin Gardner, a long-time favorite author of those who enjoy mathematical puzzles and essays, has written (originally in 1964 and in an extensively revised version in 1990) one of the best books ever created about mathematics, physics, and their intersection in the concept of symmetry. *The Ambidextrous Universe* (now entitled *The New Ambidextrous Universe*) was occasioned by a groundbreaking scientific discovery in 1957 that parity is not conserved. You'll have to read the book to find out not only what this dull-sounding phrase means but why it was so important. Gardner takes us on a fascinating journey of more than three hundred pages that begins with a chapter on mirrors and explores symmetry and handedness in mathematics (starting at the simple level of Lineland and Flatland), art, nature, and the human body, gradually leading the reader into the arcane land of particle physics, entropy, time-reversed worlds, and superstrings. This book is both thrilling and highly accessible, and leaves readers with not only a deep understanding of what symmetry and asymmetry are all about at many levels but a sense of what all the excitement is about on the outer reaches of modern-day physics. *The New Ambidextrous Universe* is lengthy and challenging but well worth the time.

Hard-core mathematics

No, these aren't books about the mathematics of sex! We've saved the most difficult books for last, for those readers who are comfortable with mathematics, have a reasonable background and level of understanding, and would like to read books with a fair degree of depth and breadth (and length, for that matter: the shortest of the books we describe here is 250 pages, the longest is four volumes). Still, none requires more than high-school level mathematics to understand.

Pi in the Sky (Barrow 1992) is a fascinating exploration of what mathematics is all about, a philosophical journey with a lot of mathematical content and frequent historical stops. Drawing on a wealth of references and looking at the roots of mathematics in prehistory, the author examines topics from the spread of the decimal system to the importance of Kurt Godel's work for mathematics to speculations on the relationship between God and mathematics.

The Story of Numbers (McLeish 1992) takes chronological history as its organizing principle. Beginning with a look at the early human language of number, McLeish conducts a world tour through the mathematics of pre-Columbian North and South America, Samaria and Babylon, and many other countries, then focuses on a number of individuals who have influenced modern Western mathematics (Bacon, Napier, Newton, Babbage, and Boole), and concludes with a few chapters on computers and mathematics. This is not a quick overview but rather an extensive look at how ancient number systems worked and at the theories and procedures that more modern mathematicians developed. Here are just two examples:

1. An Egyptian scribe dividing 256 by 17 would use a division table showing multiples of 17 to perform an operation equivalent to the following:

$$256 = 136 + 68 + 34 + 17 + 1$$
$$256/17 = 8 + 4 + 2 + 1 + 1/17$$
$$= 15\ 1/17$$

2. John Napier invented the logarithm around the year 1600, based on his insight that two numbers expressed as powers of the same base can be multiplied by adding the powers. For instance, 8 x 16 = 128 can also be expressed as $2^3 \times 2^4 = 2^7$.

Journey through Genius (Dunham 1990) looks at the history of Western mathematics as seen in twelve of its great theorems, from Hippocrates' Quadrature of the Lune (construction of a square equivalent in area to a given crescent) around 440 B.C. to Cantor's work with the transfinite realm in 1891. This is perhaps the most technical of the books we have described, since much of it consists of formal proofs of the theorems (which are not necessarily easy to understand), but the book also provides a sense of who these famous mathematicians were as people and of the times in which they worked.

Finally, for those who would like a really complete mathematical library, *The World of Mathematics* (Newman 1956) is a four-volume compendium of mathematical articles and documents. Published nearly forty years ago, it is currently in print and also often turns up in used bookstores. It has sections on mathematical history and biography, number theory, applications to physical and social science, probability, philosophy of mathematics, and "puzzles and fancies." It includes both summary essays on specific topics and excerpts from classic works such as an essay by Newton on the Binomial Theorem, early life insurance tables by Edmund Halley, and *Flatland.*

A final word

We hope you have enjoyed this excursion through the world of mathematics books for adults. We had a lot of fun reexamining these books and thinking about the special contribution of each one, and we found ourselves wanting to go back and reread most of them. But the ones that actually ended up on the bedside table for immediate rereading were the two books by Edward Tufte, *The Visual Display of Quantitative Information* (1983) and *Envisioning Information* (1990), and Martin Gardner's *The New Ambidextrous Universe* (1990). Even if you don't get around to reading any of the other books, we really hope you will at least check these three out from the library and browse through them. They are thrilling examples of what mathematics can do and be.

References

Abbott, Edwin A. [1884] 1982. *Flatland: A romance of many dimensions.* Verplanck, NY: Emerson. Also available in other editions.

Barrow, John. 1992. *Pi in the sky: Counting, thinking, and being.* Oxford: Clarendon.

Davis, Philip J., and Reuben Hersh. 1981. *The mathematical experience.* Boston: Houghton Mifflin.

———. 1986. *Descartes' dream: The world according to mathematics.* Boston: Houghton Mifflin.

Dewdney, A. K. 1993. *200% of nothing: An eye-opening tour through the twists and turns of math abuse and innumeracy.* New York: John Wiley.

Dunham, William. 1990. *Journey through genius: The great theorems of mathematics.* New York: Wiley.

Gardner, Martin. 1990. *The new ambidextrous universe.* New York: W. H. Freeman.

Huff, Darrell. 1954. *How to lie with statistics.* New York: Norton.

Humez, Alexander, Nicholas Humez, and Joseph Maguire. 1993. *Zero to lazy eight: The romance of numbers.* New York: Simon & Schuster.

Ifrah, Georges. 1985. *From one to zero: A universal history of numbers.* New York: Viking.

McLeish, John. 1992. *The story of numbers.* (Originally entitled *Number.*) New York: Ballantine.

MacNeal, Edward. 1994. *Mathsemantics: Making numbers talk sense.* New York: Viking.

Monmonier, Mark. 1991. *How to lie with maps.* Chicago: University of Chicago.

Newman, James R. 1956. *The world of mathematics.* 4 vols. New York: Simon & Schuster.

Olivastro, Dominic. 1993. *Ancient puzzles: Classic brainteasers and other timeless mathematical games of the last 10 centuries.* New York: Bantam.

The paradox box: Optical illusions, puzzling pictures, verbal diversions. 1993. Boston: Shambhala.

Paulos, John A. 1988. *Innumeracy: Mathematical illiteracy and its consequences.* New York: Hill and Wang.

———. 1991. *Beyond numeracy: Ruminations of a numbers man.* New York: Knopf.

Peterson, Ivars. 1988. *The mathematical tourist: Snapshots of modern mathematics.* New York: W. H. Freeman.

———. 1990. *Islands of truth: A mathematical mystery cruise.* New York: W. H. Freeman.

Ruedy, Elisabeth, and Sue Nirenberg. 1990. *Where do I put the decimal point? How to conquer math anxiety and increase your facility with numbers.* New York: Henry Holt.

Shepard, Roger N. 1990. *Mind sights: Original visual illusions, ambiguities, and other anomalies.* New York: W. H. Freeman.

Stewart, Ian. 1992. *Another fine math you've got me into . . . . New York: W. H. Freeman.*

Tobias, Sheila. 1993. *Overcoming math anxiety.* Rev. ed. New York: Norton.

Tufte, Edward R. 1983. *The visual display of quantitative information.* Cheshire, CT: Graphics Press.

———. 1990. *Envisioning information.* Cheshire, CT: Graphics Press.

vos Savant, Marilyn. 1993. *Is it solved? The world's most famous math problem.* New York: St. Martin's.

Zaslavsky, Claudia. 1994. *Fear of math: How to get over it and get on with your life.* New Brunswick, NJ: Rutgers.

9 More Books for Children

We always knew we wanted to do a sequel to *Read Any Good Math Lately?* As soon as the manuscript left our hands, we were already discovering newly published children's books on mathematical themes (and a few older ones that we'd somehow missed). Little did we realize that just a few years later, we'd have discovered close to *four hundred* additional books to list in this new volume. We had originally planned an annotated bibliography, arranged alphabetically, but realized that it would be most useful to our readers if we arranged the books by categories, following the same topics we covered in *Read Any Good Math Lately?* Rather than annotate every book, we decided to describe the most exciting, innovative, or important books in each area and provide an accompanying bibliography of all the new books on these topics. Readers of our first volume can enliven the work they are already doing by adding newer titles, while teachers new to mathematics-oriented children's books can begin with the latest ones available. One other comment: we have listed books by author name, not even attempting to include the names of the illustrators, since our major concern is that readers be able to find the books. However, the contribution that illustration makes to these books is extraordinary. Mathematical knowledge is often highly visual, and many of the concepts presented in these books could never be conveyed in words alone. Also, good-quality illustration helps readers bond emotionally and aesthetically with a book.

Classification

Classifying objects or ideas into categories is an important foundation for mathematical work in both arithmetic and geometry; counting and the arithmetic operations that follow it rely on grouping, while geometry relies on understanding the properties of categories of shapes. Classification is at its heart both intuitive and logical: making instinctive connections about what belongs together and being able to talk more formally about similarities and differences. *Duck* (Lloyd & Voake 1988) is a charming story of a toddler who calls all animals "duck" and all vehicles "truck"; he's corrected by his grandmother when he's wrong and kissed by her when he's right. Young school-age children might enjoy reminiscing about how similarly simple their own classification schemes used to be!

Most of the books we have discovered that promote discussion of classification are about animals, probably because animals are so diverse, in such interesting ways. In *A Mother for Choco* (Kasza 1992), a little bird looking for a mother learns about categories by what they *don't* include; a giraffe can't be his mother because she doesn't have wings; the penguin has wings but not big round cheeks like Choco, and so on. Similarly, the young animal who asks other animals, *Is Your Mama a Llama?* (Guarino 1989) finds out about what llamas are *not* like ("She grazes on grass, and she likes to say, 'Moo!'/I don't think that is what a llama would do.") *Dinosaurs, Dinosaurs* (Barton 1989) and *All Kinds of Feet* (Goor & Goor 1984) explore classification more explicitly: Barton by using descriptive features to help young children think about different types of dinosaurs ("There were dinosaurs with horns and dinosaurs with spikes. . . . There were fierce dinosaurs and scared dinosaurs.") and Goor and Goor by looking at animals' feet in terms of how form reflects function: Polar bears' feet are broad and flat to distribute their weight so that they won't sink into soft snow, are covered with fur so they won't slip, and have claws to help them dig into and climb icebergs. Bats, by contrast, have feet made for flying, with long, thin toe bones to give shape to the wing created by skin stretched between them. Two books by Hana Machotka (1991, 1992) similarly look at the varied forms and functions of animals' feet and noses. When children have explored books like these, which provide a framework for talking about classification, they can then apply these frameworks to knowledge they gain about animals from other books.

The most versatile new book focusing on classification is *My First Number Book* (Heinst 1992; also discussed in Chapter 7), which is really a first mathematics book. Young readers are presented with large double-page spreads of photographs artfully arranged across areas of white space and asked to think about classification in various ways. The first photos are of matching pairs (left and right handprints, identical twins), while the next ones show partners like rabbit and carrot, knife and fork. As children move through the book, they are asked to sort sets of objects into subsets (blue and yellow cars) and to establish one-to-one correspondence (puppies and collars) in a gradual move into concepts of equivalent sets, greater and fewer, ordering, and, eventually, numbers. This book, which also deals with counting, measurement, addition and subtraction, shape, and other mathematical concepts, is notable not only for the aesthetic quality of its illustrations but for the appropriateness of its concept development. Of the new children's books on mathematical topics, it is the one that would be most valuable to have in a kindergarten or first-grade class (perhaps even several copies).

Counting

Counting books, like alphabet books, are published in great numbers every year because they are a unique genre, an opportunity for authors and especially illustrators to play around within a specific format with its own special constraints and make it their own. Like writing a poem, creating a counting book provides the challenge of creating a new permutation within an established prototype.

The first group of new counting books we discovered might be called "plain old counting books," those that go from one to ten, and sometimes higher, with good clear illustrations for each number. *1,2,3 Thanksgiving* (Nikola-Lisa 1991) is an especially nice starter book, because its simple story of a family Thanksgiving is accompanied by very clear representations of numbers and objects. For instance, when "Big Sister slices six skinny squash," in addition to the six squash in the main picture, the numeral 6 and a row of six squash appear at the top of the page. (Alert readers will also notice the numeral 6 in the loop of an electrical cord and will enjoy looking for the hidden numerals in all the other pictures.) *Feast for 10* (Falwell 1993) similarly uses the counting framework to tell the story of a family meal, in this case counting from 1 to 10 once while shopping for the meal and again while cooking and eating it. Since the pictures are somewhat less stylized than those in *1,2,3 Thanksgiving,* the counting of objects is slightly more challenging; rather than six squash clearly laid out in a row on a counter, readers are shown "seven dill pickles stuffed in a jar" that are indeed jammed together rather than carefully arrayed.

Two additional books use low-key animal themes to count from one to ten. In *Animal Sleepyheads: 1 to 10* (Cole 1988), the reader sees a series of somnolent animals, from "1 sleepy bunny curled up soft and snug" to "10 sleepy mice squeezed in just one bed." A little livelier story animates *When One Cat Woke Up* (Astley 1990), where the title character steals two fish, fights with three teddy bears, and so on. A two-page spread at the end of the book recapitulates the numbers of objects by laying them out in an array.

An animal book that is definitely *not* low-key is *The Right Number of Elephants* (Sheppard 1990), where we discover the usefulness of pachyderms for everything from pulling a train out of a tunnel (ten are needed) to "impress[ing] the neighbors with a quick circus" (five) to being a friend (just one). These elephants are not shy; they race and rollick and fill up the page.

Two other books, *The World from My Window* (Samton 1985) and *One White Sail* (Garne 1992), are very similar visually and would be interesting to present to children together. Both use bold shapes and bright colors to portray stylized numbers of objects in the natural world. In Samton's book, each picture contains echoes of the previous one, so that the five fish in the foreground on one page appear smaller and in outline when we see six trees on the next page. At the end of the book, readers see a two-page spread that recapitulates all the previous pictures, the animals and scenery spread out across the world. Garne's book is even brighter, as befits the strong sunlight in the Caribbean where it is set. The illustrations are strongly stylized, with "five blue doors in the baking hot sun" pictured with friezes of fish and palm trees underneath, while we see "nine steel drums sing a soft sweet tune" surrounded by a picture-frame design of musical notes.

The Numbers (Felix 1991) is an especially ingenious take on the simple counting book. A number of little mice seem to emerge right out of the paper of the pages of the book, paper that they have chewed on until it forms the shapes of numbers as large as they are. The number of mice on the page always matches the most recently chewed-out number. (This is one in a series of similar "mouse books" by the same illustrator.)

Finally, two other counting books begin with a much larger animal. *One Gorilla* (Morozumi 1990) starts with a scene of the gorilla sitting under a tree and goes on to show other "things I love," such as "four squirrels in the woods" and "ten cats in my garden," always accompanied by the charming, oddly ubiquitous gorilla. One wouldn't expect a book with the title of *The Life-size Animal Counting Book* (van Noorden 1994) to start with a big gorilla but it does. The book, although large-format, isn't big enough to show this primate from head to toe, but does manage a delightful close-up of head and paws with some of the gorilla's body seen in foreshortened form in the background. The book progresses to larger numbers of gradually smaller animals, with the nine guinea pigs being especially cute; it goes beyond ten to show us twenty butterflies and a hundred creepy crawlers laid out in an aesthetically pleasing array that makes them very easy to count. The appropriate number of ladybugs also appears around the border of every two-page spread.

An interesting new set of books for developing number concepts is the Count Me In series (Aertssen 1994; van Eeden 1994; van Loon 1994), recently translated from the Dutch. Each book has a numerical concept (such as recognizing sets of various sizes or getting a sense of larger numbers) embedded in a simple story. The intention is that children will notice and talk about the details in the pictures in ways that will spontaneously lead them to think about early number concepts. Counting rhymes are another good way to help young children think about numbers; they are especially valuable in helping children learn the sequence of numbers. *Tickle-toe Rhymes* (Knight 1989) is a collection of original rhymes, each one focusing on a different animal in a series of groupings from one through five. The busy cartoonlike illustrations encourage the reader to find each group (which add up to fifteen animals per poem). Michael Katz has selected *Ten Potatoes in a Pot and Other Counting Rhymes* (1990) from familiar sources as well as less common ones. The rhymes are arranged in order of quantity, with "baa, baa, black sheep's" three bags full coming early in the book and "eleven comets in the sky" near the end.

Counting books are not just for the very youngest of readers; many recent ones are meant to be pored over at length, offering a challenge to find and count objects that are not necessarily in plain sight. *Norman Rockwell's Counting Book* (Taborin 1977), an older book that may still be available in libraries, is a little more challenging than the usual number book because the pictures weren't originally designed for counting. The compiler's inspired selections lead us to interesting sets; for instance, Rockwell's famous painting of a young soldier whose neighbors and redheaded family spill out of their tenement apartments to welcome him is captioned "17 neighbors greet returning soldier." A special treats at the end of the book is three of

Rockwell's April Fool's pictures, in which the reader is invited to count the mistakes, like dolls with real human faces and flowers growing out of the floor. *From One to One Hundred* (Sloat 1991) also rewards close attention; it has a two-page spread for each number from one to ten and then by tens up to one hundred, with small pictures at the bottom indicating what can be counted; for instance, a winter scene contains fifty snowflakes, fifty huskies, fifty people, and so on.

Two books bring a sense of humor to themes that are not obviously about counting, at least at first glance. *One Day, Two Dragons* (Bertrand 1992) appears just to be about two little dragons who have to go to the doctor and get shots. But we soon realize that the numbers that fit so easily into the first line of the story ("One day, two dragons caught a cab to Three Bug Street") continue throughout the story, getting bigger as we go along. Sometimes the numbers lead to something countable in the picture ("Seven chairs in the waiting room were empty"), sometimes not ("The receptionist could talk for thirteen years about shots that tickle"). *When Sheep Cannot Sleep* (Kitamura 1986) doesn't look like a counting book at all; it seems to be merely a story about the creature that most of us count when *we* can't sleep. But we soon realize that the pictures of the insomniac sheep's wanderings are full of increasingly larger numbers of objects and that we can count (for instance) the fourteen colored pencils he discovers and the fifteen pictures he draws with them. The book comes to a satisfying end as he lies in bed thinking about his friends and relatives; an accompanying picture leads the reader, if not the protagonist, to finally count sheep.

Pigs from 1 to 10 (Geisert 1992) and *World of Wonders* (Ockenga & Doolittle 1988) can perhaps best be described as counting puzzle books; Geisart's story of a quest to find a mysterious cavern has the numerals from 0 to 9 hidden in the design of each of its monochrome pictures. For instance, in one of them, some stones falling through the air form the shape of a 2 while the ends of two logs look like a figure 8. Those who are fond of numbers will be delighted to see that the pigs' quest leads them to a series of strange rock formations in the shape of numerals, of which they make giant wooden copies to carry home. *World of Wonders* is a series of photographs of collections of objects for the numbers 1 through 12, with the object being to identify and count all the objects scattered throughout the picture. Keys to each picture at the back of the book show the care that the authors have taken to assemble appropriate items for each number. For instance, the photo for 5 has slips of paper with the names of the five senses, peppers representing the book *Five Little Peppers and How They Grew,* nickels, a pentagon, five golden rings, as well as other objects with no special connection to "fiveness," for a total of thirty-nine sets or concepts.

One last group of newer counting books uses the counting book format to inform the reader about other topics, often related to science or social studies. Jim Haskins has added *Count Your Way Through India* (1990a) and *Count Your Way Through Israel* (1990b) to his country series. These are social studies more than mathematical books, but do a nice job of picking interesting facts related to numbers. For instance, the India volume discusses the three pieces of furniture that Gandhi owned (a mat, a cot, and a spinning wheel) and why, while the Israel book explains the significance of the seven branches of the menorah. *The Wildlife 1 2 3* (Thornhill 1989) and *Mother Earth's Counting Book* (Clements 1992) use the counting-book format to explore nature themes. Thornhill's book uses vivid colors to illustrate animals from one panda to one thousand tadpoles, with a paragraph of information about each animal at the end of the book. Clements, counting up to ten and back down again, explores features of our planet such as two poles, four oceans, and seven continents; the back of the book gives information about the area of each ocean, about the islands (those chosen include one from each ocean), and about the other illustrations. The theme is a strongly ecological one about the unity and diversity of the planet.

Addition and subtraction

Teachers who want to explore a variety of models of addition and subtraction with young children will continue to find diverse representations of these operations in newer children's books. *Amelia's Nine Lives* (Balian 1986) starts with a situation equivalent to one (Nora's pet cat) but goes to zero when Amelia disappears. Amid talk of cats having nine lives, everybody in the neighborhood drops off cats that look like Amelia, but Nora just keeps crying. Finally, after over a week, with nine black cats crawling all over Nora's family, she finds the *real* Amelia, who looks, purrs, smells, and feels right . . . and is accompanied by four kittens! ("'Does that mean cats have fourteen lives?' asked [younger brother] Ernie.") The text is written so that readers can predict how many cats each new picture will show. *The Cat's Midsummer Jamboree* (Kherdian & Hogrogrian 1990) uses a predictable story pattern to model the addition of consecutive units to create increasingly bigger groups, with the added feature (since the addends are animals playing musical instruments) of introducing the musical terms *duet, trio, quartet, quintet,* and *sextet.* (When joined by a seventh animal, "the musicians became/a jamboree in a tree.") *The Bus Stop* (Hellen 1988) uses ordinal numbers to tell the simple story of people lining up for a bus ("First comes Mrs. Bishop. . . . Second is Jane Jackson."). The book uses cut pages so that each new standee flips over to join the others in line and when the bus comes (its page flipping over on top of them), we see all seven people through its cut out windows.

Many books that explore concepts of subtraction combine it with addition. *Arthur's Tooth* (Brown 1985) deals with a "take away one" situation intimately familiar to children: losing a tooth. The protagonist of *Bea's 4 Bears* (Weston 1992) takes readers through a very simple subtraction and addition process as she starts with four teddy bears and then strews them all over the house and yard until she can't find any of them and has "ZERO bears!"; she eventually retrieves them all and ends up, satisfyingly, with her original four. *Six Sleepy Sheep* (Gordon 1991) uses a tongue twister text (try saying "Soon one sheep snoozed. . . . Six sleepy sheep slumbered") to explore various names for six. As the sheep fall asleep one at a time, the pattern can be seen as repeated subtraction (six awake minus one asleep equals five awake, and so on) or as additive combinations (four awake and two asleep is the same six as three awake and three asleep). *Ten Bears in a Bed* (Richardson 1992) uses a pop-up format to explore a familiar subtraction rhyme; the reader uses pull tabs to knock each consecutive bear out of bed. All ten bears are always visible so that the progressive combinations (10 + 0, 9 + 1, and so on) can be easily constructed. Another bedtime addition/subtraction story is *Ten Out of Bed* (Dale 1993), about one child and nine stuffed animals. The number out of bed playing games keeps decreasing by one as the animals fall asleep; a small picture in the bottom corner of each page shows the animals asleep on the pillows, their number, of course, increasing by one with each new page. The most delightful new take on subtraction is *Ten Sly Piranhas* (Wise 1993); this school of vicious fish, drawn as roly-poly pink creatures with big toothy grins, loses a member on every page because piranhas cannot—alas!—even trust one another.

Multiplication

A relatively small number of new children's books deal with multiplication or related concepts (and we found none with division themes). Following *Two Feet* (Pascoe 1991) on their adventures in the world can help young children begin to think about sets of two. Noah's Ark is a perennial setting for animals in pairs, although the one seen in *Two by Two,* a 1984 story by Kathryn Hewitt, resembles a modern cruise ship and may be upsetting to traditionalists. *Piggies* (Wood & Wood 1991), featuring Don Wood's inimitable heightened illustrations, establishes pairs of fat, smart, long, silly, and wee little piggies perched on matching pairs of a narrator's life-size fingertips, then follows them through adventures of hot and cold, dirty and clean, skipping and dancing. Children just learning to count by twos will see the obvious two-by-two connection.

Three well-thought-out books explore multiplication concepts at a higher level. *One Hundred Hungry Ants* (Pinczes 1993) presents alternative arrays for one hundred, as the title creatures realize they'll reach the food at a picnic more quickly if they're in two rows of fifty, or better yet ten rows of ten, rather than one long line of a hundred. *Sea Squares* (Hulme 1991) uses a seashore setting to explore square numbers. Some of the choices are obvious: four seals have four feet each, for a total of sixteen, and of course 8×8 is represented by "eight eight-legged octopuses kicking in the ocean,/Stirring up the currents in a watery commotion." Other square numbers are created by giving animals big meals: seven pelicans each have seven fish in their pouches, and nine tubfish are each preparing to eat nine clams. Carol Schwartz's beautiful pictures have borders of seashells on the left side and a preview of the next page's picture on the right. *Each Orange Had 8 Slices* (Giganti 1992) is an ambitious book that presents visual representations of set-within-set models of multiplication. For instance, the first page in the book shows three flowers, each with six petals, with two bugs sitting on each petal. The text then asks readers to determine first the number of flowers, then the number of petals, and finally the number of black bugs in all. The answers are, respectively, 3, 18 (3×6), and 36 ($3 \times 6 \times 2$). The book wisely does not answer the questions or even provide advice about how to find out, leaving readers to explore the problems in their own ways. The pictures (by Donald Crews) are all laid out so that the answers can be found by counting yet also clearly show the equivalence of the sets, thus helping children recognize (or discover) that repeated addition or multiplication is possible. Teachers should be aware that a few of the questions are a little tricky: one scene is of three ducks, each followed by four baby ducks, each duck saying "quack, quack, quack." The total number of quacks is *not* $3 \times 4 \times 3$ but $(3 + (3 \times 4)) \times 3$ for a total of 45 quacks, since not only the baby ducks but the adults are quacking. The picture makes this clear, but adults need to be careful not to jump too quickly to an algorithm rather than letting children explore the pattern by themselves.

Fractions

The Teacher from the Black Lagoon (Thaler 1989) includes the concept of one half as a small part of its story. The narrator, on the first day of school, is shocked to discover that his teacher is a real monster, the kind that breathes fire. When a student responds to her assignment of two hundred pages of fraction problems by saying, "We've never had fractions," the teacher smirks, "This is a whole boy." After taking a big bite, she adds: "This is half a boy. Now you've had fractions." *The Little Mouse, the Red Ripe Strawberry, and the Big Hungry Bear* (Wood & Wood 1984) tells the simple story of a mouse who, afraid that a big bear is going to eat his strawberry, cuts it in half, gives half away, and eats the rest himself. *Eating Fractions* (McMillan 1991) is the story of two children, a luscious meal, and several fractions. A whole (such as a pizza) is shown on one page, then divided, then eaten by the children. Words and schematic representations are shown under each whole and each fractional part. Recipes for the meal are provided at the end of the book. *Half and Half* (Nelson 1990) is the story of a peddler who buys half of the sixteen pies made by a local pie maker (thus introducing the set model of fractions). He then sells or trades off half his remaining pies until only one is left, which is divided into halves and then halves again (thus representing both set and area models of fractions). *Fraction Action* (Leedy 1994) has more of an instructional format, a series of five lessons about fractions told in comic strips. A teacher demonstrates a variety of simple fraction concepts to her students: both the area and set models are included, using examples for 1/2, 1/3, and 1/4. The concept that the parts must be equal is also explored. This book and McMillan's would be good companion pieces when introducing fractions for the first time.

Big numbers

Children love to explore their fascination with big numbers. We'll discuss a number of relevant books, in the order of how big the numbers get! *The Wolf's Chicken Stew* (Kasza 1987) explores "hundredness" as a wolf tries to fatten up a chicken for eating by leaving a hundred pancakes, a hundred doughnuts, and a hundred-pound cake on her porch on successive nights. To his surprise, she doesn't eat them herself but feeds them to her large brood of chicks, who give the wolf a hundred kisses as thanks for his generosity. *Pumpkins* (Ray 1992) is the story of a farmer who, in order to raise money to save a field, plants seeds and harvests 461,212 pumpkins, which he distributes around the world by renting 1,400 trucks, 37 boats, 800 airplanes, and 100 flying carpets. Charming lists of place names recount some of the places where the pumpkins ended up ("in Kiev, Killarney, Khartoum and Tashkent, in Quito, Quebec, Cairo and Cadiz"). The book jacket reveals that the author was inspired by her work in conservation; she herself bought a field to prevent its development.

Moving up the number line to *A Million Fish . . . More or Less*, Patricia McKissack (1992) tells the tale of Hugh Thomas, who catches three fish and then a million more on the Bayou Clapateaux in Louisiana, but on the way home loses most of them to talking alligators and raccoons and some very hungry crows and cats. When he arrives home with only three fish, we realize that the story he is about to tell Papa-Daddy and Elder Abbajon about what happened to the rest grows out of their own tradition of storytelling. *One Million* (Hertzberg 1993), though not designed especially for children, is a wonderful way to help them understand what a million really looks like, since it contains a million dots, 5,000 to a page for 200 pages. To make this rather repetitious book a little livelier, each page singles out two or three numbers to connect with statistics. For instance, there are 63,360 inches in a mile; there were 244,723 British battle deaths in World War II; there are 650,782 people named Young in the United States; and the diameter of the sun is 864,000 miles. *One Million* will be of tremendous interest for children just to browse through and can also be used to generate discussion about how some of the statistics were arrived at and how accurate they are. (For instance, the number of inches in a mile is 63,360 by definition, while the diameter of the sun expressed as miles can only be a rough estimate, and the number of Youngs in the United States is constantly changing.) Hertzberg also provides an excellent introduction ("Five Thousand Words About One Million Dots") that provides an interesting overview of big numbers for adults. By the way, if you'd like your students to see what a billion dots look like, just buy a thousand copies of *One Million*!

Jumping to multimillions, *The Giant Jam Sandwich* (Lord 1972) tells what happens when four million wasps fly into the town of Itching Down, threatening to make everyone's summer pretty miserable. Fortunately, a baker realizes that the wasps' favorite food (strawberry jam) might be used to entice them, and the title sandwich, the size of a field, is created. The facing pages showing the wasps swooping down on the open-faced sandwich and then being smushed by the second slice of bread are especially satisfying, and birds end up feasting on the whole sticky mess so that nothing is wasted. It might be fun to estimate the size of the bread slices and number of wasps per square foot, as well as to determine how much the loaf of bread probably weighs and what the ingredient list would look like. A similar mass-quantity food story, although with smaller numbers, is *The Biggest Birthday Cake in the World* (Spurr 1991), in which the richest man in the world wants his fortieth birthday celebrated with a giant cake. *Land of Dark, Land of Light*

(Pandell 1993), although mainly about seasonal patterns of animals that live in the Arctic, introduces some large numbers in describing the profusion of life of the Arctic spring: we see crowded pictures representing the migration of tens, hundreds, thousands of birds and caribou, as well as animals suffering from some of the millions of mosquitoes that swarm.

Geometry

A large number of new children's book explore geometry topics, in part because geometry encompasses so much, from basic knowledge of shapes and of concepts like left and right to applications in art and architecture. Our discussion of these books focuses on five major areas: spatial orientation; shapes, both simple and sophisticated; shadows, reflections, and visual illusion; pattern and art; and architecture.

SPATIAL ORIENTATION

Books to help younger children explore concepts like up and down or left and right often have a very simple focus. *Look Up, Look Down* (Hoban 1992) uses a number of very different pictures to explore what you might see looking in one of these two directions. Hoban's pictures are composed in visually interesting ways: a break in a pavement is photographed on a diagonal as a backdrop for ants swarming around a piece of fruit, and an upward look through a tree's network of branches is placed across from a photo of weeds growing through the patterned holes in a circular grating. *Left or Right?* (Rehm & Koike 1991) uses photographs to ask a series of left-or-right questions of gradually increasing difficulty. The first page shows a picture of one child, then asks if he is on the left or right in a picture of two children. A question late in the book asks the reader to pick out a specific leaf from a display of others that look quite similar, and to discern that it is on the left when it is actually closer to the center of the page than to the edge. *Wheel Away!* (Dodds 1989) uses a number of spatial orientation terms as it follows a runaway bicycle wheel down, through, in, and over a varied landscape. The wheel is shown at the right-hand edge of every two-page spread, but a row of brightly colored dots shows its path, so that young readers have a precise visual referent for each spatial term. *If at First You Do Not See* (Brown 1982) and *Once upon Another* (MacDonald & Oakes 1990) both—in very different ways—play around with spatial orientation by using pictures that can be viewed upside down as well as right side up. *If at First You Do Not See* is the story of a caterpillar who keeps landing on what appear to be food sources, but he discovers (as do we as we follow the text around the edge of the page) that they are really people or creatures of one kind or another. For instance, two ice cream cones, when seen upside down, turn out to be clowns with cone-shaped hats. *Once upon Another* uses a single set of illustrations to tell two familiar fables, with the book turned upside down and read in reverse order for the second story. The pictures, which are collages of scraps of colored paper, are abstract enough that the fuzzy orange hare in one story becomes a lion when the book is turned upside down, while the purple blob of a tortoise becomes a little mouse. The pictures are *very* abstract; teachers will want to give children plenty of time to interpret them.

Two books play around in other ways with spatial orientation concepts. *The Moon Comes Home* (Salter 1989) travels with a little girl on a nighttime car ride home as she explores the continuity of the moon in relation to everything else around her. Grandmother's house gets smaller and then is left behind, cars "whoosh back like waves beside the long ship of our car," she has the illusion that the car is standing still while the trees race past backward, fenceposts blur into a wall, while all along the moon stays constant and still in the sky above. The style of the illustrations reinforces the sense of a dreamy, slightly surrealistic experience. *The Wrong Side of Bed* (Keller 1992) is even more surrealistic; for little Matt, getting up on the wrong side of the bed means that the whole world has temporarily turned upside down. To get down the stairs to breakfast, he has to leap *up* to, cling to, and climb up the banister; when he has nothing to step on outside the school bus door, he falls off into the big wide universe, where he floats for a while until he eventually comes back down and falls into bed. The illustrations are appropriately distorted and magical.

SHAPES

Books about shape help readers explore the contours and configurations of the world around us, as well as the role of shape in abstract mathematics. *Think About Shape* (Pluckrose 1986) is a fairly typical beginner book, using photographs to explore both names and properties of shapes. (Triangles can be arranged in a tiling pattern with no empty spaces, while we can clearly see that the same is not true for circular coins.) *Shapes in Nature* (Feldman 1991) uses photographs of scenes in nature and matching black outlines to help attune children to the shapes all around us. For instance, triangles are seen in mountains, fins, ice, and teeth. *Spirals, Curves, Fanshapes and Lines* (1992) is one of Tana Hoban's most exciting shape books because the pictures are diverse and the shapes involved take so many forms. Using both found and posed arrangements, Hoban invites readers to wonder at the fanshapes of a peacock's tail and an array of dozens of carrots, as well as the rapidly expanding spiral of a shell and the curvy lines of a tuba. *Circles* (Ross 1992), by contrast, focuses on only a single shape, but finds an amazing number of things to say about it and do with it. Aimed at upper elementary and middle school students, *Circles* also has chapters on spheres, discs, cylinders, cones, and spirals and is both an information book and an activity book. For instance, in the disc chapter, readers are invited to bake cookies in both disc and ball shapes to compare cooking times and taste, as well as to make a "super flyer" out of paper plates. We also learn about the history of wheels and about why no animals have ever evolved wheels instead of legs. This is an outstanding book.

The spherical shape of the earth is explored in *How We Learned the Earth Is Round* (Lauber 1990), which tells what conclusions the Greeks drew from observing the apparent rising and falling of ships on the horizon and the curved shadow on the moon during eclipses. This book also includes activities and experiments using spheres and other shapes. The same concept is explored from a psychological perspective in *Anno's Medieval World* (Anno 1980), which starts out by showing people standing on absolutely flat land, which gradually begins to take on the curvature of the earth as the author describes the evolution of human understanding that our planet is a sphere. By the end of the book, when the first explorers have set off to sail around the world, the people in the pictures are standing on a globe.

Shape: The Purpose of Forms (Laithwaite 1986) explores why particular shapes are used for particular functions. The point of view feels like an engineer's, with a section on how shapes are made (molding, cutting, forming) and many pictures of manufactured objects, such as a joint that moves in ways similar to the human hip. *By Nature's Design* (Murphy 1993) is perhaps the most exciting of the new shape books, and the one of most interest to adults. Created for the Exploratorium science museum in San Francisco, *By Nature's Design* explores six geometric patterns found in nature: spirals and helixes; meanders and ripples; spheres and explosions; branching; packing and cracking; and fractals. The fine-art photographs and the text are both outstanding; we learn how design in nature arises out of necessity (when water and wind flow along the path of least resistance) and efficiency (when sap travels through a system of branches to reach all the points in a large area while moving along the shortest possible distance). Each section of the book introduces the geometrical principle involved, then follows up with a dozen or so pages of photographic examples and commentary. Although most of the text is beyond the range of elementary school children, the pictures are extremely accessible and teachers can easily absorb and share the concepts. Most adults will learn something new from this book.

SHADOWS, REFLECTIONS, AND VISUAL ILLUSION

Shapes can be explored in shadows or mirror reflections, or in visual illusions—the exciting outer fringes of what we know and can do with shape.

In *Bear Shadow* (Asch 1985) a little bear out fishing discovers, just as many children do, that he can't escape his shadow, which seems to be scaring the fish away. He hides behind a tree, nails his shadow to the ground, and digs a hole for it to fall into, but he still can't get rid of it and finally makes a deal that if his shadow will let him catch a fish, it'll get a fish too: a shadow fish! *Shadow Geometry* (Trivett 1974) is a much more sophisticated treatment of shadows: a series of activities through which readers can explore how the shapes of shadows vary as the placement of the object and the light source change in relation to each other.

Mirror Magic (Simon 1991) examines the basic properties of mirrors and includes a few activities such as making a simple periscope and kaleidoscope.

Mirrors (Zubrowski 1992), an activity book developed by the Boston Children's Museum, is more elaborate, consisting of many games and experiments woven through explanations of how mirrors work and how they are used. In one very interesting game, one player builds a maze following specified criteria and the other must place two mirrors in such a way that a flashlight directed into the maze from a fixed point will cast light on a picture. Experiments with plane, transparent, and curved mirrors help older children explore many subtle features of reflection.

Curved mirrors are a source of anamorphic pictures, a type of visual illusion that is explored in a few new books. *Hidden Pictures* (Bolton 1993) is an exploration of illusion in the world of art, focusing especially on the kind of anamorphic pictures that are unviewable until a mirrored cylinder is placed at a particular spot on the page and the reflection in the cylinder reveals the true image. Nearly half of the two dozen pictures in the book are this type of anamorphic image; most of the others are paintings with double or hidden images (one of the book's examples of a double image is Salvador Dali's picture of a room that is also a face, with a sofa for lips, draperies for hair, and so on). The author, who teaches art history, has also included information about the artists' intentions and the historical context of many of the pictures. *Arithmetic* (Sandburg [1933] 1993), a classic poem, has been illustrated by Ted Rand with a series of anamorphic pictures, some of them involving the use of a mirrored cylinder and others that are seen without distortion by holding the book up to one's eye and looking across the image from a labeled point, thus foreshortening the elongated illustration. Sandburg's poem has a charmingly odd tone to it ("If you ask your mother for one fried egg for breakfast and she gives you two fried eggs and you eat both of them, who is better at arithmetic, you or your mother?"), making it an inspired choice for this unusual rendition. Both books include a sheet of Mylar to make a mirrored cylinder, and both provide instructions for making your own anamorphic drawings.

Some other books examine what might be called "classic" optical illusions, such as the two circles that appear to be different sizes because of the different-size circles that surround each one and the figure/background picture that can be seen as either a vase or two faces. *Picture Puzzler* (Westray 1994) depicts a number of the most familiar illusions in a bright folk-art style in which they stand out clearly. (The use of color in this book and others enlivens the presentation of these common illusions, which have usually appeared in black-and-white collections.) Many of the same optical illusions appear in *Opt* (Baum & Baum 1987), in which they are worked into a story set in an imaginary kingdom of illusions; the illusions are explained at the end of the book, along with suggestions for creating one's own. (*Opt* was the featured book on a recent *Reading Rainbow* program; a videocassette of the show can be ordered by calling 800-228-4630.) *The Optical Illusion Book* (Simon 1976) contains more text and focuses on how the illusions work. Younger readers would enjoy the first two books and older children could appreciate all three. *Pentamagic* (Pentagram Design 1992) has classic illusions and a little bit of everything else as well: simple magic tricks, color afterimage illusions, and a few anamorphic pictures (again, a sheet of Mylar is included). There are 150 separate displays in the book; Pentagram Design is known for its vivid graphics, and this book will reward many hours of attention.

Two books show samples of the illusionary work of illustrators known for their playfulness with shape. *The Unique World of Mitsumasa Anno* (Anno 1977), a compilation done at a relatively early stage of Anno's career, includes his own interpretations of several classic illusions and other oddities like a pair of Dalmatians whose patterns are reverse images of each other and a planet that is part moon, part earth. The forty pictures each reflect a distinct aspect of a creative visual mind. Readers might enjoy comparing Anno's impossible staircase with the ones found in *The Pop-up Book of M. C. Escher* (Blaze International Productions 1991). Books of Escher's weird and complex explorations of shape and pattern have become a mini-industry (one can usually buy Escher T-shirts, ties, and socks at NCTM conferences), but this book is unique. Eight pieces of paper engineering, each different in conception and execution, are an ideal tribute to Escher's vision, carrying it into an additional dimension. Brief texts reflect on the essence of each picture.

Finally, no discussion of visual illusions would be complete without a discussion of the new craze for 3-D illusions. At the time of this writing, *Magic Eye* and *Magic Eye II* (N. E. Thing Enterprises 1993, 1994) have been on the best-seller lists for months and *Magic Eye III* (1994) has just been published. Made possible by new computer technology, these slightly-out-of-synch images reveal a 3-D image when you make your eyes go out of focus in a certain way. Although some people find them easier to see than others (all the books provide instructions for learning to see them), these pictures are magical and a truly new category of optical illusion that should be included in any exploration of the topic. The *Magic Eye* collections have the best images, but other books, such as *Stereogram* (Horibuchi 1994) have many pictures and extensive background information. (*Stereogram* has many images that are seen correctly only with the more difficult cross-eyed technique, which appears to be more common in stereograms from Japan.)

Pattern and art

Geometry provides the foundation for various aspects of art; shapes and the relationships between them create particular aesthetic effects and underlie the theory of artistic composition. A few recent children's books explore the relationships between art and geometry from multiple perspectives. At a simple level, designs and minisculptures can be created by the arrangement of shapes such as tangrams (Ernst & Ernst 1990) and through origami and other kinds of paper folding (Aytüre-Scheele 1990; Huber & Claudius 1990). *Eight Hands Round* (Paul 1991) uses an alphabet-book format to illustrate twenty-six different patchwork patterns. Although the geometrical features of patchwork aren't addressed directly, the level of detail in the pictures makes it easy to explore how shapes such as squares, triangles, and hexagons can be fitted together to make an amazingly diverse collection of quilt patterns. In *Picture This* (1991), Molly Bang conducts an exciting exploration of the aesthetic and emotional aspects of shape and composition. Using simple cut paper shapes and just a few colors (black, white, red, and mauve), she thinks through different ways of staging the story of Little Red Riding Hood. Each left-hand page is a discussion of how we react to the composition on the right-hand page. For instance, Red Riding Hood is represented by a small red triangle, while three long black triangles are arranged to make the head of a wolf. When the wolf's eye is a red lozenge, it seems to be staring right at Red Riding Hood, and the way it echoes her redness makes it especially scary. The second half of the book uses the same format to explore more general principles, such as the emotional effect on the viewer of sharp points as opposed to curves.

A Short Walk Around the Pyramids and Through the World of Art (Isaacson 1993) is primarily an art appreciation book, but in a few cases focuses on how geometry creates particular artistic effects, as in the simple, stable shapes of the pyramids and the harmonious effect that is created when identical shapes are repeated throughout the buildings and layout of an entire town (a Spanish village of simple white boxlike houses arrayed along a hillside, for example). *Perspective* (Cole 1992), from the deservedly popular Eyewitness Art series, explores that most mathematical of artistic techniques, using both diagrams and reproductions of paintings. Topics discussed include the "invention" of perspective, the powerful effects of foreshortening, and the creative uses to which perspective has been put in the work of artists from different countries over several centuries. The trademark Eyewitness format of spreading multiple pictures and blocks of text across the page make for an exciting exploration of the relationship between mathematics and art. *The Art Pack* (Frayling, Frayling & Van der Meer 1992) is a box of wonders between the cover of a book. Paper engineering and other special features are used to explore how artists achieve their effects and how to interpret the resulting images. A surprisingly large amount of this short but complex book relates to the mathematics of art: there are pop-up screens that show how a three-dimensional image can be converted into a two-dimensional one with perspective; images of running horses on a paper wheel that can be spun to create the illusion of movement; a pop-up Parthenon with an overlay of its Golden Section proportions; and much more. *The Art Pack* was designed for adults (and a few of the art reproductions contain nudes), but it is one of the most exciting books around for exploring some of the mathematical principles underlying art.

ARCHITECTURE

The most practical of arts is architecture, and mathematics is central to how buildings are put together and why they stay up. There are a large number of new architecture books for children; the ones discussed below offer some direct exploration of the design and mathematical (particularly geometric) principles involved; the reference list also includes architecture books without a specifically geometric focus.

For younger readers, *The Clever Carpenter* (Alley 1988) explores the concept of artistic vision in the story of a carpenter who is unappreciated by his community because he builds structures that reflect his quirky views of the relationship between function and aesthetics—a dresser has drawers shaped like socks and T-shirts and a playground slide looks like a fancy roller coaster.

Three recent books use illustrations of real houses to develop the concept that houses are built in many different ways. At the simplest level, *Houses and Homes* (Morris 1992) shows a number of houses from around the world that contrast across features like size, building material, and shape. *This Is My House* (Dorros 1992), written for slightly older readers, shows houses in various parts of the world and includes a paragraph about how each house is built for or fits into its environment. *The House I Live In* (Seltzer 1992) has a narrower geographical focus, looking at diverse houses across the United States, and talks at length about the specifics of history, geography, and design that affected the form each house took. For instance, stone houses in Pennsylvania were built when early farmers had to remove an abundance of stones from fields before plowing, and the bay windows of San Francisco's Victorian houses provided more accessible views of San Francisco Bay than flat windows would have.

Two books by Gail Gibbons, who is known for her informational books for younger readers, explore the details of architectural construction. *How a House Is Built* (1990a) takes us through the erection of a wood-frame house from the architect's design and the digging of the foundation through the final touches of plumbing, electrical wiring, and landscaping. *Up Goes the Skyscraper* (1990b) does the same thing for a much larger building. Books for older readers provide even more detail about the construction of specific kinds of structures. *A Skyscraper Story* (Wilcox 1990) provides an interesting contrast to the Gibbons book on the same topic; in addition to being more detailed as befits its older audience, it is illustrated with photographs and is about the building of a specific skyscraper, Norwest Center in Minneapolis (the book has a foreword by the architect, Cesar Pelli). Photographs taken from varied distances and at different stages of construction are excellent counterparts to a text that explains, for instance, why elevators are crucial to the building of such a tall structure and how the internal structure of the building rather than the walls are what holds it up. A particularly interesting feature for the mathematically minded is a "shopping list" of the materials used to build Norwest Center: eight acres of glass (enough to cover twelve football fields) and 33,000 cubic yards of concrete (enough to fill fifty-eight railroad cars). *Bridges* (Robbins 1991) explores features such as diagonal trusses, arches, and peaked roofs (on covered bridges) that make these beautiful structures work so well.

Another excellent architectural book for young readers is *Frank Lloyd Wright for Kids* (Thorne-Thomsen 1994). The book nicely weaves together the life of this famous architect with numerous hands-on activities. Readers learn about Wright's early years on a Wisconsin farm, his love of nature, and his fascination with a set of geometric shapes known as Freobel blocks. Black-and-white photographs of his famous houses, such as Fallingwater and the Frederick C. Robie House in Chicago, as well as architectural drawings and floor plans, are other interesting features. Numerous activities throughout the book emphasize important architectural ideas, such as symmetry, pattern, and the use of basic geometric shapes. For instance, readers are given instructions on how to build a cantilever, how to create a model of Fallingwater with graham crackers, and how to make a model textile block from plaster.

Stephen Biesty's Incredible Cross-sections (Biesty 1992) is a wonderful oversize collection of cutaway views of buildings (e.g., a castle, an observatory, and the Empire State Building) and other structures (e.g., an oil rig and a steam train), making this an exploration of not just architecture but also engineering. Numbers in many cases supplement the information about design; for instance, displayed right beneath a picture of an ocean liner is a number line showing length in feet and below that seven Statues of Liberty laid end to end as a basis for comparison; another set of pictures shows the roughly one thousand crew members and two thousand passengers that the ship holds, grouped in arrays to make their numbers more visibly comparable. (Brown 1992, Fleisher & Keeler 1991, and Wilkinson 1993 are similar books that would work well in conjunction with this one.) Another book that relates architecture to broader engineering principles is *Nature by Design* (Brooks 1991), which explores the architecture created by animals, in many cases making direct connections to the form and function of human structures. Brooks is careful not to anthropomorphize; in his first chapter he comments that

> *attributing humanlike intentions to an animal can keep us from looking at the animal's sense of itself in its surroundings—its immediate and future needs, its physical and mental capabilities, its genetic instincts. . . . [Yet] animal structures let us have it both ways—we can be struck with a strange wonder, and we can empathize right away too. (p. 7)*

Throughout the book he connects readers to animal architecture not through attributing human intentions to these creatures but by appreciating the absolute rightness of their structures for the environments of which they are part.

Finally, for exploring in detail how architecture and engineering help humans create structures that defy the downward pull of gravity, *Building* (Salvadori 1979) takes readers through a series of simple constructions using ordinary materials like string, paper, and small weights to examine how to compensate for the forces like tension, compression, and wind that act on buildings. (*What It Feels Like to Be a Building* [Wilson 1988] also develops a sense of these forces by helping readers imagine their own bodies experiencing the forces operating on structures such as an arch.) The fifteen chapters of *Building* explore every major architectural structure in terms of its underlying geometrical principles. It is also a good introduction to architectural principles for teachers and for older students who can read the book on their own, and could be used to plan projects for younger children as well.

Measurement

Measurement pervades our lives and our thoughts: How fast do I run? When will I be as tall as my big brother? How big *were* those dinosaurs anyway? How many days until summer vacation? It is therefore no surprise that there are many, many new children's books that relate to one aspect or another of measurement. Since there are so many of these books, we will discuss a limited number of books under seven subtopics: comparisons; the measurement process; maps and mapping; animals; length, weight, and volume; money; and time. The reference lists at the end of the chapter provide additional titles and include two additional categories: cookbooks, which provide practical experiences in measuring; and several books about pumpkins (which for some reason seem to be currently popular), all dealing with size or measurement in some way.

COMPARISONS

Three books for younger readers show children (unfortunately, all boys!) thinking about their sizes in comparison to the world around them. Angus, in *Angus Thought He Was Big* (Graham 1991), thinks he is big until he meets Ernie, a tall clown, and keeps refining his notion about what bigness is as he encounters an elephant, a circus, cities, mountains, the world, and finally outer space. In *How Tall Are You?* (Nelson 1990), the world the child compares himself to remains constant while his own size changes. As he grows from the age of one to the age of six, he notices that he is becoming taller than some of his toys and pets. *George Shrinks* (Joyce 1985) puts a surrealistic spin on children's smallness in relation to the world around them: the title character wakes up small one morning (about the size of a mouse) and tries to grapple with the list of tasks his parents have left him. (It's fun to wash the dishes when you can use a sponge as a surfboard!) It's the environment that dwarfs the normal-sized people in the similarly eccentric *June 29, 1999* (Wiesner 1992), in which Holly Evans's research on the effects of extraterrestrial conditions on vegetable growth goes sadly awry and the whole country is inundated with broccoli as big as houses and red peppers that have to be anchored like giant hot-air balloons. (Adults will appreciate the "wisely abandoned" Potatoland, with its giant sculptures of Reagan, Nixon, and Carter.) A new series of four books by Anita Ganeri (all 1992) uses paired questions and pictures to explore comparisons in the world around us. The wealth of information provided offers many opportunities for further explorations. For instance, rather than just telling which planets spin the fastest and the slowest, Ganeri (1992b) compares the rotation speeds if one were standing on earth or on Jupiter and also points out that Jupiter spins 580 times to Venus's one. The illustrations are often clever; the four-millimeter "smallest wheels ever"—those inside pre-quartz movement wristwatches—are blown up here (1992a) to the size of the picture of the biggest wheels (twice as high as a horse), which belong to a dump truck.

THE MEASUREMENT PROCESS

The books in this category deal in one way or another with the human process of measuring: How do we decide what to measure? How do we go about it? What results do we get from different kinds of measuring tools? *Counting on Frank* (Clement 1991), discussed at length in earlier chapters of this book, takes us inside the mind of a mathematical thinker as he calculates how many of his dog could fit into his bedroom and how high toast would shoot up from a toaster as big as a house. One of the real delights of the book is how it helps us look at the whole world around us mathematically. In *Sam Baker, Gone West* (Raphael & Bolognese 1977, adapted from the Tolstoy story "How much land does a man need?") a greedy man is promised all the land he can walk around in one day. He is torn by indecision as he tries to walk as far outward as he can, yet still leave enough time to make it back to his starting point before nightfall. The twist at the end is Tolstoy's; we find out that a hole in the ground six feet long is ultimately all the land a man needs. (Narode [1994] has written about the different versions of this story and how it can be used in the classroom.)

Ten Mile Day and the Building of the Transcontinental Railroad (Fraser 1993; also discussed in Chapter 7) tells the true story of a feat of measurement and engineering, the day in 1869 when a team working in Utah was challenged to lay an unprecedented ten miles of track on the western section of the transcontinental railroad just days before it was to join up with the eastern section. Although this is not primarily a mathematical story, numbers appear throughout the book, along with maps and illustrations that would stimulate readers to create, for instance, a chart coordinating time and distance or a combination of writing and art exploring the placement of all the materials in the ten historic miles of track. The following excerpt from the text shows how integral numbers are to this true story:

> *The railhead was ten miles, fifty-six feet farther east than it had been the previous evening. . . . A total of 3,520 rails, twice that number of fishplates, 28,160 spikes, and 14,080 nuts and bolts had been placed to complete the job. The eight track layers were declared heroes and were featured in later histories. Each had lifted over 125 tons of iron.*

Moving ahead in time to the latest in measurement technology, two books use thrilling illustrations and accompanying text to explore the greatly magnified universe of the electron microscope. *Magnification* (Norden & Ruschak 1993) is the more spectacular, since it combines microscope technology with paper-engineering technology to create some delightful surprises. (The first page greets you with a pop-up ladybug 620 times normal size.) After a brief explanation of how microscopes work, the book offers pop-up and lift-the-flap examples ranging from dust bunnies to ticks to a housefly's foot at different magnifications. In some cases, we peek under a flap to guess what we've just seen at many times life size, while in others the same item appears at different magnifications above and below the flap. (The flap showing Velcro is held closed by pieces of Velcro affixed to the appropriate halves of the picture.) While *Magnification* totally entrances us in a mere fourteen pages, *Microaliens'* (Tomb & Kunkel 1993) seventy-five pages provide a more in-depth view of the same topic. Six chapters show magnified images ranging from denizens of the air (bees, pollen, bird feathers) to the cells inside our bodies. This book, which will help students learn about parts of our world too small to be seen with the naked eye, is also an exploration of the frontiers of how we measure.

MAPS AND MAPPING

Maps are one of the more interesting applications of measurement, since they are an interpretation of our world as well as a representation of it and since there are so many choices involved in creating a map (what scale? what balance between natural features like topography and human features like roads? how much detail?). *As the Crow Flies* (Hartman 1991) is a nice introduction to the idea that a map is a mental representation. We see an eagle, a rabbit, a fish, and a crow in their relationships to the world around them, followed by a map that would serve each of them. (For instance, the rabbit's map follows a path from burrow to garden.) At the end, the moon shines over a "big map" that pulls together all the others.

A number of other books address elements of creating and reading maps, typically providing short essays on a number of topics. For example, *Around and About Maps and Journeys* (Petty & Wood 1993) uses the image of a child floating over his neighborhood in a hot-air balloon to point out that a map is like the view from above, then compares his largely pictorial map with a more complete street plan of the same area. *Maps and Globes* (Knowlton 1985) takes a (literally and figuratively) more global perspective, using the history of maps, at first based on an incomplete knowledge of the world, to show how modern maps all begin from an understanding of the spherical shape of the earth. *Let's Investigate Marvelously Meaningful Maps* (Carlisle 1992) has especially good sections on weather maps, charts of the oceans, and the process of mapmaking.

Pictorial Maps (1991), by Nigel Holmes, is a wonderful reference. Holmes has been graphics director of *Time* magazine since 1978, and the book contains a diverse collection of maps for students to browse through and is a valuable information source for the teacher. Holmes includes about every kind of map illustration imaginable, some of them purely graphic (a swimming pool in the shape of the United States for a Holiday Inn advertisement), some historical (a 1547 chart of the coast of North America), and some an inspired blend of graphic design and information (a bird's-eye view of West 53rd Street in Manhattan, created for the Museum of Modern Art). Holmes also includes a technical chapter on matters such as projections, scale, and symbols. (Warning: Before bringing this book into a classroom, you may want to excise the last map in the book, which looks like a map but is actually a detailed diagram of sexual intercourse!)

ANIMALS

Many animal books explore measurement by comparing animals to each other. *How Big? How Fast? How Hungry?* (Waverly 1990) compares other cats to the house cat; the tiger is bigger (six hundred pounds as opposed to eight), the cheetah is faster (it can reach speeds of seventy miles per hour versus the house cat's thirty), and the lion is hungrier (it can eat seventy-five pounds of meat at a time, whereas the house cat eats one fifth of a pound).

Some animal books explore measurement by illustrating animals life size. *Large as Life: Daytime Animals* (Cole 1985a) and *Large as Life: Nighttime Animals* (Cole 1985b) present charming images of animals in their environments and also include further information at the end of the book about the size, habits, and habitats of each animal.

Children are always curious about the sizes of dinosaurs since we can't, of course, see them at the zoo. *Patrick's Dinosaurs* (Carrick 1989a) takes an ingenious approach; every time his brother uses an analogy to explain the size of a dinosaur, Patrick visualizes the dinosaur in the here and now, and the illustrations echo his thoughts. For instance, when Patrick is told that a stegosaurus was bigger than a car, "in his mind the lane of cars was a line of walnut-brained stegosauruses. The plates on their backs swayed like sails as they plodded along." When his brother tells him that a tyrannosaurus was two stories high, "he peeked into his bedroom. Sure enough, the ugly head of the tyrannosaurus almost filled his window." The tone of the pictures is a charming blend of fear and whimsy. Bernard Most, who has created several dinosaur books, uses a similar technique in *How Big Were the Dinosaurs?* (1994), showing, for instance, a diplodocus that was as long as a basketball court with its head in one basket and its tail in the other. He uses the same format in *The Littlest Dinosaurs* (1989), but is able to put these creatures in homier settings since they are so much smaller. (The tylocephale was about the length of a comfortable sofa, and the six-foot-long ovirapotor, whose name means "egg thief" is shown raiding the refrigerator.) It is interesting to compare Most's cartoonlike illustrations with Carrick's more realistic ones.

LENGTH, WEIGHT, CAPACITY, VOLUME

A few new books deal with single aspects or types of measurement. *Supergrandpa* (Schwartz 1991) tells the true story of sixty-six-year-old Gustav Hakansson, who in 1951 rode 1,761 kilometers in the Sverige-Loppet, the longest bicycle race in Sweden's history. *One-Eyed Jake* (Hutchins 1979), an exploration of principles of weight and water displacement, is the amusing story of a pirate captain; his crew hate him but, afraid of his anger, they have to trick him to leave his employ. One by one they get away. One-Eyed Jake robs the passengers of a ship of all their jewels, whose weight threatens to sink his own boat, but he tosses the cook, who is heavier than the jewels, onto the other ship (which is just where the cook had hoped to find a job). Similarly, the bosun is tossed onto a cargo boat to compensate for the weight of stolen feathers and the cabin boy ends up on a fishing boat. When the cabin boy throws the key to the cabin back to Jake, it adds just enough extra weight to sink the ship!

The Mitten (Brett 1989) tells the story of a lost mitten whose stretchiness enables it to expand in capacity from the size of a young boy's hand to a temporary warm home for a mole and then, crowding in one at a time, a rabbit, a hedgehog, an owl, a badger, a fox, and even a bear. When a mouse joins the throng, however, its whiskers tickle the bear and the resulting sneeze shoots the mitten into the air and sends the animals flying. *Knowabout: Capacity* (Pluckrose 1988) is a more focused look at capacity that uses photographs to model how we fill empty spaces in order to measure and compare how much they hold.

For exploring volume, *Carrot Holes and Frisbee Trees* (Bodecker 1983) is a charming novella about a couple who just want to be ordinary gardeners but end up growing carrots so large that they are most useful as shade trees when they are still in the ground and as lumber after they are pulled. And the seeds of these carrots make good Frisbees. (The final picture of a carrot on a flatbed truck looks remarkably like a giant redwood.) *Spaces, Shapes and Sizes* (Srivastava 1980) examines volume more formally, suggesting a number of experiments using sand, popcorn, toys, and apples.

MONEY

Recent (or recently discovered) children's books on money topics fall into three major categories: stories about earning money, renditions of the story of money, and consumer-oriented books. *Willis* (Marshall 1974) tells the story of a group of animals who need to earn nineteen cents to buy a twenty-nine-cent pair of sunglasses. Their enterprises are not very successful, however; a rhinoceros is not at all pleased by their spontaneous repainting of her house, they're failures as lifeguards because they don't know how to swim, and they eat all the merchandise they're supposed to be assembling at a candied-peanut factory. Fortunately, they eventually use their unique talents to put on a show and earn enough to buy four pairs of sunglasses, in the process communicating a nice message that "everyone is good for something." *The Magic Money Machine* (Nelson 1990) is about a boy who saves a stack of pennies, groups them by ten, and then finds they're too heavy to carry to the store. However, a friend supplies a magic money machine to exchange pennies for dimes and dimes for dollars. *How the Second Grade got $8,205.50 to Visit the Statue of Liberty* (Zimelman 1992) starts out as a straightforward account by the class treasurer but soon turns into a satire as the class's profits get depleted by parking tickets, a cat's falling into the tub of lemonade for their lemonade stand, and so on. Just as the reader despairs that the second grade will ever get to New York, they foil a bank robbery and claim a hefty reward. This book may not emphasize the virtues of thrift and hard work, but it's a pretty funny read! *What's Cooking, Jenny Archer?* (Conford 1989) is a short novel about a budding cook who, upon being offered a friend's lunch money if she'll make his lunch every day, sets out on a rapidly expanding small business ("$1.50 times 5 days = $7.50. $7.50 times four people = $30.00. Thirty dollars a week! Just for making four extra lunches"), with disastrous consequences as ingredients use up a lot of her money, recipes fizzle, and her dog eats the $5.50 worth of meat that she'd set on the counter for chicken sandwiches. The financial calculations throughout the book keep the reader in tune with the mathematics of running a small business.

Three recent books (two of them with the same title) give young readers a sense of the history and uses of money. *Round and Round the Money Goes* (Berger & Berger 1993) is aimed at younger readers than the other two (and is indeed part of a series of books for early readers). In a relatively short space it explores the nature of money as a universal exchange medium; how money grew out of bartering and eventually became more abstract; how money is made; and explanations of earning, spending, saving, interest, and credit. Carolyn Kain's *Story of Money* (1994) focuses especially on history, finishing with an overview of money in today's world as well as some social aspects such as what taxes are used for and relationships between rich and poor countries. Betsy Maestro's book with the same title (1993) has a strongly historical and global feel; the first third of the book is devoted to methods of exchange that preceded the first coins; throughout, maps and pictures represent many countries of the world and their money. Appendixes include information about unusual money, descriptions of the pictures on each American bill, and the names of currency units of thirty-two countries.

The Monster Money Book (Leedy 1992) is an introduction to consumer issues for young readers, written in comic-strip style. The members of the Monster Club add up their dues money and, in thinking about what to spend it on, consider issues of quality, price, investment, charitable donation, and banking. *Caution! This May Be an Advertisement* (Gay 1992), written for a teenage audience but probably usable in upper elementary and middle school, offers an up-to-date overview of the psychology and business of advertising and focuses on informing and enlightening young consumers by helping them understand the techniques that are being used on them. One particularly interesting story is that of the invention and marketing of the ever-popular Flintstones chewable vitamins.

TIME

There are dozens of books on time, some of them embedding time concepts into picture books, some using the sweep of history to tell a story, and some focusing on information and exposition. In *The Completed Hickory Dickory Dock* (Aylesworth 1990), we find out what happens *after* "the clock struck one, and down he run," all the way up to "silvery, bilvery beams. The mouse had wonderful dreams. The clock struck twelve, now dream some yourselves." *Train Leaves the Station* (Merriam 1992) uses times of the day as part of a counting rhyme. ("Salt in the ocean, clay in the bricks, train leaves the station at six-o-six.") *Today Is Monday* (Carle 1993) uses the days of the week and a food for each one to create a cumulative text ("Saturday, chicken/Friday, fresh fish/Thursday, roast beef . . ."), with music for singing it provided at the end. *The Best Time of Day* (Flournoy 1978) explores the human context of the hours of the day, following young William through waking up, doing chores, eating meals, playing, and other events of a busy day, through Daddy's coming home (the time alluded to in the title), a pleasant evening, and bedtime. *Only Six More Days* (Russo 1988) tells a story about the psychological dimension of time for about-to-be-five-years-old Ben, who fills the days until his birthday by counting party favors, listing party games, and clearing off shelf space for his presents.

Three slightly longer picture books deal with seconds, hours, and the course of a year respectively. *Thunder Cake* (Polacco 1990), a story about making a cake before a thunderstorm arrives on a grandmother's farm (getting eggs from the chicken, milk from the cow, and so on), features a race against time as a young girl counts off seconds between lightning flashes and thunder to judge how far away the storm is. *Nine O'clock Lullaby* (Singer 1991) is a wonderful tour of the world through its time zones, with 10 P.M. in Puerto Rico featuring "sweet rice, fruit ice, coconut candy. Papa playing congas, Tío his guitar," while at 11 A.M. in Japan, "in the pond grandfather floats a tulip so the fish can greet the spring." *Farm Boy's Year* (McPhail 1992) recreates a month-by-month diary of an imagined farm child a century ago in New England, with sledding in January, fishing in April, and hunting in November.

A number of books explore the passage and effects of time by following a single site through history. John S. Goodall (1979, 1990, 1992a, 1992b, 1992c) has created a series of primarily wordless books that explore largely English settings in different time periods. For instance, half-pages provide multiple views of *The Story of an English Village* (1979) from the fourteenth century to the late twentieth century, while *The Story of the Seashore* (1990) shows Britons at the beach in peace and war, in good weather and bad, at home and abroad. *The Big Tree* (Hiscock 1991) follows a maple in upper New York State from its sprouting in 1775 (the year of Paul Revere's ride) to the present day, with informational side trips that explore the process of photosynthesis, the nature of sap, and the annual process of budding and leafing. *Everything from a Nail to a Coffin* (Van Rynbach 1991) tells the true story of a more human endeavor, a small-town store built in 1874 that has gone through several changes of name and owner but still exists today. Multiple pictures of the store's interior carry us from the days of penny candy and soda fountains to today's hardware and computers. *Life Story* (Burton 1962), by the well-known author/illustrator of *The Little House*, takes the broadest possible historical scope, presenting the history of life on earth as a five-act play (with a prologue covering the time from the birth of the sun to the depositing of sedimentary rock). Act 1 stars trilobites and other invertebrates, Act 2 the dinosaurs, and so on, up through Act 5, which explores the present time through day and night and the seasons of the year. Most of the double-page spreads show a globe with a caption indicating how long ago the scene took place. Although Burton's paleontological data is bound to be a bit dated, the sweep and scope of this book make it special.

Franklyn Branley has written three books that help young readers learn about specific aspects of time, two of them—*What Makes Day and Night* (1986) and *Sunshine Makes the Seasons* (1985)—new editions of earlier volumes in the Let's-Read-and-Find-Out Science Book series. *What Makes Day and Night* asks readers to imagine themselves seeing our planet from out in space and uses multiple diagrams of the earth to show how the spatial relationship between the earth and sun creates the daily cycle of light and dark. Readers are also invited to conduct a demonstration using themselves as the earth and a lamp as the sun. *Sunshine Makes the Seasons* extends the same principle to following the course of light and dark throughout the year, using an orange (with a pencil stuck through it to simulate the earth's axis) to explore the effects of a tilted axis. *Keeping Time* (1993) is a more comprehensive look at time and is aimed at older readers. It has chapters on scientific aspects of time ranging from the length of a day to a simple explanation of the time distortions predicted by the theory of relativity. It also features extensive discussions of socially constructed features of time such as daylight savings time, the names of the days, and the evolution of our calendar. Simple projects show readers how to make a sundial, a number of simple clocks, and a model of the International Date Line.

Two recent books provide comprehensive overviews of time for younger and older readers. *My First Book of Time* (Llewellyn 1992), from the same publisher as *My First Number Book* (Heinst 1992), uses a large-scale format to help readers learn to tell time in both digital and analog formats, as well as to explore concepts like day and night, days of the week, and the kinds of growth that can be seen in days (seeds), weeks (a duck), and years (people). A fold-out clock with movable hands appears at the back and is referred to throughout the book as an aid in answering questions and solving puzzles. *Big Book of Time* (Edmonds 1994), which grew out of the author's study of children's conceptions of time, uses double-page spreads to explore not only the usual concepts of hours, months, and years but also the meaning of spans such as moments (defined psychologically as a fleeting event or change in state such as the moment when lightning hits a tree), the role of personal and historical decades in our lives, and the big bang, when time first began. This wonderful book, which begins with "now" and ends with "forever," connects us to the philosophical and magical aspects of time.

Puzzles and games

Math puzzles continue to be made into books as new puzzles are invented and old ones are recycled for new audiences. A particularly lively new entry is *Puzzlooney!* (Ginns 1994), which uses a cartoon format to present puzzles that mostly involve the use of logic and in most cases include some numerical aspect. For instance, a picture of eight oddly decorated currency notes is accompanied by directions to grab the one that's worth the most money, keeping in mind that: "A bill with a picture of a woman on it is worth triple the printed value. Divide the value by two if the printed value is an even number. A bill with a seven anywhere on it is worth nothing." *The Great Book of Math Teasers* (Muller 1989) is a lively collection of short problems at various levels of difficulty and covering a variety of mathematical topics. This book would be enjoyable for puzzle fans in the upper elementary grades, and it is a useful resource for a "puzzle of the week" to share with a class. An easy puzzle asks how long it will take thirty hens in four coops to hatch thirty eggs if twenty hens in three coops hatch them in eighteen days. (The answer is eighteen days; the hatching process can't be speeded up!) A harder puzzle asks the reader to calculate the value of the sequence $2 - 4 + 6 - 8 + 10 - 12 + 14$ up to 210.

Some puzzle books focus on a particular topic or theme. *Map and Maze Puzzles* (Dixon & Parekh 1993), a British book that is available in the United States, presents a series of beautifully designed maps of imaginary places with accompanying puzzles that involve mazes, codes, and logic and are couched in language that will appeal to readers who enjoy fantasy. ("On the way to Lollo Rosso, a sinister stranger, the Long Knight of Howles, invites Sir Gelfrid and Hildegarde to supper at his fortress.") *Math Fun with Money Puzzlers* (Wyler & Elting 1992) mixes straight puzzles ("What is the greatest number of coins you can have and still not make change for a dollar?") with consumer information (what the interest rates on bank loans and credit cards add up to in actual cash spent, and even what the 20 percent a week in interest that a loan shark might charge comes out to!).

Math puzzles can be turned into a form of magic for young readers to try out on their friends. *Math-a-magic* (White & Broekel 1990) describes some twenty tricks under the headings "The trick," "How to do it," and "The Math-a-magic secret." An example is "Super Memory," where the magician asks a friend to write down and then slowly read off a list of fifteen digits, circle one of them, then read off the remainder in any order, after which the magician names the circled number. The trick is to mentally add the numbers in each list, then determine the difference. (How nice, in these days of calculators, to value mental arithmetic!) The similarly titled *Math-emagic* (Blum 1991) includes calculator, card, memory, and other tricks, along with some "Funny Stuff" like the picture of the three and a half of clubs that is meant to be photocopied, glued onto a joker, and put in an envelope for the finale of a trick in which you claim to produce a card with half the face value of the already revealed seven of clubs. A promising new series of books is based on the children's television show *Mathnet. The Case of the Unnatural* (Connell & Thurman 1993), the first book of several available in this series of paperback originals, solves a mystery while incorporating three types of math problems and puzzles: batting averages, guess my rule (determining functions), and an alphanumeric code.

Some adult books are of interest here. *Ask Marilyn* (vos Savant 1992), by the author of the popular "smartest-woman-in- the-world" column in *Parade* magazine, includes two chapters of excellent puzzles, many of them accessible to children. One of the best of these is the game show puzzle: "You're given a choice of three doors. Behind one door is a car, the others, goats. You pick a door, say #1, and the host, who knows what's behind the doors, opens another door, say #3, which has a goat." Should you switch to door #2? Vos Savant not only answers the puzzle but prints a wide selection of the letters that were sure she was wrong. (By the way, yes, you should switch.) A sequel, *More Marilyn,* published in 1994, also includes a number of brain teasers and logic puzzles. *A Gallery of Games* (Marchon-Arnaud 1994) gives especially clear pictures and instructions for making a variety of simple games, many of which could be constructed as class projects. The multiple versions of several games are charming, such as checkerboards made out of matchboxes or a beach mat, created to fit on a page divider, or built in the sand out of stones and shells. *Favorite Board Games You Can Make and Play* (Provenzo & Provenzo 1981) provides patterns and rules for many of the classic games such as Nine Men's Morris, mancala, and fox and geese. Some of those included, such as Snakes and Ladders and backgammon, are already widely available (and perhaps overfamiliar) in commercial versions, but many of the others will be new to children and are often quite simple to construct.

Jack Botermans and Jerry Slocum (sometimes working with other authors) have produced a series of attractive illustrated collections of games and puzzles, with detailed instructions for their construction. Slocum and Botermans are true aficionados; Slocum has a personal collection of over 18,000 mechanical puzzles. Although these books are written for adult audiences, the number and quality of illustrations make them accessible to children. *The World of Games* (Botermans et al. 1989) is the most comprehensive, describing some 150 games from hopscotch to lacrosse to dice games, in many cases with instructions for making them. *Puzzles Old and New* (Slocum & Botermans 1986) is an exhaustive collection of an amazing variety of puzzles and includes many, many photographs of historic and modern puzzles (e.g., old sliding block puzzles and dozens of variations on Rubik's cube). Patterns are given for many of the puzzles. Although some of them are beyond the range of elementary school children (making them involves hardwood and bandsaws), others can be made of cardboard and other simple materials. Solutions to many of the puzzles, including popular ones like the Soma cube and the Tower of Hanoi, are provided in the back of the book. (Warning: A puzzle on p. 114 has an offensive name, the Jolly N——.) The most recent book by these authors, *New Book of Puzzles* (Slocum & Botermans 1992), is especially nicely designed, presenting 101 puzzles, many of which children can create. Any one of these three books would be a wonderful addition to a classroom.

References

CLASSIFICATION

Anno, Mitsumasa. 1989. *Anno's faces.* New York: Philomel.

Barton, Byron. 1989. *Dinosaurs, dinosaurs.* New York: Scholastic.

de Hamel, Joan. 1987. *Hemi's pet.* Boston: Houghton Mifflin.

Goor, Ron, and Nancy Goor. 1984. *All kinds of feet.* New York: Crowell.

Guarino, Deborah. 1989. *Is your mama a llama?* New York: Scholastic.

Heinst, Marie. 1992. *My first number book.* New York: Dorling Kindersley.

Kasza, Keiko. 1992. *A mother for Choco.* New York: Putnam.

Lacey, Elizabeth. 1993. *What's the difference? A guide to some familiar animal look-alikes.* New York: Clarion.

Lloyd, David, and Charlotte Voake. 1988. *Duck.* New York: Lippincott.

Machotka, Hana. 1991. *What neat feet!* New York: Morrow.

———. 1992. *Breathtaking noses.* New York: Morrow.

Pearce, Q. L. 1992. *Why is a frog not a toad?* Los Angeles: Lowell House.

Trapani, Iza. 1992. *What am I? An animal guessing game.* New York: Whispering Coyote.

Wu, Norbert. 1993. *Fish faces.* New York: Henry Holt.

COUNTING

Aertssen, Kristien. 1994. *Count on me.* Count Me In series, no. 4. New York: Annick.

Arnholt, Catherine. 1992 *The twins, two by two.* Cambridge, MA: Candlewick.

Ashton, Elizabeth. 1991. *An old fashioned 1 2 3 book.* New York: Viking.

Astley, Judy. 1990. *When one cat woke up: A cat counting book.* New York: Dial.

Bertrand, Lynne. 1992. *One day, two dragons.* New York: Clarkson Potter.

Brett, Jan. 1990. *The twelve days of Christmas.* New York: Putnam.

Brown, Paula. 1993. *Moon jump: A countdown.* New York: Viking.

Carroll, Kathleen. 1992. *One Red Rooster.* Boston: Houghton Mifflin.

Charlip, Remy, and Jerry Joyner. 1975. *Thirteen.* New York: Four Winds.

Clements, Andrew. 1992. *Mother Earth's counting book.* Saxonville, MA: Picture Book Studio.

Cole, Joanna. 1988. *Animal sleepyheads: 1 to 10.* New York: Scholastic.

Darwin, Susan, Beth Grout, and David McCoy, eds. 1992. *Look both ways: City math.* Alexandria, VA: Time-Life for Children.

Duntze, Dorothée. 1992. *The twelve days of christmas.* New York: North-South.

Falwell, Cathryn. 1993. *Feast for 10.* New York: Clarion.

Felix, Monique. 1991. *The numbers: A story of the little mouse trapped in a book.* Columbus, OH: American Education.

Fleming, Denise. 1992. *Count!* New York: Henry Holt.

French, Vivian. 1991. *One ballerina two.* New York: Lothrop, Lee & Shepard.

Garne, S. T. 1992. *One white sail.* New York: Simon & Schuster.

Geisert, Arthur. 1992. *Pigs from 1 to 10.* Boston: Houghton Mifflin.

Greenfield, Eloise. 1993. *Aaron and Gayla's counting book.* New York: Black Butterfly.

Harshman, Marc. 1990. *Only one.* New York: Dutton.

Haskins, Jim. 1990a. *Count your way through India.* Minneapolis: Carolrhoda.

———. 1990b. *Count your way through Israel.* Minneapolis: Carolrhoda.

Hirschi, Ron. 1992. *Hungry little frog.* New York: Cobblehill.

Holder, Heidi. 1987. *Crows: An old rhyme.* New York: Farrar, Straus & Giroux.

Johnson, Angela. 1991. *One of three.* New York: Orchard.

Johnson, Odette, and Bruce Johnson. 1992. *One prickly porcupine.* New York: Oxford.

Katz, Michael J. 1990. *Ten potatoes in a pot and other counting rhymes.* New York: Harper & Row.

Kitamura, Satashi. 1986. *When sheep cannot sleep: The counting book.* New York: Farrar, Straus & Giroux.

Kneen, Maggie. 1992. *Twelve days of Christmas: A revolving picture book.* New York: Dutton.

Knight, Joan. 1989. *Tickle-toe rhymes.* New York: Orchard.

Linden, Ann M. 1992. *One smiling grandma: A Caribbean counting book.* New York: Dial.

Maris, Ron. 1987. *In my garden.* New York: Greenwillow.

McGee, Barbara. 1991. *Counting sheep.* Buffalo, NY: Firefly.

Morozumi, Atsuko. 1990. *One gorilla: A counting book.* New York: Farrar, Straus & Giroux.

Nightingale, Sandy. 1992. *Pink pigs aplenty.* San Diego: Harcourt Brace Jovanovich.

Nikola-Lisa, W. 1991. *1,2,3 Thanksgiving.* Morton Grove, IL: Albert Whitman.

Ockenga, Starr, and Eileen Doolittle. 1988. *World of wonders: A trip through numbers.* Boston: Houghton Mifflin.

Pallotta, Jerry. 1991. *The icky bug counting book.* Watertown, MA: Charlesbridge.

Rosenberg, Amye. 1992. *Ten treats for Ginger.* New York: Simon & Schuster.

Samton, Sheila. 1985. *The world from my window.* Honesdale, PA: Boyds Mills Press.

Schade, Susan, and Jon Buller. 1991. *Hello! Hello! A counting book.* New York: Simon & Schuster.

Sheppard, Jeff. 1990. *The right number of elephants.* New York: Harper & Row.

Sloat, Teri. 1991. *From one to one hundred.* New York: Dutton.

Smith, Cara L. 1990. *Twenty-six rabbits run riot.* Boston: Little, Brown.

Sullivan, Charles. 1992. *Numbers at play: A counting book.* New York: Rizzoli.

Taborin, Glorina. 1977. *Norman Rockwell's counting book.* New York: Abrams.

Thornhill, Jan. 1989. *The wildlife 1 2 3: A nature counting book.* New York: Half Moon.

van Eeden, Maria. 1994. *The robbers five—or is it six?* Count Me In series, no. 3. New York: Annick.

van Loon, Paul. 1994. *A party at Manny's.* Count Me In series, no. 1. New York: Annick.

van Noorden, Djinn, ed. 1994. *The life-size animal counting book.* New York: Dorling Kindersley.

Wood, Jakki. 1992. *Moo moo, brown cow.* San Diego: Harcourt Brace Jovanovich.

Yoshi. 1991. *1, 2, 3.* Saxonville, MA: Picture Book Studio.

ADDITION AND SUBTRACTION

Balian, Lorna. 1986. *Amelia's nine lives.* Nashville, TN: Abingdon.

Bogart, Jo Ellen. 1989. *10 for dinner.* New York: Scholastic.

Brown, Marc. 1985. *Arthur's tooth.* Boston: Little, Brown.

Carlson, Nancy. 1984. *Harriet's Halloween candy.* Minneapolis: Carolrhoda.

Dale, Penny. 1993. *Ten out of bed.* Cambridge, MA: Candlewick.

Enderle, Judith R., and Stephanie Tessler. 1992. *Six creepy sheep.* Honesdale, PA: Caroline House.

Everett, Percival. 1992. *The one that got away.* New York: Clarion.

Gordon, Jeffie R. 1991. *Six sleepy sheep.* Honesdale, PA: Boyds Mills.

Hellen, Nancy. 1988. *The bus stop.* New York: Orchard.

Kherdian, David, and Nonny Hogrogrian. 1990. *The cat's midsummer jamboree.* New York: Philomel.

Mahy, Margaret. 1975. *The boy who was followed home.* New York: Dial.

Merriam, Eve. 1993. *12 ways to count to 11.* New York: Simon & Schuster.

Richardson, John. 1992. *Ten bears in a bed.* New York: Hyperion.

Samton, Sheila. 1991. *On the river: An adding book.* Honesdale, PA: Boyds Mills.

———. 1991. *Moon to sun: An adding book.* Honesdale, PA: Boyds Mills.

Schertle, Alice. 1985. *Goodnight, Hattie, my dearie, my dove.* New York: Lothrop, Lee & Shepard.

Showers, Paul. 1991. *How many teeth?* Rev. ed. New York: HarperCollins.

Weston, Martha. 1992. *Bea's 4 bears.* New York: Clarion.

Winer, Yvonne. 1985. *Mr. Brown's magnificent apple tree.* New York: Ashton Scholastic.

Wise, William. 1993. *Ten sly piranhas: A counting story in reverse (A tale of wickedness—and worse!)* New York: Dial.

Wylie, Joanne, and David Wylie. 1984. *A more or less fish story.* Chicago: Children's Press.

Young, Ed. 1992. *Seven blind mice.* New York: Philomel.

MULTIPLICATION

Chwast, Seymour. 1993. *The twelve circus rings.* San Diego: Harcourt Brace Jovanovich.

Giganti, Paul, Jr. 1992. *Each orange had 8 slices: A counting book.* New York: Greenwillow.

Hewitt, Kathryn. 1984. *Two by two: The untold story.* San Diego: Harcourt Brace Jovanovich.

Hulme, Joy. 1991. *Sea squares.* New York: Hyperion.

Parish, Peggy. 1974. *Too many rabbits.* New York: Macmillan.

Pascoe, Gwen. 1991. *Two feet.* Hocksville, NY: Newbridge Communications.

Pinczes, Elinor J. 1993. *One hundred hungry ants.* Boston: Houghton Mifflin.

Wood, Audrey, and Don Wood. 1991. *Piggies.* San Diego: Harcourt Brace Jovanovich.

FRACTIONS

Leedy, Loreen. 1994. *Fraction action.* New York: Holiday House.

McMillan, Bruce. 1991. *Eating fractions.* New York: Scholastic.

Nelson, Joanne. 1990. *Half and half.* Cleveland: Modern Curriculum Press.

Thaler, Mike. 1989. *The teacher from the Black Lagoon.* New York: Scholastic.

Wood, Don, and Audrey Wood. 1984. *The little mouse, the red ripe strawberry, and the big hungry bear.* New York: Child's Play.

BIG NUMBERS

Hertzberg, Hendrik. 1993. *One million.* New York: Times Books.

Kasza, Keiko. 1987. *The wolf's chicken stew.* New York: Putnam.

Lord, John V. 1972. *The giant jam sandwich.* Boston: Houghton Mifflin.

McKissack, Patricia. 1992. *A million fish . . . more or less.* New York: Knopf.

Pandell, Karen. 1993. *Land of dark, land of light: The Arctic National Wildlife Refuge.* New York: Dutton.

Ray, Mary L. 1992. *Pumpkins.* San Diego: Harcourt Brace Jovanovich.

Spurr, Elizabeth. 1991. *The biggest birthday cake in the world.* San Diego: Harcourt Brace Jovanovich.

GEOMETRY: SPATIAL ORIENTATION

Brown, Ruth. 1982. *If at first you do not see.* New York: Henry Holt.

Dodds, Dayle Ann. 1989. *Wheel away!* New York: Harper & Row.

Hill, Eric. 1980. *Where's Spot?* New York: Putnam.

Hoban, Tana. 1992. *Look up, look down.* New York: Greenwillow.

Keller, Wallace. 1992. *The wrong side of bed.* New York: Rizzoli.

MacDonald, Suse, and Bill Oakes. 1990. *Once upon another.* New York: Dial.

McMillan, Bruce. 1992. *Beach ball—left, right.* New York: Holiday House.

Rehm, Karl, and Kay Koike. 1991. *Left or right?* New York: Clarion.

Salter, Mary Jo. 1989. *The moon comes home.* New York: Knopf.

GEOMETRY: SHAPES

Anno, Mitsumasa. 1980. *Anno's medieval world.* New York: Philomel.

Carle, Eric. 1992. *Draw me a star.* New York: Philomel.

Feldman, Judy. 1991. *Shapes in nature.* Chicago: Children's Press.

Hoban, Tana. 1992. *Spirals, curves, fanshapes and lines.* New York: Greenwillow.

Karlin, Bernie. 1992. *Shapes: Circle.* New York: Simon & Schuster.

———. 1992. *Shapes: Square.* New York: Simon & Schuster.

———. 1992. *Shapes: Triangle.* New York: Simon & Schuster.

Laithwaite, Eric. 1986. *Shape: The purpose of forms.* Science at Work. New York: Franklin Watts.

Lauber, Patricia. 1990. *How we learned the earth is round.* New York: HarperCollins.

MacKinnon, Debbie. 1992. *What shape?* New York: Dial.

Murphy, Pat. 1993. *By nature's design.* An Exploratorium Book. San Francisco: Chronicle.

Pluckrose, Henry. 1986. *Think about shape.* New York: Franklin Watts.

Ross, Catherine S. 1992. *Circles.* Toronto: Kids Can Press.

Van Fleet, Matthew. 1993. *Match it: A fold-the-flap book.* New York: Dial.

Wylie, Joanne, and David Wylie. 1984. *A fishy shape story.* Chicago: Children's Press.

GEOMETRY: SHADOWS, REFLECTIONS, AND VISUAL ILLUSION

Anno, Mitsumasa. 1977. *The unique world of Mitsumasa Anno: Selected illustrations 1968–1977.* London: The Bodley Head.

Asch, Frank. 1985. *Bear shadow.* New York: Simon & Schuster.

Baum, Arline, and Joseph Baum. 1987. *Opt: An illusionary tale.* New York: Viking.

Blaze International Productions. 1991. *The pop-up book of M. C. Escher.* Petaluma, CA: Pomegranate.

Bolton, Linda. 1993. *Hidden pictures.* New York: Dial.

Horibuchi, Seiji, ed. 1994. *Stereogram.* San Francisco: Cadence.

N. E. Thing Enterprises. 1993. *Magic eye: A new way of looking at the world.* Kansas City, MO: Andrews and McMeel.

———. 1994. *Magic eye II: Now you see it. . . .* Kansas City, MO: Andrews and McMeel.

———. 1994. *Magic eye III.* Kansas City, MO: Andrews and McMeel.

Pentagram Design. 1992. *Pentamagic.* New York: Simon & Schuster.

Sandburg, Carl. [1933] 1993. *Arithmetic.* San Diego: Harcourt Brace Jovanovich.

Simon, Seymour. 1976. *The optical illusion book.* New York: Morrow.

———. 1991. *Mirror magic.* Honesdale, PA: Boyds Mills.

Trivett, Daphne. 1974. *Shadow geometry.* New York: Crowell.

Westray, Kathleen. 1994. *Picture puzzler.* New York: Ticknor & Fields.

Zubrowski, Bernie. 1992. *Mirrors: Finding out about the properties of light.* New York: Morrow.

GEOMETRY: PATTERN AND ART

Aytüre-Scheele, Zülal. 1990. *Beautiful origami.* New York: Sterling.

Bang, Molly. 1991. *Picture this. Perception and composition.* Boston: Little, Brown.

Cole, Alison. 1992. *Perspective.* Eyewitness Art. New York: Dorling Kindersley.

Ernst, Lisa, and Lee Ernst. 1990. *The tangram magician.* New York: Abrams.

Frayling, Christopher, Helen Frayling, and Ron Van der Meer. 1992. *The art pack.* New York: Knopf.

Huber, Johanna, and Christel Claudius. 1990. *Easy and fun paper folding.* New York: Sterling.

Isaacson, Philip M. 1993. *A short walk around the pyramids and through the world of art.* New York: Knopf.

Paul, Ann W. 1991. *Eight hands round: A patchwork alphabet.* New York: HarperCollins.

GEOMETRY: ARCHITECTURE

(Note: This listing also includes some adult reference books.)

Alley, R. W. 1988. *The clever carpenter.* New York: Random House.

Balaban, Richard. 1976. *The mystery tour: Exploring the designed environment with children.* Washington: Preservation Press.

Balterman, Lee. 1991. *Girders and cranes: A skyscraper is built.* Morton Grove, IL: Albert Whitman.

Bare, Colleen. 1992. *This is a house.* New York: Cobblehill.

Barton, Byron. 1981. *Building a house.* New York: Greenwillow.

Biesty, Stephen. 1992. *Stephen Biesty's incredible cross-sections.* New York: Knopf.

Blackwell, William. 1984. *Geometry in architecture.* Berkeley, CA: Key Curriculum Press.

Blumenson, John. 1977. *Identifying American architecture: A pictorial guide to styles and terms, 1600–1945.* Nashville, TN: American Association for State and Local History.

Brooks, Bruce. 1991. *Nature by design.* New York: Farrar, Straus & Giroux.

Brown, David. 1992. *The Random House book of how things were built.* New York: Random House.

Carter, Polly. 1992. *The bridge book.* New York: Simon & Schuster.

D'Alelio, Jane. 1989. *I know that building: Discovering architecture with activities and games.* Washington, DC: Preservation Press.

Darling, David. 1991. *Spiderwebs to skyscrapers: The science of structure.* New York: Dillon.

Dorros, Arthur. 1992. *This is my house.* New York: Scholastic.

Fleisher, Paul, and Patricia Keeler. 1991. *Looking inside machines and constructions.* New York: Atheneum.

Gibbons, Gail. 1990a. *How a house is built.* New York: Macmillan.

———. 1990b. *Up goes the skyscraper.* New York: Holiday House.

Hawkes, Nigel. 1990. *Structures: The way things are built.* New York: Macmillan.

Morris, Ann. 1992. *Houses and homes.* New York: Lothrop, Lee & Shepard.

Munro, Rosie. 1987. *The inside-outside book of Washington, D.C.* New York: Dutton.

———. 1989. *The inside-outside book of London.* New York: Dutton.

———. 1992. *The inside-outside book of Paris.* New York: Dutton.

Robbins, Ken. 1991. *Bridges.* New York: Dial.

Salvadori, Mario. 1979. *Building: The fight against gravity.* New York: Atheneum.

Seltzer, Isadore. 1992. *The house I live in: At home in America.* New York: Macmillan.

Thorne-Thomsen, Kathleen. 1994. *Frank Lloyd Wright for kids.* Chicago: Chicago Review Press.

Wilcox, Charlotte. 1990. *A skyscraper story.* Minneapolis: Carolrhoda.

Wilkinson, Philip. 1993. *Amazing buildings.* New York: Dorling Kindersley.

Wilson, Forrest. 1988. *What it feels like to be a building.* Washington, DC: Preservation Press.

MEASUREMENT: COMPARISONS

Berenstain, Michael. 1991. *Faster, slower, higher, lower.* Racine, WI: Western Publishing.

Ganeri, Anita. 1992a. *The biggest and smallest.* Hauppauge, NY: Barron's.

———. 1992b. *The fastest and slowest.* Hauppauge, NY: Barron's.

———. 1992c. *The first and foremost.* Hauppauge, NY: Barron's.

———. 1992d. *The longest and tallest.* Hauppauge, NY: Barron's.

Graham, Amanda. 1991. *Angus thought he was big.* Hicksville, NY: Newbridge Communications.

Joyce, William. 1985. *George shrinks.* New York: Harper & Row.

Nelson, Joanne. 1990. *How tall are you?* Cleveland, OH: Modern Curriculum Press.

Sawicki, Norma J. 1989. *The little red house.* New York: Lothrop, Lee & Shepard.

Thaler, Mike. 1988. *In the middle of the puddle.* New York: Harper Trophy.

Wiesner, David. 1992. *June 29, 1999.* New York: Clarion.

Woaters, Anne. 1991. *This book is too small.* New York: Dutton.

Zolotow, Charlotte. 1987. *I like to be little.* New York: HarperCollins.

MEASUREMENT: THE MEASUREMENT PROCESS

Briggs, Raymond. 1970. *Jim and the beanstalk.* New York: Coward-McCann.

Clement, Rod. 1991. *Counting on Frank.* Milwaukee: Gareth Stevens.

Fraser, Mary Ann. 1993. *Ten Mile Day and the building of the transcontinental railroad.* New York: Henry Holt.

Lowery, Lawrence. 1969. *How tall was Milton?* New York: Holt, Rinehart & Winston.

Narode, Ronald. In press. Communicating mathematics through literature: Money, greed, area, and irony in Tolstoy's "How much land does a man need?" In

Communication in Mathematics, K–12, edited by Portia Elliot (1996 yearbook). Reston, VA: National Council of Teachers of Mathematics.

Norden, Beth B., and Lynette Ruschak. 1993. *Magnification.* New York: Lodestar.

Raphael, Elaine, and Don Bolognese. 1977. *Sam Baker, gone west.* New York: Viking.

Smulders, Frank. 1994. *Bigger than biggest.* Count Me In series, no. 2. New York: Annick.

Tomb, Howard, and Dennis Kunkel. 1993. *Microaliens: Dazzling journeys with an electron miscroscope.* New York: Farrar, Straus & Giroux.

MEASUREMENT: MAPS AND MAPPING

Carlisle, Madelyn W. 1992. *Let's investigate marvelously meaningful maps.* Happauge, NY: Barron's.

Hartman, Gail. 1991. *As the crow flies: A first book of maps.* New York: Bradbury.

Holmes, Nigel. 1991. *Pictorial maps.* New York: Watson-Guptill.

Knowlton, Jack. 1985. *Maps and globes.* New York: Harper & Row.

Lye, Keith. 1991. *Measuring and maps: Projects with geography.* New York: Franklin Watts.

Makower, Joel. 1992. *The map catalogue.* New York: Vintage.

Petty, Kate, and Jakki Wood. 1993. *Around and about maps and journeys.* Hauppauge, NY: Barron's.

Weiss, Harvey. 1991. *Maps: Getting from here to there.* Boston: Houghton Mifflin.

MEASUREMENT: ANIMALS

Carrick, Carol. 1989a. *Patrick's dinosaurs.* New York: Clarion.

———. 1989b. *Big old bones: A dinosaur tale.* New York: Clarion.

Cole, Joanna. 1985a. *Large as life: Daytime animals.* New York: Knopf.

———. 1985b. *Large as life: Nighttime animals.* New York: Knopf.

Most, Bernard. 1994. *How big were the dinosaurs?* San Diego: Harcourt Brace Jovanovich.

———. 1989. *The littlest dinosaurs.* San Diego: Harcourt Brace Jovanovich.

Tison, Annette, and Talvs Taylor. 1989. *Animals large and small.* New York: Grossett & Dunlap.

Van Allsburg, Chris. 1988. *Two bad ants.* Boston: Houghton Mifflin.

Waverly, Barney. 1990. *How big? How fast? How hungry?* Milwaukee, WI: Raintree.

MEASUREMENT: LENGTH, WEIGHT, CAPACITY, VOLUME

Bodecker, N. M. 1983. *Carrot holes and Frisbee trees.* New York: Atheneum.

Brett, Jan. 1989. *The mitten.* New York: Putnam.

Hutchins, Pat. 1979. *One-Eyed Jake.* New York: Greenwillow.

Pluckrose, Henry. 1988. *Knowabout: Capacity.* New York: Franklin Watts.

Schwartz, David M. 1991. *Supergrandpa.* New York: Lothrop, Lee & Shepard.

Srivastava, Jane. 1980. *Spaces, shapes and sizes.* New York: Crowell.

MEASUREMENT: MONEY

Adams, Barbara. 1992. *The go-around dollar.* New York: Four Winds.

Berenstain, Stan, and Jan Berenstain. 1983. *The Berenstain Bears' Trouble with money.* New York: Random House.

Berger, Melvin, and Gilda Berger. 1993. *Round and round the money goes: What money is and how we use it.* Nashville, TN: Ideals Children's Readers.

Conford, Ellen. 1989. *What's cooking, Jenny Archer?* Boston: Little, Brown.

Cribb, Joe. 1990. *Money.* Eyewitness Books. New York: Knopf.

Gay, Kathlyn. 1992. *Caution! This may be an advertisement: A teen guide to advertising.* New York: Franklin Watts.

Godfrey, Neale. 1991. *The kid's money book.* New York: Checkerboard.

Hill, Elizabeth S. 1991. *Evan's corner.* Rev. ed. New York: Viking.

Kain, Carolyn. 1994. *The story of money.* New York: Troll.

Leedy, Loreen. 1992. *The monster money book.* New York: Holiday House.

Maestro, Betsy. 1993. *The story of money.* New York: Clarion.

Marshall, James. 1974. *Willis.* Boston: Houghton Mifflin.

Nelson, JoAnne. 1990. *The magic money machine.* Cleveland: Modern Curriculum Press.

Shelby, Anne. 1990. *We keep a store.* New York: Orchard.

Zimelman, Nathan. 1992. *How the second grade got $8,205.50 to visit the Statue of Liberty.* Morton Grove, IL: Albert Whitman.

MEASUREMENT: TIME

Allen, Jeffrey. 1975. *Mary Alice, Operator Number 9.* Boston: Little, Brown.

Allison, Linda. 1975. *The reasons for seasons: The great cosmic megagalactic trip without moving from your chair.* Boston: Little, Brown.

Aylesworth, Jim. 1990. *The completed hickory dickory dock.* New York: Atheneum.

Berger, Barbara. 1984. *Grandfather twilight.* New York: Philomel.

Branley, Franklyn M. 1985. *Sunshine makes the seasons.* Rev. ed. New York: Crowell.

———. 1986. *What makes day and night.* Rev. ed. New York: Crowell.

———. 1993. *Keeping time.* Boston: Houghton Mifflin.

Bruchac, Joseph. 1992. *Thirteen moons on turtle's back: A Native American year of moons.* New York: Philomel.

Burton, Virginia L. 1962. *Life story.* Boston: Houghton Mifflin.

Carle, Eric. 1993. *Today is Monday.* New York: Philomel.

Cave, Kathryn, and Terry McKenna. 1989. *Just in time.* New York: Clarkson N. Potter.

Cohen, David. 1992. *America: Then and now.* Mill Valley, CA: Cohen.

Demers, Jan. 1986. *On Sunday I lost my cat.* Worthington, OH: Willowisp Press.

Dijs, Carla. 1993. *What do I do at 8 o'clock?* New York: Simon & Schuster.

Edmonds, William. 1994. *Big book of time.* New York: Readers Digest Kids.

Fleischman, Paul. 1991. *Time train.* New York: HarperCollins.

Flournoy, Valerie. 1978. *The best time of day.* New York: Random House.

Goodall, John S. 1979. *The story of an English village.* New York: Atheneum.

———. 1990. *The story of the seashore.* New York: Margaret McElderry.

———. 1992a. *Great days of a country house.* New York: Margaret McElderry.

———. 1992b. *The story of a farm.* New York: Margaret McElderry.

———. 1992c. *The story of a castle.* New York: Margaret McElderry.

Gould, Deborah. 1988. *Brendan's best-timed birthday.* New York: Bradbury.

Grossman, Bill. 1990. *The guy who was five minutes late.* New York: HarperCollins.

Hiscock, Bruce. 1991. *The big tree.* New York: Atheneum.

Krasilovsky, Phyllis. 1979. *The man who tried to save time.* New York: Doubleday.

Lionni, Leo. 1992. *A busy year.* New York: Knopf.

Llewellyn, Claire. 1992. *My first book of time.* New York: Dorling Kindersley.

Maestro, Betsy, and Giulio Maestro. 1990. *Temperature and you.* New York: Dutton.

McPhail, David. 1992. *Farm boy's year.* New York: Atheneum.

Merriam, Eve. 1992. *Train leaves the station.* New York: Henry Holt.

Murphy, Jill. 1986. *Five minutes' peace.* New York: Putnam.

Nelson, Joanne. 1989. *Time to run.* Cleveland, Ohio: Modern Curriculum Press.

Ockenga, Starr. 1990. *A book of days: Then and now.* Boston: Houghton Mifflin.

Polacco, Patricia. 1990. *Thunder cake.* New York: Philomel.

Russo, Marisabina. 1988. *Only six more days.* New York: Puffin.

Rylant, Cynthia. 1987. *Birthday presents.* New York: Orchard.

Sherrow, Victoria. 1990. *Wilbur waits.* New York: Harper & Row.

Shook, Michael, and Robert Shook. 1992. *It's about time!* New York: Penguin.

Singer, Marilyn. 1991. *Nine o'clock lullaby.* New York: HarperCollins.

Trivett, Daphne, and John Trivett. 1979. *Time for clocks.* New York: Crowell.

Turner, Gwenda. 1990. *Once upon a time.* New York: Viking.

Van Rynbach, Iris. 1991. *Everything from a nail to a coffin.* New York: Orchard.

Viorst, Judith. 1992. *Sunday morning.* New York: Atheneum.

Wallace-Brodeur, Ruth. 1992. *Home by five.* New York: Margaret McElderry.

Ward, Cindy. 1988. *Cookie's week.* New York: Putnam.

Whelan, Gloria. 1988. *A week of raccoons.* New York: Knopf.

Wiesner, David. 1991. *Tuesday.* New York: Clarion.

Wood, A. J. 1992. *Errata, A book of historical errors.* New York: Simon & Schuster.

MEASUREMENT: SEVERAL BOOKS ABOUT BIG PUMPKINS

Gillis, Jennifer S. 1992. *In a pumpkin shell: Over 20 pumpkin projects for kids.* Pownal, VT: Storey Communications.

Kroll, Steven. 1984. *The biggest pumpkin ever.* New York: Scholastic.

McDonald, Megan. 1992. *The great pumpkin switch.* New York: Orchard.

Ray, Mary L. 1992. *Pumpkins.* San Diego: Harcourt Brace Jovanovich.

Silverman, Erica. 1992. *Big pumpkin.* New York: Macmillan.

Titherington, Jeanne. 1986. *Pumpkin, pumpkin.* New York: Greenwillow.

MEASUREMENT: COOKING

Anderson, Gretchen, and Karen Milone. 1985. *The Louisa May Alcott cookbook.* Boston: Little, Brown.

Barchers, Suzanne I., and Patricia C. Marden. 1991. *Cooking up U.S. history: Recipes and research to share with children.* Englewood, CO: Teacher Ideas Press.

Barrett-Dragan, Patricia, and Rosemary Dalton. 1992. *The kid's cookbook.* San Leandro, CA: Bristol.

Bruno, Janet. 1991. *Book cooks.* Cypress, CA: Creative Teaching Press.

Carle, Eric. 1990. *Pancakes, pancakes!* Saxonville, MA: Picture Book Studio.

Cefali, Leslie. 1991. *Cook-a-book.* Hagerstown, MD: Albyside Press.

Copage, Eric. 1991. *Kwanzaa: An African-American celebration of culture and cooking.* New York: Morrow.

Dooley, Norah. 1991. *Everybody cooks rice.* Minneapolis: Carolrhoda.

Douglas, Barbara. 1985. *The chocolate chip cookie contest.* New York: Lothrop, Lee & Shepard.

Krensky, Stephen. 1992. *The pizza book.* New York: Scholastic.

Wilkes, Angela. 1989. *My first cook book.* New York: Knopf.

Williamson, Sarah. 1992. *Kids cook!* Charlotte, VT: Williamson.

PUZZLES AND GAMES

Blum, Raymond. 1991. *Mathemagic.* New York: Sterling.

Botermans, Jack, Toneny Burrett, Pieter van Delft, and Carla van Splunteren. 1989. *The world of games.* New York: Facts on File.

Connell, David D., and Jim Thurman. 1993. *The case of the unnatural.* Mathnet™ Casebook no. 1. New York: Children's Television Workshop/Freeman.

Dixon, Sarah, and Radhi Parekh. 1993. *Map and maze puzzles.* London: Usborne.

Ginns, Russell. 1994. *Puzzlooney! Really ridiculous math puzzles.* New York: W. H. Freeman.

Keller, Charles. 1991. *Take me to your liter.* New York: Pippin.

Marchon-Arnaud, Catherine. 1994. *A gallery of games.* New York: Ticknor & Fields.

Muller, Robert. 1989. *The great book of math teasers.* New York: Sterling.

Olivastro, Dominic. 1993. *Ancient puzzles: Classic brainteasers and other timeless mathematical games of the last 10 centuries.* New York: Bantam.

Provenzo, Asterie B., and Eugene F. Provenzo. 1981. *Favorite board games you can make and play.* New York: Dover.

Slocum, Jerry, and Jack Botermans. 1986. *Puzzles old and new: How to make and solve them.* Seattle: U. of Washington Press.

———. 1992. *New book of puzzles: 101 classic and modern puzzles to make and solve.* New York: W. H. Freeman.

vos Savant, Marilyn. 1992. *Ask Marilyn.* New York: St. Martin's.

———. 1994. *More Marilyn: Some Like It Bright.* New York: St. Martin's.

White, Laurence B., Jr., and Ray Broekel. 1990. *Math-a-magic: Number tricks for magicians.* Morton Grove, IL: Albert Whitman.

Wyler, Rose, and Mary Elting. 1992. *Math fun with money puzzlers.* New York: Julian Messner.

———. 1992. *With a pocket calculator.* New York: Simon & Schuster.

If you have discovered other books we may not know about, or if you would like to share some of your stories about how you have used mathematical children's books in the classroom, please drop us a line in care of Heinemann.

Credit lines continued from page ii